Down The Tube

Down The Tube

THE BATTLE FOR
LONDON'S UNDERGROUND

CHRISTIAN WOLMAR

AURUM PRESS

First published in Great Britain
2002 by Aurum Press Ltd
25 Bedford Avenue, London WC1B 3AT

A catalogue record for this book is available from the British Library.

ISBN 1 85410 872 7

1 3 5 7 9 10 8 6 4 2
2002 2004 2006 2005 2003

Designed by Geoff Green Book Design
Typeset in Stone Print by M Rules
Printed in Great Britain by MPG Books Ltd, Bodmin

Contents

This book is dedicated with love to Tony Bevins and Keith Harper, two old hacks, who are sadly missed and would have thoroughly enjoyed this tale.

Acknowledgements

This book would not have been possible without the cooperation I received from all sides of this controversy. A request for interview was only turned down by a couple of people, and I did not bother asking Gordon Brown. Otherwise, everyone was prepared to help, which was extremely gratifying. There are, of course, a whole host of people to thank for whom anonymity is more important than an acknowledgement, including many who still work for the Underground.

Of those I can name, I would like to thank, in no particular order: Josephine Grant at the London Transport Museum, who let me clutter up her office for long periods, and her colleagues in the library; Steve Norris who has helped me with almost every book on transport I have written, although we have the odd disagreement; a wide variety of people at Transport for London, including Maggie Boepple, Jay Walder, Lesley McLeod, Steve Polan, Peter Hendy, Susan Kramer, Bob Kiley and Ken Livingstone; Martin Callaghan, Jon Smith and the press office at London Transport who were all extremely helpful, even though they suspected that the book might not entirely endorse their argument; Bill Mount for a lesson in reading consultants' reports; my pal Roger Ford who keeps me sane during the lonely days; Rupert Brennan-Brown, one of the best PRs in the business; Nigel Harris and the team at *Rail*, even though they call me the electrician for my skill at plugs; Ron Rose for neck massages; and Brendan Martin, Peter Ford, Sir Alastair Morton, Denis Tunnicliffe, Neal Lawson, Tony Travers, John Fowler, Phil Kelly, Rupert Brennan-Brown, Tony Ridley, John Self, Mike Horne, Jerry, Steve and McM. And there are, of course, those whom I have forgotten.

Special thanks go to Stephen Glaister and Jon Shaw for reading the manuscript and making many helpful comments; Piers Burnett at Aurum, for having the idea; and Andrew Lownie, my agent, who stood by me in difficult times. The errors and omissions remain, of course, my responsibility.

And none of this would have been possible without my partner, Scarlett McGwire, who was particularly supportive when the deadline came and went, and, of course, my wonderful children, Molly, Pascoe and Misha.

NOTE: I have used the words London Underground and Tube interchangeably, rather than confining the use of 'Tube' to the deep tube lines. For comments and reactions, my email address is xian@pro-net.co.uk

CHAPTER ONE

A day in the life of the Tube

To exlore the bowels of the London Underground system is easy. There are little anonymous doors with incomprehensible coded index numbers off almost every corridor which, when opened, reveal the very Edwardian soul of the system: redundant lift shafts, abandoned machinery that would cost far too much to remove, electrical equipment stored in tiny, low ceiling rooms built in an age before six-footers were commonplace, and much more. The Underground people are only too happy to show visitors these nooks and crannies, as it is part of their continuous propaganda war for more resources to renew the system.

Camden Town is a perfect place to show how every day the Underground is stretched close to breaking point. The station was originally built in 1907 to accommodate the Charing Cross, Euston and Hampstead railway, but when in the 1920s the two sections of what is now the Northern Line merged, it had to be reorganised but largely within the existing confines. Therefore it has throughout its history been too small to accommodate the ever-increasing numbers using it. On the surface, the entrance is on a narrow peninsula at a junction between two busy one-way streets that is far too small to accommodate what has become one of the most heavily frequented stations on the network. There are 50,000 daily users on an average weekday but the real nightmare is at weekends, which were, until the 1980s, so sleepy that nearby Mornington Crescent was only a Monday to Friday station. Now, Camden Market has become one of London's most popular tourist destinations and a staggering 70,000 use it every Saturday and Sunday, which means that special contraflow systems have to be used, forcing those joining the Tube at Camden Town to go down the ninety-six steps of the winding staircase that envelops the long-disused lift shaft, made redundant in 1927 when the escalators were built. At the busiest time, on Sunday afternoon, the station entrance is closed, as the flow is too big, and passengers wanting to get into the network are diverted instead to nearby Chalk Farm and Mornington Crescent.

The staggering, and not completely understood, renaissance in Tube passenger numbers is well illustrated by the recent history of Mornington Crescent, which was closed for six years in the 1990s and nearly shut permanently because it is just at the other end of the High Street from Camden Town and was thought to be superfluous to requirements. But Tube usage has almost doubled in that time, and Mornington Crescent, whose evocative name has even spawned an eponymous and deliberately incomprehensible game on the radio programme *I'm Sorry I Haven't a Clue*, is now an essential part of the system.

The two fundamental problems of the Tube, the pressures caused by growth and the lack of investment, are forever entwined. When Tony Ridley took over as managing director of London Underground in 1980, he was expected to manage the decline. It was, incidentally, the same mistake that was made a decade later when the railways were privatised and expected gradually to wither away. The growth has been nothing short of phenomenal. The very success of the Tube in increasing passenger numbers, from under 500 million annually a couple of years after Ridley took over to today's throughput of double that, is responsible for many of the failings of the system. If there were more room on the trains, tracks, platforms, escalators, if the steady throng of people abated even just for a bit as it did on Sundays a few years ago, then the task of those trying to keep the system moving, let alone improve it, would be so much easier.

It is important to keep that recent history in mind. The massive investment programme which everyone agrees is needed would be unnecessary if the system were not so much in demand. There are several apparent reasons for the increase in usage but no satisfactory and definitive explanation. London's population stopped declining in the mid-1980s and the economy has, apart from the four-year recession that started in 1989, grown throughout that period. Then there is the introduction of more simplified ticketing, especially the Travelcard in its various mutating forms that became more and more useful. Right at the beginning of this period, there was the Fares Fair policy, introduced by Ken Livingstone as leader of the Greater London Council. Even though Fares Fair was revoked by the Law Lords following a legal challenge by the London Borough of Bromley, and then only partially reinstated, it had a big impact on growth because it introduced the Travelcard which made travelling round the capital considerably cheaper for those making several journeys. Once someone has paid for a Travelcard, the car is seen as an extra expense, rather than, as is usually the case with public transport, the other way around. With free travel for weekly Travelcard holders, weekends, which used to be a slack period for the Underground, have now become its busiest time at some stations. Worsening road congestion and rising tourism are other factors that have contributed to the massive growth, but there is no entirely convincing explanation for the scale of the increase during the 1990s. This is why the rise in usage was, in fact, largely unpredicted and therefore weakened the case for extra cash for investment in the eyes of the Treasury officials who controlled the purse strings. That was one cause of the constant underinvestment in the Tube in the post-war period, but, as we shall see (Chapter 3), not the only one.

Back to Camden Town. There are long-term plans to redevelop the station. Indeed, various such schemes have been in the offing since the 1930s but, according to the London Underground managers showing me round, there are always objectors – the local civic society, the traders, the council, even the local church. It is clearly a prime piece of real estate and the station redevelopment would more than pay for itself if an office block were to be built over it, but that would involve wrecking the classic lines of the station built by Charles Yerkes (the American entrepreneur who was responsible for creating much of the Tube network) with the characteristic, though not easily visible, maroon tiles of the original station. The station concourse consists of little more than a draughty corridor, open at both ends to the elements and the traffic noise. The little shop is closed in preparation for a small extension but behind the station there is still a hoarding hiding one of the few remaining legacies to the 'Luftwaffe's handiwork', as Jeff Mills, the group station manager, a lifetime Tube man who has climbed through the ranks during his thirty-six years of service, put it. The fact that this land has remained unused for over half a century when, clearly, the station is far too small to cope with the demand can only be attributed to the vagaries of property development and planning consent added to the unexpected huge growth at the station.

There are still no ticket gates at Camden Town because there hasn't been the room to put them in. Now, with the closure of the shop, a bit of extra space has been created and gates will be installed, though not in an entirely satisfactory way purely because of the architectural limitations of the station. The installation of gates at nearly all inner London stations during the 1990s is a success story, one of the reasons for the rise in ticket sales, since they make evasion more difficult. Indeed, the Friday before I visited Camden Town in February 2002, a team of revenue protection officers had descended on the station and issued 137 notices to prosecute, which demonstrates just how many people are dodging the fare because they know Camden is not protected by gates.

The installation of the gates at Camden Town is part of a complex Private Finance Initiative project called Prestige, undertaken by TranSys, which won the contract in 1998, and can be seen as a precursor, though much more simple, of the Tube PPP which is explained in detail in Chapter 8. Indeed, the term PFI is somewhat synonymous with Public Private Partnership (see Chapter 7 for a history of both concepts), though the latter is many dimensions more complicated. The basic concept of PFI is for companies to be awarded contracts to build an asset and look after it for a long time afterwards – usually twenty-five to thirty years – and to be remunerated through an annual payment rather than an overall sum at the beginning. TranSys, which is a consortium of four companies – W.S. Atkins, EDS, ICL and Cubic Corporation – is a £1bn plan to gate – or regate – all the Underground's 274 stations, allowing smart card technology to be used. The ticket PFI appears, so far, to be on time and is due to go 'live' early in 2003 but has occasionally led to difficult situations and hurried work. According to Howard Collins, the service delivery manager for the Jubilee, Northern and Piccadilly lines, another long-term Underground man with twenty-five years' experience and an obvious pride in his fiefdom, 'We are under pressure to do things quickly from our project managers, who are under pressure from TranSys, who are under pressure from their bankers.' TranSys gets more money if new machines are installed quickly and more people use the system, and is, according to Collins, therefore always in a hurry to install them, even in cases where they may not be adequate, as some stations are simply too small or badly designed to cope. Collins says that this can lead to compromises, but that London Underground always has the final say as far as safety is concerned. Thus, at Southgate on the Piccadilly Line, the ticket barriers had to be taken out and reinstalled because they were proving a safety hazard. As we shall see, these are the types of issues raised time and again by opponents of the Tube PPP.

At Camden, you don't really need to go behind the scenes to discover the inadequacies of the station. They are all too apparent in the complex web of cramped tunnels that link the two sets of platforms which sit above one another. Camden Town is an inexplicable labyrinth for the tourist visitors to London who will not realise that the reason why southbound trains go along both the Bank and Charing Cross sections of the Northern Line from both the two southbound platforms, rather than being separated, is a result of the complex history of the line, built as two separate entities and then merged rather haphazardly. This means, as seasoned north Londoners know, that southbound passengers have to look at the indicators in the cramped area at the bottom of the escalators, and occasionally take a risk on their accuracy to see whether it is worth running to try to catch a train which the dot matrix indicator flashes as 'here' or whether to give up to wait for the next one. Heading north is an equally hit and miss experience, as passengers are encouraged to take the first train and then change at Camden Town to get to the right branch, which involves bustling through a narrow corridor often filled with a contraflow of people making the opposite transfer.

London Underground has, at various times, considered separating the two sections of the line so that one southbound platform serves the Bank branch, with the trains from High Barnet, and the other the Charing Cross with the trains from Edgware, but that would create such a throng of people forced to change at Camden Town that the idea has been rejected, even though the consequent simplification would end those interminable stops in the complex of tunnels between Euston and Camden Town while trains wait for those on the other branch to cross their path

Howard Collins points out that the station is rather brighter than it has been for a decade or two thanks to a recent £1.3m refurbishment, undertaken because insalubrious Camden Town, created originally to house railway workers, has now become a trendy showcase for London thanks to the popularity of the market. The platforms have been resurfaced, the walls given a lick of paint and the tiles replaced with colours carefully selected to match the original. It is much more pleasant, but the underlying problems still show through. Mills points out the wet patch where the paint is already flaking on the ceiling of Platform 2: 'We just can't stop the water getting through,' he says glumly. Collins remarks that London Underground is the second biggest shifter of water in London after Thames Water.

Of course, in the non-public areas where paint is at a premium and the fight against damp is less urgent, the fetid atmosphere is much worse. The control room tucked away between the platforms deep in the entrails of the station is cramped, not least because it contains the remnants of the long-abandoned lift shaft, and there is a faint musky smell of rats' piss. Its entrance is half hidden behind the remnant of an Ionic column, a feature of the station originally built by Yerkes and now painted in a bluey mauve colour that is out of place with the design: 'We don't get the choice of the full Dulux range and this is the best the architect could do,' says Mills whose artistic sensibilities have, quite understandably, been affected by the crassness of the choice. The control room doubles as a mess room, though staff are unlikely to want to hang around much in the fetid atmosphere, and there is even a tiny 'customer reception area' to deal with lost property and the like where, on cue, a couple of teenage girls pop in because one of them has left her season ticket on the train. There are a couple of computer terminals but these are not linked in with the rest of the Underground system, so most of the communication is by telephone and fax. There is not even any room to stick up a notice, because the walls are so cluttered with pipes and ducts and the ceiling almost touches our heads. Ideally, says Mr Mills, 'we would have a control room at ticket hall level which would enable us to control the entrance to the station more quickly'. And, of course, it should be kitted out with modern communication equipment to cope with the 110 trains per hour which call at the station during peak times.

The Camden Town control room is principally concerned with what happens at the station, but the staff also have an important role in keeping the trains running: 'When did you last go into the tunnel, Iqbal?' asks Collins of the controller on duty. 'A couple of weeks ago,' comes the reply from the diminutive, bearded, middle-aged fellow. That happens when the signal fails and therefore goes automatically red and sets the points against a train. A track man then has to 'scotch and clip' points – open and lock them – to enable trains to pass over them, overriding the red signal. Otherwise the service comes to a halt until the points can be properly repaired, which could take hours. It is a skilled operation, as getting it wrong can lead to a derailment. That shows the Tube is a much more integrated system than the national railway where station staff, working for operators, never venture onto the track as that is the realm of Network Rail and its contractors. Collins stresses that, even with the PPP, which separates the infrastructure from the day-to-day operations, 'these guys will still do things like sort out points. They have a much more active role in keeping the trains running than their counterparts on the national railway.'

As if to confirm that point, Iqbal relates how he had to sort out a train the previous night after a passenger 'under the influence of drink' had tried to jump out of the moving train as it left the station from the gap between two carriages as the doors had shut and he had realised he had missed his station. This brought the train to an emergency stop and, quite amazingly, the hapless wretch was unhurt. But Iqbal and his team, together with the driver, got the train working as rapidly as possible. 'The man was arrested,' he added with some satisfaction.

There are a couple of station controllers on duty, most of whose time is spent checking the CCTV monitors fed by forty-four cameras dotted around the station or wandering round the entrails of the station checking for fires. This is a legacy of the Fennell report, produced in the aftermath of the King's Cross fire in 1987, which revealed a catalogue of failing managerial procedures (see Chapter 4). The fire started underneath an escalator but the inquiry also revealed that inflammable materials were kept randomly in all kinds of storerooms. So now, every three hours, Iqbal and his fellow station controllers have to check these spaces, where, far from there being a fire risk, the reek of dampness is so strong that it seems to date from when the Edwardian builders of this line dug out the space. There is more opening and closing of doors than in the average prison because another Fennell recommendation specified that every nook and cranny had to be sealed off with a fire resistant door, even though most of these little cells are empty and will always remain unused.

These procedures are, of course, a monumental waste of time and money, the typical kind of overkill imposed in the aftermath of accidents by inspectors not versed in the subtleties of risk assessment. These people's energy could be spent much more usefully making contact with the public and helping smooth their journeys. Indeed, Collins says there are negotiations with the fire brigade and the Health and Safety Executive to reduce this burden and release the staff from this task, but such issues are controversial because if the media get hold of them, they would publish scare stories about passengers' lives being put at risk.

Mills shows me the engine room for the escalators, which, again in line with Fennell, is spotless and tucked away between yet another trio of locked doors. There is barely a drop of oil, and what there is drips slowly onto a collection tray in order to minimise the fire risk. The escalators, though, have not been fully replaced since they were installed a cool seventy-five years ago, and the DC motors, lumbering and inefficient but simple and reliable, display plates that proclaim they were built in 1974.

Escalators are one of those emblematic features of the Tube. Their presence – and their failings – seem to characterise everything that is good and bad about the system. They are a wonderful invention, allowing far faster access to the platforms – each has the potential to carry 13,000 people per hour – than lifts or stairs. They have a solidity that exemplifies the engineering skills of the Underground's creators.

Yet they always seem to be going wrong. They are built for a twenty-five-year life and are comfortably capable of lasting much longer. But they do fail and sometimes spectacularly. In 1999 cracks were found in the drive shaft of an escalator, and dozens of a similar design, mostly on the Northern Line, for which no spare parts could be found, had to be taken out of service for weeks, causing some stations to be closed due to safety concerns. The same thing happened again the following year at several busy stations, and in May 2002 fifty-one escalators on the new section of the Jubilee Line had to be shut down, some for several weeks, after a design fault was uncovered which could lead to a sudden stop when the escalator was operating in a down direction – but this time people were allowed to walk down the stalled escalators and therefore stations were kept open. This zeal by the safety authorities may be excessive but has to be understood in the context that the Underground's most recent major accident, the King's Cross disaster which killed thirty-one people, was caused by a fire under an escalator, probably started by a lighted match from a smoker. Given that escalator breakdown causes much more inconvenience than the mere hassle of having to walk up or down the stairs, why, as a *London Review of Books*[1] article asked, 'does it take so long to mend an escalator?', a question repeated frequently by Tube passengers. The answer, as the piece explains, is a combination of the age of the equipment, the fact that they can only be worked on for four hours per day during the closure of the system and the increasing safety requirements. These are factors which dog the maintenance of the whole Tube system.

The escalators at Camden Town were made by Otis and are still serviced by that company. 'We have had a relationship with Otis for eighty years,' says Mills. 'They provide all the engineers who service these escalators. They have people who know our system better than we do. They will normally get here within an hour of being called out.' The PPP, even though it is only 'shadow running', has created a layer of management separating Mills from Otis, as he now has to go through go through the 'infraco' – the infrastructure company for the Jubilee, Northern and Piccadilly lines, which will become privatised once the PPP deal is operating – who in turn call out Otis, but he stresses that 'that does not matter on the ground'.

The use of private contractors has been a feature of the Underground ever since it was built and therefore the debate about privatisation has often started from the wrong premise. It is about the dividing line, the interface as it were, between the private and public sectors, rather than the overall structure of the organisation. Collins recalls that when he first joined the Underground there was a food preparation centre in Croydon which made pies – 'very good they were too' – for all the canteens across the system: 'We made everything, which was crazy because we were in all sorts of businesses that we were not expert in.'

Now things have gone to the other extreme. Since September 1999, the Underground has been 'shadow running' as if it were divided up in the way that the PPP will split it up. In other words (as explained in Chapter 8), there are three infrastructure companies each covering a group of lines, and one operator, London Underground. Of course, the 'infracos', as they are universally called, are still controlled by London Underground, but they have been run as separate concerns since the reorganisation came into effect. This means that the cleaners are controlled by the infracos, who in fact contract out the work, so it is at two removes from operators such as Collins and Mills. And the way they now work is performance oriented rather than defined in terms of a fixed number of hours. Mills explains: 'We can no longer order cleaners to do something directly. It is more hands off. But we can complain to their supervisors at the infraco that the station is dirty, and their company risks a fine if it is below the standards they are supposed to meet.' The cleaners no longer have a specific time at which they must work, but to keep the station clean they may well have to be there most of the day. But it is up to the infraco how the work is run and managed. It is the brave new world of 'output specifications' and 'performance regimes' with which all London Underground's staff must familiarise themselves.

As we head south from Camden Town, I ride in the cab of a Northern Line train down to the Embankment. The trains are new and are full of exciting kit. At each station, CCTV cameras at each end of the platform beam their high quality images directly into the cab, allowing the driver to open and close the doors without leaving his seat, which is on the left-hand side of the cab, even if the platforms are on the other side. The cameras have other safety uses, too, as the driver can spot if anyone has fallen on the track as the train is leaving the platform: 'That has happened a couple of times,' says Peter Neal, the manager in charge of the Northern Line who has joined us for the trip.

The trains still have drivers who actually operate the trains rather than, as on the Victoria Line, built in the 1960s, sitting at the front of the train simply to reassure the passengers, while in reality doing nothing other than opening and closing the doors since the train is controlled automatically. The Central Line, too, has automatic trains which started running without a driver in 2001, but the Northern Line did not have sufficiently modern equipment to allow centrally controlled running: 'It will come in the next few years when the signalling is redone,' says Neal. There are, though, no guards: they were finally dispensed with after years of battles with the unions (see Chapter 4).

The Northern Line trains are the product of another PFI project, one with a patchy record. Instead of buying a precise number of trains, under the £400m contract London Underground specified that it needed a given number of fully operational train sets – initially eighty-six, later to be ninety-six – every morning from the manufacturer, Alstom, out of the 106 provided. At first the contract worked badly and performance deteriorated. The deal highlights the difficulty of transferring risk to the private sector, the key aim of the PPP. When the contract was drawn up, the liability of the contractor, on the insistence of the banks, was capped – reputedly at £20m, though the figure is 'commercially confidential' – which meant that once performance had reached this nadir, there was no incentive for Alstom to improve the service. London Underground decided that rather than trying to pursue the company, it would adopt a softly-softly approach that essentially meant paying extra to ensure the trains were fixed. The story demonstrates that, as we will see several times in this book, transferring risk to the private sector is fraught with difficulties and complexities. Eventually the deal has proved successful – but not in the way originally envisaged, as risk has not been transferred. Collins says, 'even Dick Murray [the *Evening Standard*'s veteran transport correspondent] admits that the Northern is no longer the Misery line [the moniker the paper gave it during the 1990s].' This, again, as we shall see (Chapter 7), is a simpler version of the PPP contract which defines the output not as bits of hardware such as trains or signalling equipment, but in terms of trains per hour or lost customer hours. Again, however, the Northern Line PFI is a much, much simpler concept than the Tube PPP.

So in the corner of the control room for the Northern and Victoria lines at Coburg Street, just next to Euston station, there is John, wearing an Alstom logo on his shirt, who works for the train manufacturer rather than for London Underground. His desk seems to have been punitively chosen, squeezed in between a wall and the line controllers, and Neal says that as with the controllers, there is someone on duty twenty-four hours a day to ensure that faults with the train equipment can be dealt with as quickly as possible: 'Sometimes a driver will just phone up for advice about a fault which he can deal with himself after I have talked to him,' says John. The control room in Coburg Street is not as dingy or cramped as the station office at Camden Town but the technology is much the same. Nevertheless, the Underground is economical on signallers. The whole 36-mile length of the Northern Line is controlled by just four men – 'we have very few women here,' admits Neal – as most of the work is carried out automatically by the computers which set the route for each train as the last one clears the track ahead.

Another journey in the cab of a Northern Line train and a change at Embankment takes us to St James's Park, the station underneath the headquarters at 55 Broadway, that evocative address which should be a theatre rather than a solid art-deco office block housing London Underground's senior management. As you enter the building from the station concourse, you pass a series of archaic brass and glass displays, one for each line, which log the passing of each train on a circular paper graph that is replaced each day. It was a successful 1930s attempt at monitoring performance which, of course, is long redundant but is kept running as a reminder to the HQ staff who pass it every day of the age of the system which they must manage. Here, too, there is a control room, a more modern one which deals with major incidents and distributes system-wide information to the various lines. Amazingly, this centre was only created after the Fennell report into the King's Cross disaster highlighted the lack of such an emergency control centre: 'There was a bloke in a room with a few telephones but nothing else,' says Collins. As ever, the centre is better served than the outposts and the control room is fitted up with the spanking new technology that is so glaringly missing from Camden Town and the other outer reaches of the system. The control centre is really a back-up, ready to spring into action for major incidents that may affect more than one line. On the day I visit, little is happening but it does not take much to show that the system is creaking under the twin strains of age and intensive use. The bald picture is given in the passenger charter figures for each line provided by the Underground. In the year ending 31 March 1998 trains ran 95.5 per cent of scheduled kilometres and this fell to 91.6 per cent in the year to March 2001, rising slightly to 92.9 per cent during the following twelve months. In other words, seven out of 100 trains are not running, excluding those which have to be cancelled as a result of special events and engineering work, at a time when demand continues to rise.

But for the real story of people's day-to-day experience of the system, one has to turn to the pages of *Underground News*, the monthly magazine of the London Underground Society produced for Tube enthusiasts. Each month it has a particularly well-informed section of half a dozen pages outlining every major incident on the Tube that has caused a substantial delay during the past month. There is a story to tell every day, with barely half a dozen entries a year simply noting that the day 'was really uneventful with only mundane matters occurring'.

Take just one day, a bad one admittedly, but illustrative of the way incidents have a lengthy knock-on effect and of the diversity of the causes, with roots both in the failing infrastructure and the day-to-day problems of coordinating thousands of staff.

Thursday 2 May 2002 started badly and was one of those days where virtually every line on the Underground suffered from a disruption. The Victoria Line between Victoria and Brixton did not begin operating until just before 9 a.m. because of defective track at Vauxhall, forcing thousands of south Londoners to find alternatives routes into work. The Metropolitan's furthest extremity, Chesham, was also out of action because of a track circuit failure (track circuits controlled by small currents going through the rails indicate the position of a train and therefore must always be functioning). More seriously, another track failure, where the District Line meets the Circle Line underneath the City, cut off services for over an hour from 10.20, fortunately just after the morning peak had ended. The Metropolitan then entered the evening peak with three separate signal failures all in the open air section and this was compounded by a broken-down train at Baker Street, the heart of the line, at 5.10 p.m. Half an hour later, evening District Line services, which were also being used by National Rail passengers because a fire at Barking resulted in the closure of Fenchurch Street, were disrupted by the failure of a signal at Plaistow. The Piccadilly Line, ever busy in the evening as it serves the West End, joined the fray with three Signals Passed at Danger (which involve resetting the signals and replacement of the driver either immediately or at the next station), a situation exacerbated by crew shortages at Acton Town. This caused trains to be running an hour late in the evening peak and the least used section between Arnos Grove and Cockfosters was run as a shuttle service in order to put more of the depleted number of trains on the rest of the line. And, finally, the Jubilee Line service was suspended north of Wembley Park for an hour from 8 p.m. because of yet another signal failure. Only the Central and the Northern had an uneventful day and most of the problems could be laid at the door of ageing equipment and thus the underinvestment, chronicled in Chapter 3, which has dogged the Underground ever since World War II.[2]

Indeed, that kind of day on the Tube shows just why the need for major investment in the system is not in dispute. It is merely the way that it is being delivered that is contentious. The work that is at the root of the dispute over the PPP largely takes place at night, hidden from public view and consequently ignored. On a dry, cool evening in March 2002, London Transport allowed me on to the track to see the work of these night teams. There were four of us on the visit, including press officer Allan Ramsay and two women from the JNP infraco who were observing work practices.

We meet up at Acton Town, even though the site we were going to was at Oakwood, virtually the other end of the Piccadilly line. But who needs trains at that time of night when it takes just twenty minutes to get to the other side of town. While we wait in one of those bleak, permanently lit rooms that seem to characterise twenty-four-hour offices, I note that the noticeboard reports that the shadow JNP infraco has 'lost' £22m in penalty payments in the first four months of the year. 'Oh, it's got better since then,' one of the women, noticing my interest, says.

At the station there is a clutch of white vans belonging to Transport for London and Cleshars, the heavy maintenance contractors on the line. Groups of men are busily carrying equipment down the short platform stairs. All are wearing bright orange 'hi-vi' waistcoats, the simplest and probably most effective safety measure of recent times, and you can almost tell the length of their service by the scruffiness of these vests.

We are given a safety briefing by Mick, the plump, middle-aged man who is tonight's protection master. In fact, most of the workers are qualified 'protection masters' but Mick takes on the role tonight as the senior man on the job. He has also notified the track access controller back at the Pelham Street centre near South Kensington station, who ensures that the track is clear before allowing the trains to restart. The briefing is short but not perfunctory, clearly taken seriously and not just for our presence as we have not yet been noticed when it is given. Only when we are asked for our safety certificates does it become apparent to Mick that there are visitors to the track tonight. Mick gives the time when we must be off the track, 4.35, and explains where to leave the track should there be an emergency: 'let's all be safe out there,' he says in an expression reminiscent of the famous shift briefings in *Hill Street Blues*.

There are three work sites for the twenty-five or so men tonight. There is a pattern to the work as the three sites represent the different parts of the process of replacing the old expansion joints to create continuous welded rail. Most will be at the first site where the first stage of the replacement of a couple of old-fashioned expansion joints, the joins in the rail which are tapered in order to allow for expansion and contraction caused by temperature changes, is being carried out. This is part of a long-term programme of modernisation, which allows for a smoother ride as the train no longer bumps over the joins, creating that familiar *tagada tagada* noise beloved of railway buffs but loathed by engineers tasked with keeping the trains running, and consequently reduces the cost of maintenance on the wheels.

At the first site work starts with little instruction from Tim, the 'person in charge' who is our host for the night. Almost wordlessly, the gang gets down to work, with the cutters immediately sending a stream of sparks into the night sky, which has already been lit by powerful beams set up on the trackside. Tim's main concern is that the 'new' piece of rail, which is going to be cut to replace the sections with expansion joints, needs to be turned round halfway through the job. That is because it is not a new rail at all, but one that has been previously used on one side which has been worn down by the millions of wheel flanges that have run over it in the past decade or so. The outer side has never been used and is therefore as good as new, and this means that it will be a couple of decades before that section needs replacement. It was previously a left-hand rail, so to fit it onto the right side is easy, merely a matter of heaving it into position, with the help of the little chain pulleys that have been slid along the track from Oakwood station. But getting the other side to make up the new left-hand section is much harder. As all this 'new' rail was previously a left-hand rail which has been cut into two equal halves, it has to be laboriously turned end-to-end. In tunnels, of course, that is impossible and therefore rails have to be shifted to crossovers between the tracks and turned around there. Tim assures us that it is possible to do this, 'sometimes with just inches to spare', but clearly there is a limit to the length that can be handled in that way. Beyond that, the rail has to be taken out of the tunnels, a complex job that involves using battery operated trains. And, as with all these jobs, time always weighs heavy since there is the pressure of knowing that the trains will start running again soon after 5 a.m.

Rail weighs 52 kilos per metre, so the 20-metre length that has to be manhandled is over a tonne of solid steel. Tonight's rail is so long that its ends have to be hauled over the fences carrying the cables on either side of the track and there is a lot of potential for getting fingers or feet squashed under the rail. Mick reminds people, not entirely joking, that 'I am the first aider tonight'.

Tim is quite prepared to get his gloves dirty and jumps over the cables on the side and helps swing the hefty rail round, leading the shouts of 'together, heave' that precede every shift of the rail for a few feet. It takes twenty minutes of lifting and pushing to turn the rail round. The men may mostly be labourers but that does not mean they are unskilled. Their years of experience show through in every move they make and in the quiet coordination that ensures the work is carried out in time and, most important, safely.

The main gang of twenty men was supposed to go on to replace another couple of 5-metre sections of rail, but even though the juice was turned off in time and the work both started promptly and was carried out efficiently, they were not able to do that job. Instead, they had knocked off by 4 a.m., disappearing into their white vans, off to bed. Perhaps, with slightly better planning, they could have done a bit more, but the sheer complexity of working on a long railway, mostly only accessible at stations, means that it will be difficult for the new infracos, with their profit motive at the forefront, to improve efficiency very much. Under PPP, of course, there will be fines of tens, even potentially hundreds, of thousands of pounds if either party overruns its allotted slot – London Underground for operating trains beyond the timetabled hours, the infracos for handing the track back late.

With the rail hauled around, the measurements carefully taken and the cutters and welders working quickly to fit the rail into its slot, we move along a couple of hundred yards to the next site, just four men fitting the new type of expansion joint that is used on continuous welded rail. It is around 3 a.m. and they have nearly finished their work, fitting two new joints on a site where the old type had been removed earlier that week. 'We have to do the whole thing within a week,' says Tim. A gap is deliberately left in the rail to allow for expansion and contraction until the work is completed and that should not be left too long as it is hard on the train wheels.

The third process, being carried out further up the track, so near Southgate station that it would have been much easier to get onto the track from there except that Southgate has escalators which make carrying the equipment harder, is by far the most exciting. It is a veritable firework display, as welding the rail involves cooking a mixture of magnesium, aluminium and iron filings which, when it eventually ignites, rises to a temperature of 2600°C and is poured into a pre-prepared mould. We arrive just as the mixture is about to 'take' and it does so with a blinding flash that Tim warns us not to look at. The work is being carried out by two guys in orange overalls, a pair of highly skilled welders who bear a passing resemblance to the Chuckle Brothers, but their manner, like all the gang, is quiet and efficient. Surprisingly, they do not wear goggles as they send out a stream of sparks to grind the rail down: 'It has to be done to a tolerance of 0.5mm,' the taller of the pair had explained as they waited for the half an hour it takes for the rail to cool down before they can start the grinding process. And at the end of the process, the rail looks so immaculate that you cannot see the join. Tomorrow's commuters will enjoy a slightly smoother ride.

This way of working is unavoidably expensive. In reality the men work productively for little more than three hours, even on a good night. And all sorts of failures or mishaps – a forgotten tool, a breakdown of equipment, a change in specification – can waste the whole night's work.

That is where one of the charge hands, 'John', expresses concern about the PPP: 'Don't quote me on this,' he says, 'but I do have one worry about the PPP. What if they try to make us do that bit extra?' That night his team completed two welds. The three-hour window passes quickly by once the men have walked to the site, set up their gear and, after the weld has been done, ground down the rail. It might just have been possible to do three welds, but would it have led to a botched job? 'Or,' he says, 'what if they try to bring inexperienced people off the streets and get them to do some rerailing? It won't work because they won't know what they are doing.' He is right to imply that there are no easy solutions. The efficiency with which the men took out the old expansion joints, turned one rail round and welded in the new rail was remarkable.

So will the PPP change this work? As we shall see, the PPP does not specify any clear outputs in terms of maintenance work that must be done. This is deliberate. London Underground will not be able to define a work programme to be carried out by the infracos or even tell them to undertake a particular piece of work. Therefore they could halt this type of long-term improvement programme, but the creators of the PPP are convinced that there are enough incentives on improved performance in the contracts to ensure such work continues. And therein lies much of the debate that will unfold in this book.

Clearly, over the years, not enough of these hidden improvements have taken place. This book, therefore, starts with a look at how the London Underground, once the best underground railway in the world, an example universally admired, got into its current dishevelled state.

CHAPTER TWO

Privately built becomes publicly owned

The haphazard geography of the Tube system is all too easily disguised by the wonderful simplicity and familiarity of the Harry Beck map that adorns every Underground station. That brilliant design turns an intricate web of lines strewn randomly across London into a coherent network depicted in those basic colours that resemble those on that equally comforting and familiar representation of the capital, the Monopoly board. In reality, though, the system is a messy jumble of lines with infuriating quirks that are barely fathomable by Londoners, let alone the millions of tourists and out-of-towners who use the Tube.

Why, for example, do trains heading for completely different destinations share the same platforms? I remember a childhood journey with my mother from King's Cross when we suddenly found ourselves in the open air of Royal Oak and, much to my excitement, surrounded by majestic locomotives, the Kings and Castles of the Western Region, instead of remaining in the dark tunnels to reach High Street Kensington. My mother's error was one that continues to be made today by many occasional users of the system who may, understandably, be unclear about the precise location of Harrow-on-the-Hill or Rayners Lane, a confusion that remains even though electronic dot matrix have replaced the crude and dim grey, back-lit signs. Such confusions do not arise on most subway systems in the world, where a line is just that – a direct connection between all the stations on it rather than a lottery in which the odds seem stacked against the right train coming along first.

The Northern Line is undoubtedly the most baffling, for when passengers board at one of its extremities, they face the daunting choice of 'via

Bank' or 'via Charing Cross', places that the hapless travellers may have no intention of visiting, let alone understanding their significance for their journey. There are other curiosities. Why are there two northbound Northern Line platforms at Euston both serving the same destinations with the exception of Mornington Crescent, whose destinees must seek out the platforms for the trains whose provenance is Embankment rather than Bank, as otherwise they will skip directly to Camden Town? The fact that where a train has come from determines whether or not it will stop at an intermediate station must be unique in world railway history and is a source of endless confusion to many Londoners, let alone people from the provinces coming off main-line trains at Euston who make the mistake of plunging into the depths of the Underground station before seeking advice from the staff upstairs.

There are, too, all sorts of odd vagaries on other parts of the system, such as the Circle Line that shares all its stations with other lines, and stubs that serve just one station, such as Mill Hill East and Kensington Olympia. (Sadly but sensibly, Aldwych, a one-station branch from Holborn, was shut in the 1990s.)

The explanation for all these quirks, of course, lies in the chequered history of the system which, quite astonishingly, was built largely – though not entirely, as myth would have it – with private capital at shareholders' risk. As one of the best histories puts it, 'unlike its near contemporaries, the Paris Métro and the New York Subway, financed and planned as a whole by the city authorities, the initial tube network, as a product of private company promotions subject to little or no central government interference, followed no logical plan'.[1]

The history, which cannot detain us too long here, except as a starting point to explain its current condition, is well explained in the huge bibliography generated by the Tube.[2]

A bit of history is, however, also required to illustrate that there has been much greater involvement of the private sector in both the development and the running of the Tube than might be expected, given that the railway performs such a basic public service, and to show the complex and perennially troubled relationship between government, both national and local, and the capital's transport system, a theme which will be familiar to readers of my previous book, *Broken Rails*.[3]

The bulk of the sub-surface lines (as we now must get used to calling the District, Metropolitan and Circle under the Public Private Partnership), were built in the late 19th century, starting with the section of the Metropolitan between Paddington and Farringdon, which opened on 10 January 1863, a mere three years after work started. The line, like its sub-surface successors, was built by the simple expedient of 'cut and cover' – dig a big trench, hopefully in the middle of the road which necessitates less demolition, insert the railway and all its paraphernalia, and cover it over again.

But there was no shortage of complaints, which was hardly surprising given that passengers travelled in the tunnels inside carriages hauled by steam engines. Sure, efforts were made to limit the ill effects, initially by using coke which does not give off smoke but unfortunately emits poisonous fumes so that the locomotives had to be fitted with condensing equipment to avoid having to let off steam in the tunnels. However, the drivers did not always use the condenser because it reduced the power of the engine and therefore the tunnels were, by all accounts, filled with a sulphurous miasma that made the early 'No Smoking' rule rather laughable – not surprisingly it lapsed. The carriages, fortunately, were closed right from the beginning, after tests had shown that open ones made for a nightmarish journey.

Moreover, at first, the service was not reliable, as the historian of Clerkenwell describes: 'For weeks, the stations were thronged with people desirous of riding . . . but the accommodation was somewhat scanty and the dwellers out of town, who desired a quick ride to and from the City, found that they could not depend on the railway.'[4]

Despite this early unreliability and the smoke-filled tunnels, Victorian Londoners quickly overcame their distaste for travelling where previously only sewage had run – indeed, the Prime Minister Lord Palmerston had declined an invitation to the opening, saying he hoped to remain above ground a bit longer – and crowded onto the trains. In the first year of operation there were 9.5 million users, and the following year 12 million, a staggering average of 33,000 per day for just one short section of line.

The service was a joint venture, between the Metropolitan and an existing railway company, the Great Western, which provided the rolling stock and drivers. There was, too, public sector involvement through investment by the Corporation of London, which was anxious to see the line succeed as a way of getting traffic off its overcrowded roads, an argument that has resonance today since the City Corporation is strongly supportive of the proposed Crossrail project which, coincidentally, is also intended to link Paddington with the City. The way the enterprise was funded bears some resemblance to the PPP structure in that it was a genuine partnership between the public and private sectors, but with two important differences: the railway had an integrated structure with track and operations under the same management, and, most important, there was a genuine risk of the shareholders losing all their capital, something which, as we shall see, is highly unlikely in today's PPP. The public element was provided by the City Corporation which subscribed £200,000 in share capital, having generously sold a chunk of the land, the Fleet valley, to the Metropolitan for just £179,000. The Great Western put in £175,000 and the rest, some £475,000, came from civil engineers seeking big contracts in return, and from shareholders of the Metropolitan and of the Great Northern, which connected with the new line at King's Cross.[5]

The relationship between the Metropolitan and the Great Western was strained right from the beginning by the kind of row which is widely predicted for the PPP contracts, as they have all been let to joint ventures between very different partners. According to John Glover, the antagonism between the two companies was so severe that it posed an immediate threat to the future of the line: 'Great Western proved to be an uncertain partner for the Metropolitan. The Metropolitan management was anxious to increase service frequency from the basic four trains an hour . . . but the cautious Great Western objected to the additional working costs.'[6] The pair further fell out over an allotment of shares for the Moorgate Street extension and GWR suddenly threw its teddy bear in the corner by announcing that it would no longer provide the trains after 30 September 1863, a date then brought forward to 11 August.

The Metropolitan, however, proved extremely resourceful in finding replacement trains, not something that would be feasible today. The Great Northern Railway managed to furnish the Metropolitan with sufficient stock to operate the trains, despite the added hassle of having to change gauge since the Great Western trains had used the broad 7ft ½in of its main lines, rather than the 4ft 8½in that became standard throughout the United Kingdom, the Underground and, indeed, much of the world.

Not surprisingly, the quality of service suffered again but quickly recovered thanks to Victorian resilience and the fact that the Metropolitan rapidly ordered a set of locomotives and coaches of its own. The success of the line quickly prompted interest in building others. The Metropolitan District, normally known as the District Railway, created because the Metropolitan did not have sufficient capital to embark on a new project, built a line from South Kensington to Westminster which opened in 1868. Interestingly, it was operated by rolling stock that was bought through hire purchase, not unlike the leasing arrangements which only became standard in the rail industry after British Rail privatisation in 1996–7.

With both railways expanding quickly, within fourteen years of the inauguration of the first section of the Metropolitan, all but one small section – between Mansion House and Aldgate – of what became the Circle Line had been built. The District pressed on westwards, reaching Hammersmith, Richmond and Ealing, taking broadly the shape that the line has today. The Metropolitan headed north-westward, eventually to reach deep into Buckinghamshire beyond Aylesbury, some 50 miles from Baker Street through a combination of construction and amalgamation. The line to Hammersmith from Paddington (Bishops Road), incidentally, was built by the separate Hammersmith & City railway, later incorporated into the Metropolitan, and the shuttle service to St John's Wood and Swiss Cottage, later made defunct by the construction of the Bakerloo, was also a separate enterprise.

The big two, however, were the Metropolitan and the District, and they were engaged in an endless round of battles over issues big and small. Sometimes it was just plain silly. A row over a siding at South Kensington led to a tug of war involving the Metropolitan trying to pull away a locomotive chained to the rails. The Metropolitan banned smoking, while the District allowed it, a matter which, ridiculously, even became the subject of a Parliamentary debate. Another row, over the use of a curve between Gloucester Road and High Street Kensington, was not settled until it went to court in 1903.[7] The most protracted row was over the launch and the operation of the Circle Line, which was never a separate enterprise but a joint venture of the two companies, only partly controlled by legislation.

The story of the Circle provides a diverting insight into how private sector rivals behave if left to their own devices. The idea had been that the two companies would merge and complete the Circle Line together. The two shared several directors until they went their separate ways in 1871, and joining together made obvious sense given the need to operate an integrated service on the line. However, personal antagonism between their chairmen, Sir Edward Watkin of the Metropolitan and James Staats Forbes of the District, ensured that they would remain separate entities. Indeed, as Stephen Halliday explains, it took an enterprising contractor, Charles Lucas, to bring the two together in December 1877 on 'neutral ground at his office' in order to discuss the completion of the Circle.

As with the first section of the Metropolitan, some public money did go into the Circle Line scheme, the City of London chipping in £300,000 and the Metropolitan Board of Works £500,000. So again, even though the construction of these lines is often presented as an entirely private development in the history books, it was, in effect, another Public Private Partnership. Progress was slowed by both technical and financial difficulties and the line did not open fully until October 1884. The agreement was that the Metropolitan would run clockwise on the outer track, while the District would operate the inner track in the opposite direction. As Halliday puts it, 'This apparently harmonious arrangement brought neither peace between the two companies nor an orderly service for passengers.'[8] According to the *Railway Times*, the service was abominable with trains running up to three hours late and one group of passengers even staging a break-out: 'the deluded passengers who have paid their fare make a financial sacrifice and a stampede over the banks in search of some more reliable conveyance'.[9]

With private sector competition being allowed to prevail over common sense in a way that did not even happen after British Rail privatisation, the two companies ran separate booking offices at every station and each encouraged passengers to use its own line, so that people who did not know London's geography were often shamelessly advised to take the long way round.

There was even an arbitrator, a term familiar to the cognoscenti of the PPP contracts. The poor fellow was appointed 'to hear the ripe exchange of insults which characterised the case put by each man [Forbes and

Watkin]'.[10] Sensibly, he told the companies to restrict the number of trains to eight per hour in each direction and allow for a relatively relaxed eighty minutes for the round trip, but each company accused its rival of flouting these rules by running additional trains.

These private companies forever struggled to make a profit sufficient to satisfy their shareholders while trying to build up capital to fund their new projects, but the fact that they survived was testimony both to their enterprise and to the fact that there was a huge market for their services. It is already sufficiently incomprehensible to the 21st-century mind that a sub-surface railway can be built through large sections of London using largely private capital – barring the important contributions from the City and the Metropolitan Board of Works – but it seems even more of a miracle that anyone should have embarked on the building of the deep tube tunnels on the basis of share capital and consequently in the expectation of making a profit.

The first of the deep tube lines was the City & Southwark Subway that was to become part of the Northern. Its construction was made possible by the advent and development of two important technologies, tunnelling using shields to cut through the earth and electrical traction – clearly the use of steam engines was not feasible in deep tunnels since creating ventilation shafts, as with the sub-surface lines, would have been prohibitively expensive. A couple of tunnels had already been cut under the Thames when Peter Barlow, who had, in fact, built one of them, part of an unsuccessful cable railway near London Bridge, proposed the construction of a line between the City, at King William Street, near the site of the current Monument station, and Elephant & Castle, for which parliamentary permission was quickly obtained.

Again, and unsurprisingly, the capital of £775,000 was hard to raise and the contractor had to accept part of his payment in shares but eventually work started in May 1886. By then the developers realised that the line would potentially be more profitable if it extended to Stockwell, and Parliament sanctioned the extra section. Originally the plan was to propel the trains by means of a continuous cable but this proved impractical given the length of the now extended line and the curves, and thankfully electricity was chosen as the motive power. The big mistake – but who was to know without the benefit of hindsight – was the tiny size of the tunnels which continues to dog the system to this day, but larger ones would have been impossible to fund commercially. The legacy is that the Tube is an all too apt name.

The City & South London, as it was now called, opened at the end of 1890 and proved an immediate hit, carrying over 5 million passengers in the first year, despite the underpowered and unreliable electric locomotives and the claustrophobic carriages which only had tiny windows and were forever crowded. However, despite the popularity of the service and its undoubted benefit to Londoners, profitability was poor. Investors received no dividend in the first year and only 2 per cent in the next seven thereafter, the same as they would have received through the safer expedient of simply banking the money.[11] As we shall see, the 21st-century PPP investors are expecting a rate of return nearly ten times that of their much braver Victorian forebears.

The Central, Piccadilly and Bakerloo lines all owed their origins to similar brave – perhaps foolhardy would be a more apt description – developers who managed to attract funding for their visionary schemes. Barlow's innovation had shown that it was technically possible to build Tube lines, but the enthusiasm of potential developers was constrained by the failure of what was the embryonic Northern Line to make money for its investors, and it was not until 1900 that the next line, the Central London Railway, opened from Bank (called Cornhill) to Shepherd's Bush.

Despite the lack of profit, plans to lengthen the City & South London were soon on the drawing board and, through a series of extensions and the replacement of the troublesome King William Street station with a new one called Bank, the line stretched from Euston to Clapham Common by 1907. That year, too, saw the opening of the other section of what was to become the Northern Line. Parliamentary powers had been obtained as early as 1893 but the usual difficulty in raising capital meant that work did not start until 1903. When the line opened, it ran from Charing Cross to Camden Town where it separated into the two branches, familiar to today's users, one terminating at Golders Green and the other at Archway. The fact that the railway was developed separately from the City & South London, and that operations were only merged in the 1920s to create the Northern Line, explains the haphazard arrangements which still prevail today between Euston and Camden Town.

By then, with both the embryonic Bakerloo and Piccadilly lines having opened in 1906, the Tube system was beginning to take shape. And it had already embarked on that tortuous route to integration that is clearly a vital feature of any urban network. The driving force was, oddly, a rather disreputable and licentious American, Charles Yerkes, a stockbroker whose business philosophy was to 'buy up old junk, fix it up a little and unload it upon other fellows'. That clearly applied to his purchase of the ailing District, which he obtained in 1901 through his newly created company, the Metropolitan District Traction Company, with the intention of both electrifying the line and acquiring other underground railways. He quickly bought up interests in the proposed Piccadilly, Bakerloo and Hampstead tubes, creating a new company called the Underground Electric Railways of London. In building up the system he used a lot of the latest American techniques and equipment.

Money, though, was as ever in short supply and constrained both development and rationalisation of the system. An attempt to involve the state was made by the chairman of the Underground Electric Railways Company, Sir Edgar Speyer, and his colleague, Sir George Gibb, chairman of the Hampstead line, in 1906 when the company was facing bankruptcy because of promises made by the now-deceased Yerkes to redeem £7m worth of shares in 1908. The pair offered to sell the company to the London County Council controlled by the Progressive Party, whose leading lights were the famous Fabians, Beatrice and Sidney Webb, but their efforts were to no avail, not least because the Progressives quickly lost power.

Speyer and Gibb reiterated their pleas for government support and subsidy at the opening of the Hampstead line in June 1907. At the launch banquet, attended by David Lloyd George, then president of the Board of Trade, Gibb warned that 'companies could not go on losing money without serious consequences all round'.[12] Speyer also pointed to a failing of the British system of financing railways which remains to this day – the fact that many of the beneficiaries of such developments, particularly the landowners whose holdings are served by the line and consequently rise exponentially in value, pay nothing towards their construction. The easiest way of capturing such benefits is through state involvement, as he stressed: 'While other cities rendered active help in the provision of adequate transport facilities, London stood alone in not assisting, by subsidy or otherwise, the enterprise which provided them'.[13] Speyer was eager for municipal authorities to buy shares to support railway development and for Lloyd George to regulate competition between the railway and bus operators, whose new motor buses were attracting business away from the underground lines. Lloyd George refused to countenance such notions of 'socialistic legislation' to rescue the companies.

So the underground railway companies struggled on without state support. After refinancing itself to get out of the £7m debt, which resulted in a lot of shareholders losing their money, the Underground Electric Railways Company went for more consolidation in an effort to preserve their position. The merger of the three Tube lines, brought together under one management in a subsidiary called London Electric Railways, had certainly reduced costs and it was at least able to pay small dividends towards the end of the Edwardian era. The company, now known as Underground Group and run by the redoubtable Albert Stanley, later Lord Ashfield (another American, although British by birth, and who, oddly, bears an uncanny resemblance to Bob Kiley, Transport for London's commissioner), proceeded to take over both the Central Line and the City and South London Railway (with plans to link it with the Hampstead railway to create the Northern Line) at the beginning of 1913. This meant that its only major surviving rival still operating underground rail services was the Metropolitan which, as we see below, was not to be absorbed until 1933. The Combine, as it became known, also owned extensive tram operations and in 1912 took over the London General Omnibus Company, which was by far the biggest and financially strongest bus operator, having built itself up through several acquisitions during the Edwardian years. The absorption of the buses, which had often run on deliberately competing routes, meant that the Combine had effectively created the entity that was to become London Transport twenty years later.

World War I and the subsequent economic depression inevitably led to more government involvement and, later, indirect financial support. Another big step towards integration of the Combine's various holdings was taken during the war, with the establishment of a common fund-pooling arrangement for revenue through which fares for buses, trams, the Underground and local railways were shared on the basis of a set percentage. Ashfield's strategy was to keep the struggling railway going by cross-subsidising it from the highly profitable buses. However, this did nothing to prevent continued competition from surviving and new independent bus operators and trams owned by London County Council, as well as the Metropolitan Railway, which remained fiercely independent.

London's transport was still, with the exception of the LCC trams, in private hands, but the war had softened political attitudes, with Victorian laissez-faire giving way to a greater readiness to accept a government role. There was, indeed, a Ministry of Transport for the first time. The growing unemployment caused by the end of the post-war boom prompted the government to pass the Trade Facilities Act 1921 which allowed the Treasury to underwrite investment in infrastructure. If only things were so simple today. Lord Ashfield was ready with a comprehensive plan for a series of improvements and extensions to the Underground system which, he argued, would not only improve the lot of London travellers but also provide jobs around the country in steel mills, coachworks and engineering factories. The schemes included extending all the sections of the Northern Line and integrating the services at Camden Town, extending the Piccadilly, electrification of Barking to Upminster on the District, as well as station improvements and the building of escalators. The investment was to be guaranteed by the government on the expectation that it would eventually pay for itself. Of £15m invested between 1922 and 1928, £12.5m was provided by the government.[14] It was in fact another bout of government lending to support employment, the Labour government's Development (loans and guarantees) Act 1929, which enabled the Piccadilly to be refurbished and extended to Cockfosters in the north and to Hounslow and Uxbridge in the west. Thus a pattern was set for major investment schemes for the next forty years with even the building of the Victoria Line in the 1960s being justified on the basis of creating employment.

The continued, albeit limited, competition and the lack of coordination in London's transport remained a source of irritation to Lord Ashfield who, behind the scenes, continued to lobby for an integrated system. Ashfield had long recognised one of the key home truths of railway economics which, even today, many politicians try to ignore: urban transit systems virtually always lose money even when they serve a densely built metropolis like London. As Ashfield put it to the Royal Commission on Transport which reported in 1931: 'It may be a great surprise to you to know that the Underground railways in London have never been, in their whole career, a financial success.'[15] Therefore, state help was inevitable and, with it, the end of the pretence that the Underground could be run as a conventional private company.

It was not, however, until the arrival of the Labour government in 1929 and Herbert Morrison as its Transport Minister that Ashfield's vision of a unified service could become a reality. Morrison put forward the idea of an independent and self-supporting board to run the whole passenger transport system of the greater London area. The legislation was set out in a Bill in 1931 and led to the creation in 1933 of the London Passenger Transport Board (LPTB) as a public corporation which integrated London's entire transport system since the Metropolitan (albeit very reluctantly), the various local-authority-run tram systems and the independent bus operators were absorbed as well. Even the four main-line railway companies were involved through a pooling arrangement of receipts from their London and suburban services, but they successfully resisted the idea of having a common management with the London Passenger Transport Board. As the definitive history puts it, 'Starting from opposed convictions, Morrison the Cockney Socialist and Ashfield the businessman had decided that a single agency was the only answer, and both were sufficiently flexible to adopt each other's approach to make community of view possible.'[16] The relationship between the pair and their ability to overcome their ideological differences is in sharp contrast to today's juvenile spat between Ken Livingstone and Gordon Brown over the PPP.

Indeed, Ashfield probably had the more difficult job in having to persuade his shareholders that the way forward was through public ownership. The compensation terms were generous. Their shares were to be converted to bonds paying a relatively good rate of return of 4.5–5 per cent, although there was no compensation for the years they had suffered low or no dividends. Amazingly, the proposal when published in the Bill in 1931 met with little resistance, since the Depression had softened attitudes about government intervention and, indeed, the legislation was passed with all-party support, the Labour government having fallen long before the legislation passed through Parliament. Ashfield, of course, became chairman of the new Board and Frank Pick, his long-time colleague, its vice chairman and chief executive. The famous pair complemented each other perfectly: Ashfield had demonstrated consummate management skills throughout his long career in transport, with a great ability to make the right decision at the right time, and was well used to moving in lofty political circles; Pick was the backroom boy, shy and reserved but brilliant at administration and getting things done.

This was undoubtedly the London Underground's heyday, a time when its brilliantly simple logo (a term that was unknown at the time) became a universal symbol of a modern, cheap transport system. It is a model to which Ken Livingstone aspires today, as the corporation was not only publicly owned but was able to raise money through bonds and, amazingly, did not require subsidy apart from government support for its borrowing. Investment, prompted again by government support for anti-unemployment measures, led to a host of improvements and extensions, which was spurred on by the coherence of the new system. It was unprecedented, as the definitive history puts it: 'Great plans had been made for the transport of London before; but nothing so comprehensive had been launched with real hope of achievement.'[17] Various anomalies that had been created by the separate ownership structure on the Circle were quickly sorted out, as was the mess at Baker Street on the Metropolitan. Extensions were put forward for all the tube lines, which were to assume, largely, the shape they still have today.

How this was financed is worth a bit of detail, given that raising money is one of the central points at issue in the PPP. In response to the system's enormous capital needs, the Treasury agreed that a finance corporation should be established to raise up to £45m at the best rate obtainable under government guarantee.[18] This meant that the board had the best of both worlds. It could raise money cheaply, but was not subject to the irritating day-to-day Treasury control that is so restrictive and results in bureaucratic delays. And it saved the Board a lot of money compared with having to borrow commercially: 'The interest charge paid on the Board's share of the borrowing[19] (at 2½ per cent) was some £330,000 per annum less than if the money had been raised on the market without government support.'[20] The money was being borrowed, as Ken Livingstone has sought, against future income. The only risk to the Treasury was that if the rate of return were so low that the Board could not service the debt, it would have to stump up the money; but given the high usage of the London Transport system, this seemed highly unlikely. The scheme was noteworthy in that it was not just about expansion of the network, but also about replacing the Victorian and Edwardian equipment which was now well past its use-by date. The scale of the scheme was in the same league as that of the PPP plans, but with the added merit of being planned to be completed within five years rather than thirty – and, had it not been for the interruption of war, that target would have been achieved. As it was, in the event, virtually all the planned work was carried out, either before or after the war.

The Board was a unique construct, a private–public hybrid designed to suit the flavour of the politics of the day. As Stephen Halliday puts it, 'outright nationalisation and direct government control were not yet quite respectable'.[21] The board members were not appointed by the minister as Morrison, the municipal socialist, had wanted, but instead by a committee of the great and good which included the chairmen of a bizarre motley of organisations such as the Institute of Chartered Accountants, the Law Society and the Committee of London Clearing Banks, as well as of one elected body, the London County Council. Although there were still shareholders, they only held shares with a capped (but not, interestingly, guaranteed) rate of return and were not able to hold the Board to account as with conventional companies, as there were no annual general meetings. Yet the strange system worked,[22] and the 1930s were to prove to be London Transport's finest hour, a time when it gained a reputation as the best system in the world, an example for other transit systems to follow. The intervention of World War II and the changes in the structure of transport which came in its wake started the long slow decline of the system that was to lead to the creation of the PPP.

CHAPTER THREE

The roots of decline

It was not so much World War II and the bombing that led to the long, gradual decline of London Underground but more the events in the early post-war years that were to wreak the most damage. The key factor was that London Transport, as the organisation was now called, was not only nationalised but, in the process, lost its independence without much thought having gone into the consequences of the change. Indeed, the war proved to be an abrupt end to the golden period of London Underground not only because of the lack of investment and the system's use as London's biggest air raid shelter during the conflict, but because of the changes to its structure and the lack of investment in the early years of peace.

Given that this was an era in which state intervention and control was seen as the key to a rational future, there was little protest when, rather to the surprise of many observers, London Transport was included in the legislation that nationalised the railways and much of the rest of the nation's transport infrastructure in 1948. The change went almost unnoticed; London Transport's great defenders, Ashfield, who had retired, and Pick, who died during the war, had gone. Thus, instead of the hands-off relationship London Transport had enjoyed with the government before the war, it became just one arm of the British Transport Commission (BTC), which in turn was in the iron grip of the Treasury. When it came to the limited funds available, London Transport not only had to compete with the other investment-hungry parts of the Commission – waterways, long-distance road haulage, and, most significantly, the railways which had suffered much more from the damage and lack of investment during the war – but also with all the other demands on the post-war Attlee government that, by

1947, had become mired in financial difficulties. According to Tony Travers, head of the London School of Economics Greater London Group, it was nationalisation that was to prove the undoing of London Underground and begin its long decline from the Ashfield heyday: 'The problems of London Underground really start with the nationalisation of 1948. From then on, the Tube always had to compete for resources with health and education and it was bound to lose out.'[1]

No longer was London Transport able to raise large amounts of finance for projects through the clever government-backed mechanism it had used in 1933. Instead, now, every item of capital expenditure above £50,000 had to be referred to the Commission. Not surprisingly, faced with such restrictions on investment, London Transport saw buses as a cheaper way of improving transport quickly, through the purchase of new stock and the addition of routes. Therefore it was not surprising that planned extensions, such as the Central's connection to Denham and the line linking the Northern Line's two ends through Mill Hill and out to Bushey Park, and its branch to Alexandra Palace, were scrapped – hence the existence of the funny little single-track spur to Mill Hill East, a real 'middle of nowhere destination' – but something of a miracle that the partly built extensions of the Central, both eastward and westwards, were completed by the end of the 1940s.

Throughout the first fifteen years after the war, the Tube reaped the reward of the generous investment of the 1930s but also paid the price of being so well endowed. Much of its rolling stock was new and operated by the cleanest and most modern form of traction, electrical power; the stations, many having been built or modernised just before the war, still looked new; and the headquarters at 55 Broadway, a solid and deceptively tall 1920s block adorned outside with Jacob Epstein sculptures and inside with those oak panels beloved of the English gentry, gave the impression of an organisation in a healthy financial state and far outshone the BTC's more modest headquarters on the Marylebone Road. Contrast the Underground's situation with that of the railways, bombed and battered for the past six years by the enemy and still mostly operated by dirty steam engines little different from their Victorian forebears, and desperately overused for both military and civilian purposes during the conflict. The national railways inherited by the BTC were in a parlous state with much of their 20,000 track miles in a state of disrepair and at least half the 20,000 locomotives needing refurbishment or scrapping. Given those conditions, the Tube was always going to lose out when the BTC was making its investment decisions. The system that was widely lauded as the best in the world now had to struggle for the resources needed to retain its status. As one of the best histories puts it,

> plans for extensions, new stations and rolling stock were based on the assumptions – wholly rational in LPTB days – that resources would be provided to meet the most pressing needs and that the desired improvements would be implemented. In practice, LT's proposals had to gain the approval of a BTC always mindful of the parlous physical state of BR and of a government buffeted by successive financial crises and grave shortages of capital, labour and materials.[2]

Moreover, the management no longer had the cohesive leadership of Lord Ashfield and Frank Pick to bat for an Underground system whose thirst for capital was near-insatiable. Indeed, the position was made pretty explicit by the Commission. In 1948, in response to a plan to improve London's railways, the Commission said that these schemes could not be regarded as 'directly remunerative or economically justifiable' and that 'if the planning needs of the Metropolis make such facilities essential, the labour and material which will be required must be found from sources additional to those which are at present available to the Commission, and the cost could not be met from their financial resources.'[3] Of course, there were no alternative sources of funding supply, apart from the equally broke local authorities who were in no position to embark on massive investment schemes. Therefore, 'in other words, London's transport needs were seen to be an extra . . . . This explicitly or implicitly remained the Commission's outlook throughout its life'[4] until its demise in 1963.

The 1950s, consequently, were lean years with little money available even to maintain the network, let alone for new projects. The modest pocket-sized London Transport annual reports of that era show the extent to which the system was being run down. The 1953 report, for example, records that 'capital expenditure on the railways, on station reconstruction and other works including signalling modernisation amounted to £0.3m during the year', a staggeringly low sum, although there was one other bit of good news, the completion of the delivery of new District Line rolling stock.

The buses, trolleybuses and trams, which were all desperately in need of renewal and replacement, in contrast, received £5.9m. The 1954 report mentions that £276,000 was spent 'on the provision of passing loops at Wembley Park, to improve the running of the Metropolitan and Bakerloo services and on improvements in signalling', which suggests not much else was spent. Indeed, 'other capital expenditure on stations, tracks and other non-depreciated assets' amounted to £126,000 but this expenditure was more than offset by sales of surplus property which realised £195,000. These sums, tiny even by the standards of the day, were mostly spent on realigning track lay outs, refurbishing stations and the occasional new escalator, but clearly any major schemes to improve the network, or provide new rolling stock or signalling, were out of the question. It got so bad that the reports after 1954 do not even identify new investment. As Halliday points out, in the five years from '1954–9 the value of the Underground's fixed assets increased by less than 5 per cent before depreciation, which demonstrates that the assets were being run down rather than built up'.[5] It was what economists call disinvestment.

As post-war austerity eased, it was the railways which got virtually all the available resources through the massive railway modernisation plan initiated by the British Transport Commission in 1955. Accepted with remarkable haste by the government, it envisaged spending a massive £1.24bn (over £20bn at today's prices) over fifteen years to revamp the railways through the replacement of steam with diesel and electrification, refurbished stations and improved infrastructure. There was, therefore, still nothing available for London Transport.

There was added pressure on resources for the Underground which was to be the start of a continuing trend – competition from cars and congestion caused by them was reducing the viability of bus services that, previously, had been a cash cow for the Tube. As the 1956 report admitted, 'the road services must normally support the railways financially. Historically, they have done so since the early 1920s.'

Moreover, when there was money available, it was spent on rather odd bits of tidying up rather than catering for the masses going through central London. For example, the little-used extension from Epping to Ongar was electrified in 1957 at a cost of £100,000. That decision seems to show a marked lack of judgement on the part of the management who were making the case for investment to the BTC. Not only do relatively few people live in these wilder parts of Essex, but tube journeys from there to central London, with stops every few hundred yards, are nearly unbearable. Even the 1957 annual report which reported the building of the extension admitted that 'traffic on the line is light' and too low to allow through running of the train which would have required even more investment. The extension to Ongar was to be short-lived, as it was closed in 1994, at the third attempt, by London Transport after daily ridership dropped from 750 in 1971 to just 100. Some other more sensible, though limited, work was carried out in the late 1950s, including the completion, twenty years late, of some of the schemes set out in the 1935–40 works programme, such as four-tracking between Harrow-on-the-Hill and Watford, and electrification to Amersham and Chesham.

The annual reports for the period are more interesting for what they omit than for the occasional scheme they list. There is mention of the odd lift refurbishment or escalator installation here, a platform extension or a bit of tunnel relined there, but no suggestion of major refurbishment work on any of the lines. Many discrete improvement schemes were the result of developments outside London Transport's control, such as the redevelopment of main-line stations or new traffic schemes that required changes to entrances and exits. There is no sign in any of the reports of this period of planned maintenance programmes or assessments of future needs.

Moreover, the feeling that public transport's days were numbered underpins much of the thinking of the time. There is constant reference to the growing use of the motor car and passenger numbers were stagnating or, in bad years, falling: 'The authorities, encouraged by the insidious and pervasive road lobby, at first tended to favour roadbuilding throughout the inner area as the sole and final answer to London's transport problems.'[6] The seeds of the decline of the system from which Londoners are still suffering were clearly sown in this decade of parsimony by the BTC. If any period could be identified as the source of the state of the Underground today, it is the immediate post-war period up to the 1960s when, quite literally, nothing was invested. The system has being playing catch-up since then.

The 1960s were definitely an improvement on the 1950s. The annual reports in the early 1960s, while still coyly eschewing giving actual figures for investment, have several pages listing improvements and refurbishment schemes at various stations, suggesting that at least some serious money was involved.

Although the need for new rolling stock was first accepted as early as 1951, it was not until 1954 that LT was in a financial position even to start to consider replacing the pre-1938 stock on the Piccadilly Line; and after prototypes were tested in service, the seventy-six trains ordered started coming through late in December 1959. A further order of similar vehicles meant that a total of 176 trains were built as 1959–62 stock for the Central and the Piccadilly.

This huge order at a time of parsimony demonstrates one of the recurring features of the history of investment on the Underground. The one bit of kit without which services cannot be operated is the rolling stock, and once the old trains reach a certain point of decrepitude, even the most penny-pinching government has to stump up the cash to buy new ones. But the need for new trains distorts the investment priorities and absorbs a disproportionate amount of the money available.

Secondly, another consistent pattern in the history of Tube investment is that, whether privately owned or in state hands, there has always been a tension between growing the system and maintaining the existing one. New lines are sexy and exciting – even more so than new trains with lots of plaques to unveil and ribbons to cut – while there is minimal glamour gained from patching up dingy tunnels in the dark labyrinths of the system or replacing worn-out rails. One of the unique and clever features of the New Works Programme of the late 1930s was that it focused on both renewal and expansion. Interestingly, the PPP focuses entirely on renewal. There has been consistent underinvestment in both existing and new lines, but there has been a tendency to expand rather than consolidate when money has been made available, quite possibly just for the sod-turning and ribbon-cutting opportunities this affords the politicians (though usually the successors to the successors of those who made the original decision to invest, as even small projects like the extension to Heathrow end up taking a good part of a decade). Therefore, long before any of the backlog of investment resulting from the disastrous 1950s period could be made up, most of the new resources available to London Underground were being channelled into the construction of the Victoria Line.

One of the histories of the Tube sums up the decision-making process over the new line with well-merited sarcasm:

> The story of the development of the Victoria from its appearance as Route C in the London Plan Working Party's report of 1948 to the opening of the main stem from Walthamstow to Victoria in March 1969, shows characteristic features of public handling of investment projects in mid-twentieth century Britain: general acceptance of the intention as desirable; delay for argument on constantly changing bases; final approval under temporary pressures which were largely irrelevant to the arguments.[7]

They could have added: constant rows over financing and cost overruns during construction. The line which was extended to Brixton in 1971 therefore took twenty-three years to build from its acceptance as a worthwhile project to the opening of the full line at a cost of £90m rather than the £38m first estimated for a railway that would have gone 4 miles further south to Croydon.

The way that the decision was made to build the line broke new ground in that it was the first time that cost benefit analysis methods were used. This is a methodology which attempts to assess the wider costs and benefits of a project, rather than merely examining the costs and making a crude judgement about whether these are likely to be paid back by the scheme in the long term, and is crucial to the PPP (see Chapter 8). Now de rigueur for all major infrastructure projects, it is, in short, a way of trying to calculate the wider benefits to society of a scheme as a whole by including benefits beyond the purely financial gains. It was, as it still is today, a bit of a struggle to know what to include as a non-financial benefit; so when it was lobbying for the line, London Transport put forward various factors that should be taken into account, such as being able to reduce bus and trolleybus mileage, and relieving overcrowding on the roads and, later, on other underground lines. But the art of cost benefit analysis had only just been developed and it was not until the publication of a study[8] commissioned by the Ministry of Transport which included an examination of the line's wider benefits that the case for investing in it became unanswerable.

The authors of the study found that 35 per cent of the benefits of the new line would go to motorists able to travel faster because of reduced congestion. They ascribed a value of 7s. 6d. (37.5p) per hour to a working traveller and 5s. (25p) to those making a leisure journey and therefore 'the Victoria Line, they triumphantly announced, would give a return on capital of over 11 per cent – a very satisfactory rate of return in that era of low inflation'.[9]

Bizarrely, the fear of growing unemployment was the spur that persuaded the government in 1962 to give the final go-ahead to the building of the Victoria Line, even though by the time work started in earnest, a severe labour shortage was developing and it was estimated that 'shortage of skilled labour extended the original estimate of 5½ years by one year'[10]. Irrespective of the haphazard way in which the investment decision was made, no one can sensibly argue today that London could cope without the Victoria Line – which was the first new line to provide a route through central London since 1907.

In 1963 the BTC was abolished and, in London, replaced by the new London Transport Board, under the direct control of the Ministry of Transport: a far cry from the independent days of the pre-war London Passenger Transport Board. As one history points out, 'in particular, the whole financial framework of the Board's operation had to be approved by the Minister, and any new capital beyond temporary loans had to be borrowed from the Government'.[11] The post-war period is characterised by major changes in the structure and control of London Transport at regular intervals, none of which managed to recreate anything that remotely approached the effectiveness of the pre-war arrangements, and this new set-up was to survive for only seven years.

Under the new regime, which started in 1963, capital expenditure was again itemised and it becomes clear how little was available. That year, for example, out of a total of £17.6m capital and renewals expenditure for both buses and the Underground, nearly £10m went on new rolling stock and the Victoria Line construction, £2.4m on the new Routemaster buses (some of which are still running on the streets of central London at the time of writing, summer 2002), and, with other sundry items, that left just £1.1m for improving stations, track, signalling and depots, a meagre sum even then. The level of capital spending available for refurbishing the existing system changed little over the decade as the Victoria Line ate up virtually all the money available for investment and no attention was being paid to the gradually declining system. Given that nothing much had been spent in the war, by 1970, when there was yet another change of regime with the Greater London Council being given responsibility for London Transport, there had been three decades of neglect.

During the preparation of plans for the Victoria Line, there had been much sound and fury about how the debt would be serviced but this quickly proved to be purely academic. Cleverly, when control of London Transport was handed over to the GLC by the Labour government in 1970, the genial Tory leader of the GLC, Desmond Plummer – whose name still adorns the southbound entrance to the Blackwall Tunnel – insisted that the whole of LT's £270m debt, which stretched back to the 1935 New Works Programme, be written off before he would take responsibility for the organisation. And Barbara Castle, the transport minister who initiated the legislation effecting the transfer, managed to persuade the Treasury to agree to the request.

Local control brought some immediate benefits. With the annual burden of having to service the debt lifted from the GLC and grants available from central government under the new legislation to pay for capital expenditure, LT faced a rosier future than under its previous two regimes. Indeed, the recognition by the GLC that there was an enormous backlog of investment led to the drawing up of a plan to spend £275m over the following twenty years – i.e. increasing annual expenditure on essential renewal more than tenfold – to bring the system back to a reasonable physical state. It was basic stuff with most of the money going on trains (as ever), escalators and lifts rather than the total refurbishment which many stations, now well into middle age, needed. The public did get a few improvements, as the 1972 annual report said: 'The importance of station lighting as a means of updating the appearance of stations is fully recognised and authority has been given for a major increase in expenditure on lighting improvements in 1972 and in subsequent years.'[12] Nevertheless, the work was often lackadaisical: '1980 saw the start of an extraordinarily lethargic scheme to renew the Alperton platforms with their decaying Holden era concrete lighting, signs and fencing . . . for long periods there was no perceptible activity . . . not until October 1986 was all work completed.'[13]

The plan was largely implemented, although not very coherently, and investment expenditure increased steadily but patchily over the fourteen years of GLC control. Again much was absorbed in expansion: the creation of the Jubilee Line (hewn out of one branch of the Bakerloo) and the

Heathrow extension. Surprisingly, the Tory rulers of the GLC were quite willing to see money poured into capital expenditure, although they were very reluctant to pay out any revenue support. Therefore, when the LT chairman, Sir Richard Way, was asked by Horace Cutler, who had replaced Plummer as leader, 'what he needed from the Council in terms of capital funds, Way quoted a figure of £40m; when Cutler agreed at once without demur, Way was clearly astonished and delighted'.[14]

The GLC tended to be ruled by the opposite party to that which was in control in Westminster across the Thames from County Hall and, moreover, throughout the whole history of the organisation from 1963 to 1986, the incumbent party only once retained control of the GLC in an election. As the authors of *Rails Through Clay* put it, 'Democratic control means politics, in practice, the peculiarly black and white domestic politics of Britain in which it is regarded as a sign of weakness to embrace any bi-partisan policy – "if the other side supports it, we shall have to alter it".'[15]

With the rapid succession of changes in political control at both national and local level, the decade and a half of GLC control over London Transport was, therefore, a volatile one characterised by rapid changes in policy: 'Given the will, the new organisation could have been made to work, but power moved into the hands of prickly and flamboyant personalities; small disagreements were allowed to grow into serious quarrels, and eventually the proud new edifices of municipalised LT and then the GLC itself became too much for a Conservative government to live with.'[16] There had long been deep hostility between the GLC and LT, as recalled by Tony Ridley who joined London Transport as its managing director in September 1980: 'There was open warfare between the GLC and LT. It was all over the press and was just appalling.'

Nevertheless, the fact that the state of the Tube was now the direct responsibility of politicians intent on getting re-elected certainly helped boost levels of investment. In 1970, the year that the GLC took over, investment in the Tube was just £14.6m, of which £9.5m went on the Brixton extension of the Victoria Line and rolling stock, leaving just £2.5m for the vital 'other works'. Throughout the 1970s that figure rose steadily. By 1973 the Tube was getting £35m, but again most of that was on the expansion – £11.3m on the Fleet line and £4.3m on Heathrow – and nearly £10m on rolling stock, leaving £10m for stations, signalling and construction and other. By 1979 the figures in the annual reports show that investment in the existing infrastructure at last started absorbing serious money, £30m out of the Tube's total allocation of £80m, most of which was funded by grants from central government.

The downside of political involvement is the short-termism that inevitably accompanies it. This was most compellingly demonstrated by the Fares Fair fiasco of the early 1980s that saw fares yo-yo and resulted not merely in the recasting of the relationship between central government and London Transport, but in the eventual abolition of the GLC. Investment and the long-term needs of the system again took a back seat during this period of political controversy. In May 1981 Labour won the GLC election and the Labour councillors quickly ousted the right-wing leader, Andrew McIntosh, and replaced him with the engaging but highly controversial left-winger, Ken Livingstone. The Labour manifesto had promised a reduction in fares and this was duly implemented, a cut of a third, in October 1981; followed, in a move that was to prove more significant in the long term, by the introduction of a long-mooted zonal system of fares that had been persistently resisted by successive reactionary London Transport managements.

The cut had an immediate impact, boosting the daily passenger journeys on LT buses and the Tube from 5.5 million to 6 million and reducing the number of cars coming into central London. Bromley, a Conservative-controlled outer south London borough with no Tube station, challenged the GLC's right to impose such a dramatic cut in fares because it had increased the level of subsidy raised from London ratepayers by £125m per year. Why, Bromley asked, should our residents be forced to subsidise a system which they do not use? This omitted two key arguments: that many Bromley residents did travel into central London and use the facilities and, secondly, that even those who did not were likely to benefit from the reduction in traffic congestion. Judges, not noted for the frequency with which they use public transport, ruled against the GLC both at the Appeal court and in the House of Lords.

Livingstone and his transport chairman Dave Wetzel, who nearly two decades later returned as chair of London Buses on the Transport for London board under Livingstone's mayoralty, complained that the judgement was political but, after taking legal advice, decided that the only way of complying with the law was virtually to double the fares, leaving them a third higher than when Labour had won the GLC. Passenger numbers on the Tube and the buses quickly fell to 5 million per day and traffic congestion worsened.

Then the issue degenerated into farce. There was a widespread recognition that the fares were now too high, even by the Tory government, which asked the GLC to consult the public over ways that fares could be reduced. In late 1982 the GLC put forward a 'Balanced Plan' which aimed to strike an acceptable compromise between London's transport needs and the ratepayers who had to subsidise the system, with a 25 per cent reduction in fares. But was it legal? London Transport thought not and refused to accept the GLC's order to slash the fares. So Londoners were treated to the bizarre sight of the GLC taking an organisation which it controlled, London Transport, to court over whether the Transport (London) Act 1969 allowed it to use ratepayers' money to subsidise transport. The judges broadly said yes, and the 25 per cent cut was implemented by London Transport in May 1983, pretty much restoring fares to the level of two years previously when Livingstone had taken over. Livingstone's dislike of LT managers is said to date from this episode.

This three-way battle between the local authority, central government and London Transport, with regular interventions by the judiciary, has many similarities to the row over the PPP, not least the fact that Ken Livingstone has been a key player in both. At root, both episodes demonstrate the failure of the British constitution to establish the right balance between the powers of central and local government. Local government has always suffered under the British system from the absence of any devolution of power to the lowest level of governance, and this type of perennial conflict is an inevitable consequence of this lacuna.

The Fares Fair row, which had the effect of lionising Livingstone to such an extent that he was a shoo-in for the mayoral elections a decade and a half later, undoubtedly led to the demise of the GLC. He may have lost in the courts, but he certainly won over the hearts of the people. For the Prime Minister, Margaret Thatcher, who had always disliked the upstarts of County Hall overlooking Parliament just across the Thames, it was the last straw. Bolstered by the 1983 election victory, she pushed through legislation abolishing the GLC and the other metropolitan counties, and, in what was her only nationalisation, took direct control of London Transport. As David Howell, her Transport Secretary, put it in the run-up to the election, 'We are determined that London Transport shall cease to be the political football it has become under the GLC.'[17] If that was a sincere aim, then it has been a heroic failure on the scale of the Maginot Line. Moreover, while it is a refrain also heard from many transport managers, it is wholly unrealistic. While huge sums of money are poured into public transport systems and while transport remains a vital part of the infrastructure, politics will always be involved. And so it has proved.

The fourteen-year rule of the GLC was by no means all bad. Indeed, local control has a positive side as it means that politicians can be held to account for the poor state of the infrastructure. The authors of *Rails Through Clay* summed up the achievements of that period:

> The GLC had a useful role as a catalyst in the Heathrow extension, the Jubilee Line and the long deferred modernisation of lifts and escalators. Without the bold reductions achieved in 1981 and 1983, it is doubtful whether London could have escaped into the zonal structure from the graduated fares rut so long inhabited by the 55 Broadway hierarchy. That in turn led to the popular Travelcards and a consequent healthy increase in Underground traffic.'[18]

However, one failing of the GLC was that the fares fiasco so dominated London politics for two years that the issue of investment was left on the back burner. Indeed, this highlights a wider dilemma of political control, in that transport is unsuited to decisions dictated by the necessarily short-term considerations of politicians who always have one eye on re-election, because it takes longer than a single term of office to bring about changes that the electorate will notice.

In 1980 investment had been £78m on the Tube and the annual reports had stopped breaking the figures down between spending on the existing system and on new lines. By the last year of GLC rule, this had grown to £240m for both buses and the Tube – now lumped together in the reports – and a significant chunk was absorbed by the construction of the new Docklands Light Railway. In fact, the DLR, initially conceived as a cheap and cheerful little railway, costing just £77m at its creation, grew into a more complex network, linking both the Isle of Dogs and the as yet undeveloped Royal Docks in deepest east London with a new tunnel through to

Bank station. Consequently, during the 1980s and 1990s, it absorbed increasing levels of capital in an unplanned and unexpected way, ending up costing over £1bn in today's money if the Lewisham extension (opened in 1999) is included, and a small proportion of that investment came from local landowners. Although the ownership of the DLR changed over the years as it was passed back and forth between government and London Transport, the funding represented an opportunity cost for the Underground. In government eyes, what was spent on the DLR came out of that compartment marked 'London transport' with a little 't'.

One obstacle to examining the investment pattern over the years is the way that the accounts published by London Transport change over the years. Sometimes the Underground and buses are put in all together, at other times how much investment is going on new lines or into the existing Tube is not made clear, and for a period only one outline figure was provided. These changes suggest, if one is of a Machiavellian turn of mind, that LT, or rather its political masters in the Treasury, deliberately tried to obfuscate in order to hide the paucity of capital spending or, more prosaically and more likely, they failed to understand the importance of long-term investment in the Underground. There is no doubt, as this chapter has shown, that throughout the forty-year period between the end of the war and the renationalisation of London Transport by the government, most of the Underground network suffered consistently from disinvestment. Like the National Health Service, the Underground changed from being the world's most admired system to one that was viewed in Europe and elsewhere as part of Britain's failure to come to terms with its loss of Empire and its pre-eminent role in the world.

Thanks to the dithering over the Victoria Line, followed by equally damaging delays over the Jubilee Line Extension, Thameslink 2000, the East London Line and Crossrail, London is effectively two lines behind what would be a sensible rate of growth on rational economic grounds, based on increasing population and prosperity, as well as on the rise in central London employment. The investment in the existing infrastructure can be looked at in a similar way. In a rational world, investment would have returned to pre-war levels much more quickly in peacetime, rather than the system suffering from lack of investment for thirty years.

There was one important mitigating factor for this lack of investment. The contemporary view of most transport and planning 'experts' was that the use of public transport would continue to decline in the face of competition from the car. It was only with the rejection of the proposed motorway rings by Londoners who voted in Labour, which had stood on an explicit platform of abandoning plans for the new roads, at the 1973 GLC elections that policy makers began to recognise that cars must be restrained and not encouraged in city centres. Passenger numbers, which had long hovered around 600 million per year, already a significant drop from the 720 million of 1948, fell to below 500 million in 1982 as a result of the fares increases and the recession. Nobody predicted that, thanks to the 25 per cent fares cut, a booming economy, the nightmarish conditions on the roads, and (as we shall see in the next chapter), better management of the system, they would almost double over the next twenty years, thus creating a whole different set of problems, most notably the need for even more investment.

Thatcher was in such a hurry to take over London Transport from the GLC that a Bill was introduced in the first session of the new Parliament after the June 1983 election and became law in time for the takeover to take place at the start of the 1984–5 financial year. The irony was that while Mrs Thatcher was busy privatising all the other state-owned industries such as BT, and later gas and electricity, she had just taken back London Transport into government ownership with no intention of selling it off despite the clear management problems outlined in the next chapter. Of course, Thatcher's decision to control London Transport directly, which went against the thrust of her privatisation policy, had nothing to do with improving the lot of its passengers, but was part of her ongoing battle against Labour-controlled local government. The nationalisation of London Transport was another step in the politicians' restless pursuit of an ideal form of organisation for London's public transport – a task that dates from the creation of the Tube, has gone through a dozen versions and will remain unresolved by the 'responsibility but no power' structure envisaged by the PPP.

Out went all Ken Livingstone's appointees to the board of London Transport, and in came a group of executives appointed to run the organisation, now renamed London Regional Transport, though still known to the public as London Transport. Ostensibly, it could have been a powerful pan-London authority, but, as ever, the Treasury did not allow it a free rein and it was to be subjected to all the same type of interference as its predecessor. The ethos had to change, too. The era of 'London Transport does everything', from making its own pies at its factory in Croydon to all the heavy engineering of its trains, was, at last, beginning to be challenged. The role of the Acton Works, where trains had undergone both minor and major servicing, was re-evaluated, as a study found that most of the maintenance was overpriced when compared with outside contractors. This led, eventually, to much of the work being spread out to individual line depots. Engineering was divided into 'client' and 'contractor' functions so that contracts could be let out competitively to the private sector. Indeed, for the first time, under the Act, London Underground had to seek competitive tenders for all major work.

The attempt to begin to break up the huge London Transport monolith into bite-size chunks was a recognition that while the systematic lack of investment over a long post-war period may have been the primary cause of the Tube system's decline, the deterioration was exacerbated by the lack of any coherent management system. That became all too apparent in the events that led to the King's Cross disaster and the consequent inquiry, described in the next chapter.

CHAPTER FOUR

An accident waiting to happen

Arriving at London Underground in 1980, Tony Ridley found an organisation which had all the hallmarks of a poorly-run nationalised company. In these days of overcrowded Tubes it is difficult to envisage that, at the time Ridley started his job, the Underground was declining and, indeed, in 1982 reached its nadir of 498 million passengers in a year, half today's total. The recession of the early Thatcher years had speeded up the decline, bringing passenger numbers down to a post-war low. That decline, which apart from a few peaks during economic boom years had been pretty consistent since the 1970s, was caused primarily by competition from the car and the outflow of jobs from central London, but exacerbated by a deep malaise within the organisation whose management seemed to have lost all sense of purpose.

The organisation was characterised by managerial extravagance at the top and sloth at the bottom, with both layers showing such lack of concern about the public's money that corruption seemed institutionalised. Leslie Chapman, a senior civil servant who had written a highly critical best-seller about Whitehall[1] and who was brought in by Horace Cutler, the Tory GLC leader, to impose private sector discipline, highlighted outrageous excesses of the top management in a report produced at Cutler's behest. London Transport executives were running no fewer than twenty-six chauffeur-driven limousines because, as Cutler put it, 'obviously people running the buses knew they were too inefficient to risk using them themselves'.[2] The chauffeurs' bills alone came to a total of £160,000 with the cars costing another £400,000, at a time when the organisation was supposed to be trying to cut costs. Chapman also highlighted the arrangements for the next tiers down, the 'officers' whose 'dining club' on the second floor of the elegant 55 Broadway building received an annual subsidy of just under £55,000, more than half the cost of the meals, and which Chapman called 'the most affluent luncheon club in London'. The officers' salaries were not excessive but Chapman noted that senior staff were rewarded by very expensive index-linked pensions.

At the bottom, the corruption was pettier but widespread. 'Martin', a long-time LU manager who still does consultancy and therefore wishes to remain anonymous, arrived at Maida Vale as a naive young station assistant: 'There were lots of scams – for example, shutting the station early – and you knew what pub the booking clerk would be in. I was told not to cheat too much: "No one minds if you take the price of a packet of fags, but don't overdo it." In other words, it was official. The important thing was not to rock the boat.' A set amount was expected to be paid over from the barrier taken from people like me who, like all London children of the time, gave a few pence to the ticket collector mumbling the name of the previous station down the line, and the rest was seen as a bonus on the admittedly low wages.

Some ticket collectors created a whole enterprise out of siphoning off London Transport funds on a regular basis. Another former manager recalls how one woman worked the exit ticket barrier at Baker Street, using her seniority to ensure she always obtained that duty. Indeed, it was so lucrative that she never went on holiday – a fact that proved to be her downfall. A relief station manager wondered about her lack of interest in time off and became suspicious. A police raid on her home uncovered piles of money scattered through her house. She had so much cash that she did not dare bank it and could not even spend it, and was almost relieved to be caught. Another ticket collector made the mistake of dying, and when his locker was broken into, it was found to be full of unopened wage packets with cash inside. He had lived entirely off the proceeds at the barrier.

Martin discovered the corruption was not just at the station level and was clearly systematic and widespread. In the early 1980s he was stationed at Watford at the end of the Metropolitan Line branch, the sixth least used station in the network, as most people use Watford Junction which has much faster trains to London. Because of a BR strike, Martin was suddenly faced with 600 people getting off each train, all needing to pay an excess fare as they were BR rather than LT season ticket holders. He recalls: 'There was money everywhere, on the stairs, among the tickets – they were just throwing it at me. On the first day, I collected £400. The following day, three ticket inspectors arrived and I was very suspicious of them. There were even more passengers but they paid in just £100 between them.' The next day Martin phoned the chief ticket inspector and made it clear that he was not to send the inspectors along again: 'That type of thing permeated the company. It had bureaucratic systems introduced in the 1930s and nothing had changed. No one was prepared to look at it and say, we need to change.'

The corruption was so widespread that it must have had a significant impact on the Underground's ability to invest, both by significantly reducing the fares income and through wasting a lot of money when work was undertaken. Another former London Underground manager recalls how when the lighting was renewed by the works department at 100 Petty France, the bill was for six floors when, in fact, there were only five.

Ridley, a man who wanted to make a difference, therefore struggled for nearly the whole of the 1980s with a culture that was so inimical to change: 'I found an organisation full of very loyal, very long-serving people who tended to believe that no one outside LU had anything worthwhile to say about how to run it even though the ridership had been declining for thirty years. They were insular but, in their own terms, very devoted and competent. However, they were not politically adept and failed to recognise that things had to be done dramatically differently.'[3] The Underground's problem was not so much bad management as a complete lack of it. There was a sloppy approach which contributed greatly to the decline of what had been the world's best and biggest metro system. One perennial problem was low pay among managers, which, according to Stephen Glaister, a former member of the London Transport board and now on Transport for London's board, 'was a result of Treasury refusing to allow London Transport to pay market rates for managers'.[4]

The relationship with the unions was key – and remains problematic to this day, as we see later. Ridley was bemused by the way that negotiations never got anywhere and how decisions were not implemented. Ridley felt it was a conspiracy between the management and the unions because negotiations 'just went on and on without ever getting anywhere. The annual wage round was sorted out, because it had to be, but agreements about improving productivity and performance never came to fruition.'[5] Ridley once asked a senior rail union official why negotiations foundered all the time: 'Charlie,' Ridley said, 'I can't understand how you can stand this. I've only been at it for twelve months and I'm bored to my back teeth – how do you stand it for thirty years?' The man replied: 'Let me tell you a story that old Sid Greene [a former leader of the National Union of Railwaymen] said to me when I was young. He said, "Charlie, if you've got a problem, don't solve it too quick, you will only get another couple of the buggers."' As Ridley puts it, problem solving was not part of the agenda – the idea seems to have been to keep both unions and management occupied as long as possible. Ridley continued, 'These were not evil men, they were not wreckers. They were just locked into a system where achieving things other than just keeping things going was not part of their agenda, both in the management and in the unions. However, they did keep the thing going with minimal money through thick and thin. They worked their balls off within the limits of their resources.'

Not always. The waste was legendary. Martin recalls calling in the building department to repair dripping taps in the mess room at Watford: 'This guy turns up, demanding a cup of tea, and then spent five minutes repairing the cold tap but he refused to do the hot one. "That," he said, "is for the gas fitter. More than my job's worth to touch it."' The stopcock needed to be turned off and the man would not do that. And when Martin offered to do it, the man said he would have to report that as it was against the rules. According to Martin, 'the rules had been laid down in an agreement twenty years ago and that was that'.

Horace Cutler recounts getting a letter in the late 1970s from a fitter at Acton Works, which at the time employed 1500 people, who described it to him as a kind of workers' holiday camp: 'The lowest rate of pay for an unskilled labourer is now £100 per week plus, for five eight-hour shifts. Although we clock on for forty hours, we only actually work fifteen hours – the rest of the time is taken up in one-hour tea breaks, washing-up time and a siesta on Friday afternoon. As part of a sick scheme, we are allowed up to three days off per month on full pay without medical certification. We get five weeks annual leave.' The management, he told Cutler, 'was afraid of the communist shop stewards who are allowed to sit in the canteen all day.'[6] While Cutler could hardly be termed an impartial source, the overall picture of life in the outer reaches of London Transport was confirmed by several veterans of the organisation. As John Self, who joined as an apprentice in the 1960s, put it: 'it seemed like it was a place that was going to be there for ever'.[7]

The key to making progress with the unions, Ridley was told, was one-person operation of trains because that would open up the way to significant improvements in productivity and show that change was possible. Ridley found that 'there was an agreement signed between the management and the unions seven or eight years ago to take guards off the trains but it had never been implemented because it was all too difficult'.[8] Ridley achieved that aim with eight out of ten lines being one-person operated by the end of the 1980s – the other two, the Northern and Central, had to await new trains. There were a number of strikes on the way, including one where the unions called out the whole workforce over the issue of removing guards on the seven-station East London Line which had only a handful of trains. Ridley knew he had won that dispute when over half the staff turned up and the rail union leader Jimmy Knapp rang him early in the afternoon to say, 'I'm going to do one of the most difficult things I have ever done in my life, I'm going to call off the strike.'

The lack of managerial control was felt keenly throughout the organisation. Martin recalls that there been 'no sign of management' when he joined in 1979 and found the training – which, as we see below, was criticised strongly in the report on the King's Cross disaster – to be cursory in the extreme: 'I was trained to be a station foreman – a bit about tickets, stations, operations and emergencies – but none of it was relevant. It had not changed since the 1920s and none of it was relevant.' It consisted of a bit of chalk and talk, and then a cheery 'Get on with it, lad'.

While Ridley had begun to make some headway in tackling the worst ills of the system, he was hampered by continuing industrial relations problems, and the need for increased productivity was reduced by the burgeoning post-recession income due to the increased patronage which masked significant wastage. Indeed, London Underground's most blatant inefficiencies might well have survived much longer had it not been for the fact that they resulted in rather more serious consequences than lost revenue and wasted wages. On 18 November 1987, at 7.45 p.m., fortunately after the evening rush hour, a smouldering fire underneath the Piccadilly Line escalator at King's Cross exploded into a fireball that killed thirty-one people.

The accident and the subsequent report[9] by Desmond Fennell QC forced upon London Underground changes within two or three years which might otherwise have taken a couple of decades. The transformation was long overdue, as the circumstances of the accident and Fennell's trenchant criticism illustrate. The account of the way the fire was allowed to develop and, eventually, turn into the fireball and flashover that killed those thirty-one people remains truly shocking to this day, an indictment of the way that the once great London Underground had decayed throughout the post-war period. Its relevance to the story of the PPP and the politics of today's Underground is that the failings of management which the accident highlighted inform those who want to remove control of as much as possible of the system from the public sector, which clearly failed so miserably in the run-up to the King's Cross disaster.

The fire was probably caused by a lighted match from a smoker: although smoking had been banned in the system, it was not properly policed and passengers had got into the habit of lighting up, after their enforced period of abstinence on the train, while standing on the escalator taking them out of the station. Technically, apart from in trains and in lifts, smoking was banned where 'no smoking' notices were displayed, and since there were none on the Piccadilly Line escalators, the person whose cigarette started the fire had not been in breach of the law. This opaque state of affairs was the result of a long battle between supporters and opponents of smoking, and Ridley recalls that 'I took enormous flak in banning smoking on the trains and a complete ban was out of the question.'[10] Indeed, at one point, when his namesake, Nicholas Ridley, a man virtually never seen without a cigarette, was the Transport Secretary, there had been talk of reinstating smoking on trains.

An illustration of the way that sloppy management led directly to the disaster was the state of the area underneath the escalators. The corridors and vaults had fallen into disrepair, and old equipment and rubbish, much of it inflammable, had been allowed to accumulate. By chance, Martin carried out a safety inspection of the area underneath Highgate escalators, a mere half-dozen stops up the Northern Line from King's Cross, just a couple of weeks before the disaster: 'I could not walk across from one side to the other as there was so much junk – coils of cable, old oil cans, rags and so on. It was a complete mess. And there, in the middle, its metaphorical legs in the air, was a spent fire extinguisher.'[11] Martin took photos and rang the safety rep, saying he was worried about the state of Highgate station. He was told: 'I've been banging my head against the wall about this sort of thing and nothing can be done.' The escalator underneath King's Cross, like many others around the system, had accumulated a dangerous mix of grease, grime and discarded smoking materials which was to feed the fire. There was a lack of responsibility – the staff felt it was up to the contractors and yet did not even know what company was involved. As Fennell put it, 'the client-contractor split was not properly established at the time of the King's Cross fire and the lift and escalator engineer said that he did not succeed in monitoring escalator cleaning standards to his satisfaction or have enough staff to do so'.[12] As we shall see, the management of the client-contractor interface is probably the fiercest source of controversy in the PPP debate.

The fire had started around 7.25 and was noticed within five minutes by a passenger who reported it to a booking office clerk, who was, like the vast majority of his colleagues, completely untrained in emergency procedures. The clerk rang relief station inspector Christopher Hayes who went to investigate the incident. As Denis Tunnicliffe, who became managing director in succession to Tony Ridley,[13] cruelly put it, 'the report shows that the supervisor looks down at the flames, and says "yes", but does not do anything'.[14] According to Fennell, Hayes did not inform either the station manager or the line controller but merely told a couple of police officers whom he bumped into. He failed to operate the water fog equipment which had been installed precisely in order to mitigate escalator fires. The system had been introduced soon after the war but had fallen into disuse because water spilled when it was checked, damaging the escalator equipment. Fennell points out that Hayes was 'unprepared by training and experience to take charge of the incident'.[15] He was hampered, too, by the lack of an evacuation plan. It was hardly surprising that the response of the staff was 'uncoordinated, haphazard and untrained'[16] according to Fennell.

Indeed, virtually no one at King's Cross tube station on the fateful night had received any relevant training. According to Fennell, 'only four of the

21 staff on duty said they had had any training in evacuation or fire drills'.[17] This was part of a wider phenomenon within London Underground, the promotion of people by Buggins's turn. Only 5 per cent of management posts were ever advertised externally and appointments from outside were extremely rare. As Tunnicliffe explains, the railway was run by a hierarchy of supervisors, all promoted on seniority, right to one or two levels below that of the senior management: 'I am not saying they weren't honourable people, but they were all locked into a tradition of seniority promotion and there were no real standards and very limited training.'[18] Fennell was shocked by the lack of training and skills among people in senior positions and by the way talented people were prevented from fast-tracking up the system: 'Very few staff failed the training course which qualified them for promotion after a given length of service. Conversely, there was no means for anyone who was talented and ambitious to be promoted before his qualifying period.'[19] Training, as Martin confirmed, was a lot of uninspiring chalk and talk and question-and-answer sessions, the content of which had not changed in years.

Fennell, in his most damning sentence, said that this ethos had created 'a dangerous, blinkered self sufficiency which included a general unwillingness to take advice or accept criticism from outside bodies', which, incidentally, included the London Fire Brigade whose suggestions for improvements after earlier incidents had been consistently ignored.

Staff were supposed to be regularly tested on their knowledge of emergency procedures but very few of those who failed to answer questions correctly were sent for retraining. Not only were staff untrained, they often simply weren't there. There were supposed to be five staff working in the tube hall at the top of the escalators on the night of the fire, but in fact there were only two. The evidence to the inquiry from leading railwoman Kathleen Ord revealed a culture of lackadaisical management stretching throughout the organisation: 'On this shift, I usually go for my meal relief from 19:00 to 20:30. I know I am only supposed to have a half hour meal break but it has been an accepted practice since I have been at King's Cross for the ticket collectors to take 1½ hours on late turns only. As far as I know, all the ticket collectors take this amount of time, apart from Mr Wood who only takes an hour.'[20] The fifth ticket collector who should have been on duty had been given permission to go to hospital and, after her visit, had been told by Hayes at 6.30 p.m. that evening not to bother turning up for duty even though several hours of her shift remained. Fennell, incidentally, rejected the notion that if these people had been on duty, the disaster would have been averted, because none of them had proper training. Nevertheless, he highlights the issue because of the way it reveals lax management practices, and insists that the unlucky individuals who happened to be on duty that night should not be blamed for what happened: 'I have said unequivocally that we do not see what happened on the night of 18 November 1987 as being the fault of those in humble places.'[21]

This sequence of error and inaction was damningly summed up by Fennell: 'Between 19:30 and 19:45, not one single drop of water had been applied to the fire which erupted into the tube lines ticket hall.' As a result, lots of people, including a fireman, died needlessly as they were allowed to wander towards the fire, or, as in the case of the poor manager of the bureau de change in the tube hall, were simply forgotten about when a decision to evacuate was eventually made.

At the root of all these failings was the management's attitude towards fires – or 'smoulderings' as, Fennell witheringly notes, managers insisted they should be known. This was all the more striking since there had been earlier fires with relatively serious consequences. The most worrying had been a fire at Oxford Circus in November 1984, just under three years before the King's Cross disaster. According to London Transport's 1985 Annual Report, 'the northbound Victoria Line platform at Oxford Circus station was devastated by fire, with considerable damage to other areas of the station. The cause of the fire was still being investigated; one possibility is that a discarded cigarette started the fire in a contractor's store. It was necessary to escort over 700 passengers from halted trains through the Victoria and Bakerloo line tunnels to adjacent stations.' Although fourteen people, mainly staff, suffered from the dense smoke, all but one were released from hospital the following day. Despite the fact that it was clearly a serious incident, the lessons were not learnt because fires were seen as an inevitable hazard of running such an old metro system. In fact there had been forty-six escalator fires on the Underground from 1956 to 1988, two thirds of them caused by smokers' materials. Only a minority resulted in an inquiry by London Transport, and even in cases where one was held, the resulting recommendations were mostly ignored or not implemented.

Since no one had been killed in these fires, London Underground believed that there would always be time to evacuate people safely, because the passengers themselves acted as fire detectors. Fennell highlighted the fatal complacency: 'It was a matter of some concern to me that the directors of London Underground should still subscribe to the received wisdom that fires were an occupational hazard on the Underground.'[22]

Worse, in Fennell's eyes, the management, in particular Ridley, defended that attitude at the inquiry: 'Dr Ridley did not feel able to agree with the Court that fire should be regarded as an unacceptable hazard to be eliminated, since it was considered that fires were a part of the nature of the oldest, most extensive, underground railway in the world. It was seen as unrealistic to believe that any increased effort by London Underground could get to a position where there were no fires on escalators.'[23] Ridley even argued that had he known how many fires there were on the system – which he had not prior to King's Cross – he would not have acted differently. Ridley's attempt to defend his approach to the inquiry was to prove his undoing and he resigned three days after the report's publication in late 1988, although the board urged him to stay. Ridley now admits that London Underground's failure was in not having 'a risk analysis of the operation of the total system, which is in a sense thinking the unthinkable',[24] a point made repeatedly by Fennell.[25]

Fennell found that a fundamental problem of London Underground management was that it had long been run as a series of baronies by the engineers. The chief civil, mechanical, signal and electrical engineers were the four barons who called the shots. The operational staff were perceived as being a rung below the engineers who had what Fennell called 'a proprietorial interest' in the railway. The demarcations between these disciplines meant that important issues fell into the interstices and were neglected or forgotten. Moreover, the operations director did not concern himself with engineering matters such as the state of the escalators.

Further, there had been an overall lack of attention paid to the Underground's assets. Sure, there had been a shortage of money for investment, but even when assets were bought, they were neglected. According to Tunnicliffe, who joined London Underground as managing director in 1988, it had not only been the lack of money which ensured that the condition of the system had been declining throughout the whole post-war era.

It was also, he said, the lack of attention paid to managing the assets: 'There was a tendency to buy something and then ignore it. The Underground had been decapitalised for three decades.'[26]

Fennell's devastating conclusion on the state of London Underground management would, inevitably, force the organisation to change. While he recognised that Ridley had tried to change things, only a fundamental transformation would do. As Fennell put it, 'the old idea of the engineers running a railway must be replaced with a recognition at all levels of the responsibility of providing a mass passenger transport service for the public'. Martin does not use such diplomatic language: 'Ninety per cent of what happened at King's Cross was down to bad management, not lack of money. It was not deliberate arrogance, but it was arrogance nonetheless. The disaster showed that London Underground was twenty years behind in safety and management, with no clear vision.'

Arriving in the aftermath of such a traumatic event, Denis Tunnicliffe had a strong hand when it came to insisting on change and took Fennell's recommendations as his starting point. His focus was 'ownership': 'There was no ownership, no love or care. Nobody who operated the railway felt that at any time they owned it.'[27] Tunnicliffe was a desperately needed breath of fresh air. According to one insider, 'Denis was probably the best manager in Britain to do what needed to be done, which was to be a change agent. He had to manage a culture of change which put safety uppermost and start to look at the huge process of renewing the infrastructure which was necessary. Tunnicliffe was exciting, engaging and creative, as well as outrageous, irritating and frustrating.'

Together with Wilfrid Newton, the chairman who had been recruited from Hong Kong, it was an impressive act, with Newton as the father figure controlling Tunnicliffe's excesses but allowing his creativity to flourish. Newton had been highly successful in Hong Kong, where he had run the mass transit system, and brought not only operational experience but an ability to lobby strongly for the system, which undoubtedly helped the Underground obtain increasing amounts of investment during his period as chairman that ended in 1995. It was a good team: not perhaps in the class of Ashfield and Pick, but nevertheless, for the first time in a long while, London Underground had strong leadership and a powerful case for additional resources to ensure that King's Cross did not happen again.

Tunnicliffe describes what he found at London Underground as a 'happening'. It was impossible to track down the managerial process which ensured the trains came out of the depot every morning, but since they did, there must have been one. He did not want a 'happening', he wanted a managed process.

The worst examples of the absence of clear management objectives were in the depots. According to Tunnicliffe, 'We had skilled and semi-skilled people working on trains during the night, and skilled people during the day, under separate management structures. So a train would come in and the semi-skilled people would work on it and if it did not work by the morning, it did not go out. Then the skilled people would clock on and go for breakfast while the supervisors decided which trains to work on. Meanwhile the train stayed in the depot during the peak hours and nobody was arranging to get the sick train to the depot at the right time with a plan of work.'[28] He reorganised the whole system, creating six-person multi-skilled teams which radically improved productivity.

Tunnicliffe was a man in a hurry and quickly took the idea of 'centurions' from a former colleague at British Airways: managers who were in charge of around 100 staff and the associated infrastructure. Despite doubts that sufficient people could be found to fill 140 centurion posts, a wide variety of people ended up in these jobs, ranging from former secretaries and guards to more conventional management recruits. Below them was a newly created system of duty managers to recognise the fact that the Underground needed to be staffed 168 hours per week. To improve the sense of ownership, a system of individual management of all ten lines was created: 'I had this vision of a man – or indeed a woman – in a top hat standing at a station and seeing how their passengers were getting on. We didn't entirely succeed but we got a lot of ownership.' None of it was rocket science, but it was new to London Transport.

The response from the unions was predictable, with a series of fourteen one-day strikes in 1989. Tunnicliffe remains bemused to this day as to what they were about: 'We never quite got to the bottom of the reason, but as far as we could tell, it was caused by the commitment to manage the business, rather than just letting it drift.'[29]

Tunnicliffe's crowning achievement was the 'Company Plan', a radical attempt to refocus the business. He realised that piecemeal change would not work and that the shock of the King's Cross disaster gave him an unprecedented opportunity. He hired a consultant, a former contact at British Airways, John Loehr, who suggested that the whole organisation should be overhauled through a series of 'value analysis' teams. Behind the management jargon, there was a serious and radical idea. Thirty teams of around half a dozen people each would look at specific areas of London Underground's work and draw up plans to make improvements in that area. It was a process that took up a couple of years and vast amounts of management time. The project culminated in the teams' taking over of several floors of Telstar House, a desperately drab 1960s office block next to Paddington station, working on ways of implementing their ideas. Despite the hassle, as one manager who led three of the teams said, 'it was a very significant part of London Underground's growing up and created widespread change'.[30]

The outcome was an enormous document which 'describes a programme for radical change in pursuit of higher safety and performance standards, lower operating costs and better planned capital expenditure'.[31] Most of it was to be implemented by March 1995 and these aims were largely achieved. Note, however, the key point about lower operating costs. The Plan had two principal objectives, cutting costs and improving performance, and the number of staff was to be reduced by 5000 to 16,000, a target which was achieved through voluntary redundancy. Many employees, even some who were sympathetic to the idea that the organisation had to change, felt that there was too much emphasis on cutting costs and not enough on improving performance. As 'Frank', a middle manager who still works for the Tube, put it, 'the company plan was introduced to give the Tories a surplus on the Tube operations. It was about cutting the payroll and poisoned industrial relations.'[32] He reckons, too, that the reduction in performance in the past four years has been due to changes from the company plan: 'There used to be a planned maintenance programme to change signal relays and other electrical equipment, but this was scrapped under the plan and only equipment that failed was replaced. This was fine for a few years, but now performance is suffering and there is a big backlog.'

Much of the Plan was eminently sensible, like doing away with the nineteen grades of booking clerk. Indeed, according to Steve Norris, the minister responsible for the Tube after the 1992 election, there had been something like 1000 pay and grading agreements that were replaced by a 'simple, adult, responsible salary system',[33] and he reckoned that, overall, the total saving made by the Plan was in the order of £100m per year. Every worker was given a contract and made to sign it, which resulted in the abolition of overtime, payments for meal times and double time on Sundays. Instead, staff were expected to work a fixed number of hours. However, to many like Frank, such decisions were short-sighted: 'They cut platform assistants without realising it would have a big impact on performance because trains get delayed as they try to leave the platform. Now they are putting them back.'[34] This is borne out by LT's staffing figures which show that the number of employees has crept up, partly because of the complexities introduced by preparation for the PPP, and is again 20,000. Another manager recalled how he was desperately trying to get a piece of track work done, but every time he sent a crew, they came back having been unable to carry it out because they did not have a 'protection master', the person in charge of site safety: 'I rang the head of protection and he said that under the Company Plan, they had been told to cut the number of protection masters and he had been laying them off. I told him to go back and get some, but he said that they would have to work for another department and that it would cost more. That sort of thing was happening the whole time.' Given that there were so many changes taking place simultaneously, it was inevitable that some got in the way of each other but this example illustrates just how hard it is for such a large organisation as London Transport to get all its different parts to pull together in the same direction. Again, that was a key driver of the search for a radical new solution such as the PPP through which, London Underground hopes, such difficulties would be allowed to be overcome through the right incentives.

Tunnicliffe was able to carry through these reforms at a time when London Underground was going through one of those short periods when money from the Treasury was relatively forthcoming, not least because King's Cross enabled London Transport executives to play the safety card. The 1989–90 annual report stressed 'LUL's [London Underground Limited] first priority during the year was to implement an extensive safety programme', which required massive investment, the creation of a safety management department and lots of training.

However, the need to follow the agenda set by Fennell led to a neglect of other areas of investment. The fact that the supply of cash was always fitful remained a problem and safety proved a double-edged sword, because it channelled investment towards spending on safety-related matters that provided little or no benefit to travellers and which were sometimes completely unnecessary. The accident, therefore, led to a skewed investment pattern. Some of Fennell's recommendations resulted in an overemphasis on aspects of the system which, in reality, posed very little risk, such as the pointless regular checking of cupboards, as mentioned in Chapter 1.

Some, indeed, were not implemented, but only after lengthy consideration and much wasted expenditure and effort. According to Alan Osborne, London Underground's safety director appointed after the disaster, a lot of money was wasted in the early stages of implementing Fennell: 'One of the first things we did after King's Cross was to take all the wood off escalators. That did very little to reduce the risk compared with, say, installing sprinklers.'[35] The number of fires, incidentally, had gone down dramatically to around 1000 per year, compared with five times that number before the disaster, showing that the management's attitude about the inevitability of such incidents had been mistaken. A big escalator fire such as the one at King's Cross would now happen every 50 years compared with every ten years before the improvements. This made some of Fennell's recommendations redundant, such as enclosing each individual escalator with fire resistant walls, and this work was therefore never carried out.

Even with all the transformation achieved by Tunnicliffe and the Company Plan, London Transport remained a bureaucratic organisation unable to respond quickly to events. Peter Ford, who arrived as chairman in August 1994 from P&O, the shipping company, recalls that he was amazed at the difficulty of getting people to make decisions: 'It is a world of its own with an incredible bureaucracy and a deep-seated belief that a decision could never be made other than by committee and with people filing notes and memos to back it up. The job of prioritising what you need to do is made much harder by this vast bureaucratic process. Yet, back at P&O, I hardly ever sent a memo to Jeffrey Sterling [Lord Sterling, the chairman]. It is all about covering your tracks.'[36] Each morning, Ford found a mound of documents on his desk with the possibility 'that under all the junk, there was a vital memo from Patrick Brown, the permanent secretary at the Department of Transport, or the minister.

Those vital memos were all too frequent. The shadow of the Department hung heavily over London Transport, and behind that there was always the Treasury. Money for investment remained an endless source of angst for Tunnicliffe and his senior colleagues. As the next chapter shows, at times there was too little, followed by too much. And, as ever, it was the Treasury's overbearing influence which prevented any accurate long-term planning, and London Underground's desperate efforts to get away from that control, which led it to alternative solutions such as the PPP.

CHAPTER FIVE

Treasury rules OK

By the early 1990s, thanks to the company plan, London Underground had, at last, begun to grow up – but not enough, in the eyes of the government, to be allowed financial freedom. And it was this continued control from the Treasury which was to push its managers into developing a structure that would at last get them out of annuality, the process by which they never knew how much money they would get for investment the following year until very late in the current one.

The clearest description of the way the government machine constantly toys with London Transport, almost like a cat torturing a bird it has captured, comes from Peter Ford, who was chairman from 1994 to 1998 when he was sacked for challenging the PPP scheme. Ford recalls how every year, around the end of the first week in November, he was called to the Department to see the Secretary of State: 'It reminded me of my public school when you went to see the headmaster. The finance director and I would go in and the Secretary of State would produce an envelope and I would have to sit there and open it. The first time I did not know what to do and just sat there. After that, I realised you have to open it and read the first line of the second paragraph – the first paragraph is just niceties – and that would give you the hard number, your budget for the year.'[1]

This little meeting was both the culmination of a year's lobbying process and the start of another one. The Department expected London Transport to mount an annual campaign to try to get more money for the organisation. Ford recalls how the 'customer was the Permanent Secretary at the Department of Transport, Patrick Brown, and I would see him twice a week,'[2] but there was a regular round of other visits – the Secretary of

State every two months, the junior minister every month, and a lunch every couple of months with Steve Robson, then one of the number twos at the Treasury and a key architect of both rail privatisation and the Public Private Partnership.

Once the annual figure was given, just six months before the start of the financial year, it was unchangeable: 'You never knew what it was going to be because of last-minute changes. The figure could be, and I choose my words carefully here, plus or minus £200m from what was expected.' The former environment secretary, Lord (Patrick) Jenkin, explained why nationalised industries, like the Underground, got a bad deal: 'When you needed to shave off a hundred million or so, it was always possible to suggest that the nationalised industries should be cut a bit. It was the easiest way of saving money.'[3] Indeed, the Tube was at the end of a long and unstable chain. Transport was a balancing item for the Treasury since it involved big capital expenditure that could always be postponed with little immediate political impact. And, in turn, the Tube, ever capital hungry, was a balancing item in the Department of Transport budget. No wonder the amount available would swing up and down unpredictably.

For Ford, receiving the figure from the Secretary of State was 'the start of the hostilities for the year ahead'. He would come out of the Department to be met by Dick Murray, the *Evening Standard*'s ubiquitous transport correspondent who, having been tipped off by the Department, would promptly ask for his reaction. But he had to be careful, choosing words like 'this will be a bit tough' if the figure was good, and 'really tough' if it were bad. Making too much of a fuss at that stage was seen by the Treasury as 'unhelpful'. Indeed, the man who was supposed to be the chairman before Ford, Alan Watkins, was fired as deputy chairman of London Transport for publicly complaining over the meagreness of that year's allocation. Steve Norris, who was the transport minister in charge of the London Underground at the time, recalls the incident with some amusement: 'Watkins was a perfectly competent operator but he was out of his depth in terms of the politics. When he criticised the budget settlement, the Prime Minister [John Major] rang me to say that I had to fire him. Well, we passed the message back that he was the man chosen to be the next chairman after Wilfrid Newton, but they said that was my problem and I had to fire him anyway.'[4]

Such a crude system of annual changes is bound to lead to inefficiency. As Ford put it, 'the sheer nonsense of the whole system is that you have a system where you needed to be looking at capital expenditure over a ten to fifteen year time frame but over which you were subject to twelve-monthly changes, with wild fluctuations. Not only was it daft, it led to serious waste.'[5] Contracts were placed and then cancelled, leaving preparatory work to be junked.

But sometimes it went the other way, and more money than expected was available. The craziness of this process, apart from the almost sadistic ritual humiliation of London Transport executives by officials of the Treasury and the Department of Transport, reached its height in the early 1990s when the pendulum swung with particular force as the Tories boosted spending, partly to try to win votes in London for the forthcoming general election. Suddenly, through ministerial dithering and short-term political considerations, the London Underground found itself awash with cash, only to be thwarted in its attempts to spread spending over a reasonable period of time.

By the late 1980s London Underground had at last started to obtain serious money for investment. Gone were the days of budgets of a mere few hundred thousands for repairs. An automatic gated ticketing system had been introduced, greatly reducing fraudulent travel, sixty stations had been modernised and the total refurbishment of the Central Line, a project which would eventually cost more than £1bn, had been started. In the last five years of the 1980s, London Underground was getting an average of £290m per year (at 1990–1 prices) for investment in the existing network but this still fell far short of what was needed just to maintain the assets in their existing condition. In 1991 London Underground said it needed £750m annually for investment in the existing system until the year 2000 to make up the backlog of investment and modernise the system.

Tunnicliffe, his hand already strengthened by the need for safety improvements after King's Cross, received a further boost with the publication of a Monopolies and Mergers Commission report in June 1991. Dissatisfaction with the running of the Tube, which had begun to get overcrowded again during the Lawson boom of the late 1980s, led the Department of Trade and Industry to launch an inquiry into its operation by the MMC. It was a rather odd initiative that Tory ministers had envisaged might pave the way for the organisation to be privatised. The report, however, merely focused on the inadequacies of funding, placing the blame very firmly at the door of the government. And, ironically, the MMC report was to lead to just the sort of feast and famine period on investment of which it was so critical.

The MMC report is important in that its message is highly critical of both government and London Underground management, and, as one of the few major independent investigations by an outside organisation into the Underground, its findings are still used a decade later by those wishing to demonstrate the horrors of allowing the public sector to run important services.

The introduction to the report says it all: 'The public's perception of an erratic overcrowded and poorly maintained service in many areas is broadly correct, although the picture for the Underground as a whole is more favourable. For the most part, the deficiencies in the levels of service are the result of chronic underinvestment in both new capacity and the replacement and renewal of existing assets, an unforeseen dramatic growth in the traffic and the disruption arising from radically improved safety provisions.'[6] Moreover, the report concluded gloomily, 'the travelling public has been the principal victim of underfunding and will no doubt be so for a number of years to come'.[7]

The MMC identified the core problem in the relationship between government and the Underground, one which has also long dogged the national rail network. Rather than defining the role of the Tube network in terms of purely social goals or financial targets, the government tried to create an amalgam of both: 'Make a profit and provide a social service' seems to be the watchword of ministers whose views on the requirement for London Underground to stick to tight financial guidelines ebb and flow according to the state of the national economy and, in particular, the Exchequer.

The MMC summed it up succinctly by identifying the problem of 'the conflict between LUL's commercial objective of generating enough cash to cover both operating costs and the funding of renewals and replacements, and LRT's [London Regional Transport] and hence LUL's legal obligation to have due regard to London's public transport needs'.[8] Since passenger demand had risen by 50 per cent in the 1980s, there was a need for both renewing the core network and increasing the capacity of the system, and yet, until King's Cross, ministers had been imposing ever more stringent financial targets. As the MMC put it, 'London Underground Limited has to operate within a financial framework which does not facilitate the development of a consistent long-term policy in respect of the setting of fares and the planning and funding of investment.'[9] In particular, the funding of new lines tended to take away money from investment in the existing system.

In a message to which the government had difficulty finding a response, the MMC argued that there was a need for the government to create a system that enabled London Underground to plan its investment over a horizon of at least ten years. It was, in a way, a call for a PPP, though the concept had not yet been invented.

The situation was not, however, all the government's fault. London Underground came in for a hammering from the MMC, too: 'LUL must play its part. Its recent investment plans have been unrealistic and resulted in considerable problems when these plans failed to match the funding available and had to be scaled down.' It was even, according to the MMC, partly London Underground's own fault for not screwing enough cash out of government: 'Recent history suggests inadequate performance by LRT and LUL in getting their case across to the DTp [Department of Transport] and/or by the department in getting the case across to HM Treasury.'[10]

Tony Ridley accepts that this was partly true, recognising, in hindsight, that he had too easily followed his predecessors in simply accepting the terms of the game without sufficiently challenging them and therefore failing to demand the money the Underground system actually needed. Instead, he merely negotiated with government at the margins about the few extra million that ministers were prepared to throw his way: 'I asked for whatever I thought I could get. What I never did was to say, to fix this system, it is going to cost *x*. When I joined, I fitted too easily into thinking that you have got to make do with what you can get and argue for more, then live within what they offer. It was only towards the end of my time that we began to move from stemming the decline into coping with the massive upsurge in the number of passengers and produced a strategic plan for the future, including the two Crossrails.'[11]

Moreover, Ridley had done better than his predecessors, managing, for example, to introduce a successful ticketing system with gates at most stations, which considerably boosted revenue. But he was amazed at the way the government made such innovation difficult: 'I had to go not just to the Board but to the Government for individual items of expenditure greater than £5m. It was an example of micro-management at its worst.'

Whether London Underground would have obtained greater resources if it had asked for them more forcefully is another question. There was widespread suspicion of the way the organisation functioned, criticism that was backed by the MMC, which said: 'The efficiency with which LUL uses its present resources still leaves much to be desired.'[12] This seemed to underestimate the difficulties created by the stop-go policies of the Treasury.

Although project management, the key issue at the heart of creating the PPP, was found to have been deficient, the MMC recognised that progress was being made: 'over the past two years [LUL] has, we believe, taken steps to assess the resources required for managing the increased level of project activity arising from the significantly enlarged investment programme.' Nevertheless, the Commission had grave doubts over whether LUL could spend any extra money wisely and efficiently: 'LUL has so far failed to grapple adequately with the problems associated with cash control, particularly in regard to investment projects. This is a major task and requires a substantial change in approach.' The MMC then listed a familiar catalogue of failings by the management, ranging from not addressing productivity issues with the unions, to the complete absence of the basic management information required to run the business which characterised 'a lack of rigorous management of LUL's activities over a long period'.

The government appeared to be taken by surprise by the financial implications of the MMC report. In September 1991 the transport minister Malcolm Rifkind responded to the report, published three months earlier, by rejecting its recommendation to double investment in the Underground. Indeed, the post-Fennell bonanza had come to an abrupt end in October 1990 when London Underground announced that it would have to make emergency cuts in expenditure to avert a possible £35m overspend by the end of the financial year. The recession had reduced off peak travel and savaged property development schemes. Investment plans were quickly curtailed or abandoned while services were cut on the Jubilee and Victoria lines.

Rifkind seemed to be reiterating the 'these are hard times' line by arguing that funds of this magnitude were not available from government and nor could they be raised through fare increases, the solution recommended by the Commission. However, behind the scenes he was a skilled operator and by capitalising on the political imperative of ensuring there was not another King's Cross disaster, he managed to squeeze a record amount of money out of the Treasury. So, suddenly a couple of months later, in the November 1991 Autumn Statement, the policy changed completely. Christmas came early to London Underground with the government committing itself to increasing London Transport's grant by 60 per cent. By 1993–4, the Chancellor (Norman Lamont) promised, London Transport would have the £750m for investment in the existing network which it had told the MMC was needed each year.

LT responded that this would allow 'major structural renewal', including refurbishment of the south London Northern Line stations, large-scale installation of new escalators at several central London stations, track renewal to get rid of old-fashioned short rail, refurbishment of the Piccadilly Line and much more. For the first time, LT's managers felt confident enough to plan for a long-term and sustained high level of investment. It was to prove a mistake.

This sudden injection of hundreds of millions of pounds into the investment programme over the next three years threw the organisation into disarray. The imperative was to spend, spend, spend. By good fortune, in November 1991 when the announcement was made, London Underground was in a better state to increase its investment spending than it would have been a year or two earlier. Tunnicliffe had begun to appoint consultants to draw up business cases for sizeable capital projects precisely in anticipation of possible increases in the organisation's grant from government. Once the Chancellor had made his announcement, yet more consultants were quickly drafted in to work up more schemes and the contractual arrangements were loosened, giving contractors responsibility for managing their own work.

Inevitably, there were problems and significant waste. The six-month period between November 1991 and April 1992, the start of the financial year, was simply not long enough to crank up large new engineering projects and therefore spending in the early part of the year was much too low. There is only one worse crime than overspending the budget for investment and that is underspending it, because the money is clawed back by the Treasury at the end of the financial year and lost to the Underground for ever.

There were structural barriers to spending. There were not enough project managers, despite the attempt to give the job to anyone who was vaguely qualified and, probably most important, there was the nature of the system itself. As a former manager put it, 'the main constraint is that you are dealing with an exceedingly large pipe. You can only go in one end or the other. But if you take out all the escalators to repair them, you can't get to the station to work on replacing the pumps or whatever. That imposes a sharp physical limit on what you can do.'[13] Moreover, since King's Cross, safety requirements had become much more stringent: even small jobs like replacing lighting could now not be done without scaffolding, and generally the emergency stairs were not allowed to be used, which meant no work could be done if the escalators were not working. It was proving impossible to get all the workers on and off the network without getting in each other's way during the few early morning hours when the system was shut.

To unblock the process, a team of senior managers was created in the autumn of 1992 under the name 'Operation Strikeforce' with the aim of speeding up London Underground's spending. And it worked. By focusing on getting round the blockages with the help of Operation Strikeforce and other smaller initiatives, London Underground managed to ramp up its expenditure on investment. By the early part of 1993 it was spending £90m in a four-week period on investment, equivalent to more than £1bn per year. In fact, in the 1992–3 financial year, London Underground spent a staggering £800m on investment projects,[14] more than the target of £750m to which the government had agreed.

However, even as the organisation was spending at this ferocious rate the bonanza was beginning to come to an end. In the November 1992 Autumn Statement, which always covered the government's spending plans for the following three years, the Tories reneged on their commitments to London Transport which had been made just a year previously for the 1993–4 and 1994–5 financial years. The economic climate had changed. The expected recovery out of recession had not materialised and the government's finances had been further wrecked by suddenly having to pull out of the European exchange rate mechanism after Black Wednesday in September 1992. Cuts were inevitable.

Norris explained the process to me: 'Of the three years, the first is firm and the other two are planned. The graph always goes north so that it looks good and shows that we are going to spend more every year. But as you get to year two, you find that the firm allocation is significantly lower, and year three, which is now year two, will be higher but probably lower than it was, and year three, the new year three, will be the time when you get to the *annus mirabilis* and so on.'

Therefore, instead of the £860m which LU was expecting to receive, ministers had slashed that back to £562m. Capital investment, as the balancing item, would inevitably have to bear the brunt of that cut. Despite heavy lobbying from Norris and his boss, John Macgregor, the Treasury insisted on the reduction being made. Cutting £300m with no notice effectively left London Underground managers with no room to manoeuvre. Some of the money had been reallocated to work on the Jubilee Line, which had been delayed (see next chapter), but this was no use to London Underground, as the cash for the Jubilee Line was ring-fenced. Indeed, London Underground had embarked on the massive Central Line refurbishment and had already committed the entire amount allocated for 1993–4 by the time they heard of the cut and therefore they began dismantling plans to spend more during that year, while simultaneously still trying to increase spending for the current year. In order to try to halt the flow of spending, another set of managers was formed into a kind of anti-Strikeforce team with the task of ensuring that the spending stopped at year end. Probably nothing better sums up the nonsense of the constraints placed on London Underground than this ridiculous scenario: two teams of managers with directly opposing aims. Ultimately, Rifkind's successful lobbying may well have been counterproductive. According to Norris: 'Rifkind's blip set programmes running which consumed resources that actually should have gone elsewhere, on more basic things than renewing the Central Line.'

One of the members of Operation Strikeforce is convinced that vast amounts of money were wasted in this topsy-turvy process through 'the inexperience of project managers, reduced scrutiny given to expenditure, and the inherent stupidity of a funding regime which allowed massive projects to be started and immediately stopped or slowed down'[15]. Moreover, in the desperate rush to ensure that projects got started, priorities became distorted. Schemes which did not offer particularly good value for money were still given the go-ahead as long as they were sufficiently advanced to ensure that their cost could be counted before the end of the year. Indeed, some practices clearly exposed London Underground to corruption: contractors' bills were paid the following day, often long before the work was carried out; suppliers were given cheques for goods that had not been delivered; and the whole emphasis was on spending money, rather than on value for money.

The Operation Strikeforce manager concludes: 'I think that the same benefits could have been achieved for £500m, rather than the £793m that was actually spent if the investment had been programmed rationally rather than in this boom or bust way. If we had got the money as originally promised, we would have got new Northern Line trains much earlier and perhaps some signalling modernisation, as there was a team working on that. Some very big projects had been started and had to be stopped immediately.' Another manager from this period suggests that there is a lot of resonance with the PPP which is supposed to bring a sudden and big influx of funds into London Underground: 'There might be similarities with the PPP situation. We suddenly had all the money we wanted but this uncovered all sorts of structural weaknesses which actually stopped things happening.'[16] Indeed, experts such as Professor Stephen Glaister of Imperial College have doubts over whether the infracos will be able to spend all the money they have promised to invest in the early stages of the PPP, which will include a staggering £1bn per year from the government.

After this traumatic period of rapid changes in the amount of investment money available, Denis Tunnicliffe told the Commons Transport Select Committee, which in June 1993 examined London's transport investment needs, that major projects such as the Northern Line modernisation, another £1bn-plus project, would in future not be started without ensuring funds were available for their completion: 'We are only going to start the Northern Line when we have confidence we have got it backed through and we have the other programmes out there.'[17] He told the committee that the

Northern Line work would not start for at least three years even though some of the project had a benefit–cost ratio of five to one, a very high figure for such schemes. In order to try to achieve that, in 1993 London Underground embarked on a high profile campaign for a Decently Modern Metro which set out the need for a £7.5bn investment programme over ten years, with particular emphasis being placed on the long-neglected infrastructure. Although the campaign was unsuccessful, the Tory government, in its dying years, did give substantial increases to London Underground but never either enough or with enough consistency for Tunnicliffe to relax his relentless campaigning for more cash.

In a memorandum to the committee, the Department of Transport tried to suggest that investment levels were not so important because efficiency improvements and management initiatives 'can have as significant an influence on service performance as investment levels, and sometimes a greater one'. London Transport felt this showed the extent to which Whitehall did not understand its needs, which essentially boiled down to a long-term commitment to a high and stable level of funds for investment. Even Norris, in giving evidence to the committee, accepted that the variations in investment levels between 1992–3 and the following year had been damaging, and an 'absolutely consistent' level of funding in the two years would have been preferable.

The committee – which was Tory-dominated and chaired by the former Transport Secretary Paul Channon – recognised that investment had begun to rise from the low levels of a decade previously, but largely accepted London Underground's case that the money was not enough to maintain the network in a steady state. It recommended, probably more in hope than anticipation, that at the next Autumn Statement, 'the Government [would] commit itself to a stable programme of investment for both BR and LT' at a 'sustained and higher level which, *at the least,* will allow [BR's Network South East] and LUL to proceed with the programmes of infrastructure renewal which are necessary to maintain existing services over the medium term'.[18]

Norris now says that it is 'the lack of certainty of funding' and the role of the Treasury which are the real enemies: 'The damage which the Treasury does to Britain's infrastructure through its absurd insistence on annuality is incalculable.'[19] As London Underground's spending on investment increased over the 1980s and 1990s, the Treasury took an ever greater interest in the running of the organisation. Peter Ford reckons that his most important regular meetings and lunches were with Treasury officials who, interestingly, even had a representative, Steve Robson, on his interview board. The Treasury forced Ford to increase the fares by 1 per cent above the rate of inflation every year despite his opposition: 'It annoyed the hell out of me when the London Transport board members who used to all have free Travelcards would sit around saying that the extra money was insignificant. I would tell them that it was a significant amount to my daughter, who was training as a radiotherapist on £14,000 per year.'[20] (Ford got his revenge on the directors by taking away their cars, much to their annoyance, as he felt they should use the Tube.)[21]

The dependence on the vagaries of the Treasury is probably the single most cited reason – particularly by London Underground managers – for the Public Private Partnership. The crazy stop-go policies of the early 1990s described above had a very profound effect on London Transport managers. They all knew that the episode had resulted in massive waste and that it demonstrated that the government could never be trusted to provide a sustained level of funding. If any one event could be identified as the catalyst for the PPP, it was that fateful 1992 Autumn Statement which the whole organisation saw as a government betrayal. It was a seminal moment for the Underground's management. Tunnicliffe says it demonstrates that governments can never stick to their word, as they are at the mercy of events: 'We had Malcolm Rifkind nail his heart to the cross, promising £750m for the next three years and it dropped by 30 per cent the next year. Nobody has been able to deliver on their promises and usually when the government makes itself a promise, it breaks its word to itself.'[22]

At the time, London Transport did not see any possibility of private investment to break this cycle. Indeed, Tunnicliffe had ruled it out to the Select Committee, telling its members: 'I cannot see a scenario where the private sector would be interested. I have had my talks with the private sector and I find them remarkably risk averse. They are in the business of getting a reward for their money and they want me to make warm statements about there not being a real risk and sign them. I am so capital intensive that I find it difficult to envisage the idea of the private sector coming in, in an entrepreneurial way.'[23]

As we shall see in Chapter 7, the search for a source of stable funding by London Transport managers led them to the PPP. But the reason which probably pushed the government in that direction was London Underground's failure to keep a tight rein on the costs of the construction of the Jubilee Line Extension. In fact, as the next chapter shows, the events around the building of the JLE were rather more complex than those ministers would have us believe when they cite them in support of the PPP.

CHAPTER SIX

No celebrations for the Jubilee

The construction of the Jubilee Line Extension was a political project from the outset. Although it was called an 'Extension' it was, in effect, at 10 miles and with eleven stations, the first new Tube line for London in a generation and both its route and the timing of its building were the result of political decisions that were not necessarily made purely in the interests of improving the transport system. Even the name of the line was the subject of a political row long before any trains ran. Horace Cutler, the forceful and strongly royalist leader of the GLC, changed it from Fleet to Jubilee at a much-criticised cost to ratepayers of £50,000, in order to celebrate the Queen's 25th Jubilee in 1977, though the line was not planned to be completed until the following year. The extension was to be the subject of far more serious political rows, as right from the outset it became enmeshed in the controversy over the development of London's Docklands; then the Tory government's insistence that the project had to be partly funded by an injection of private finance delayed the start of construction; and, at the end, the Millennium Dome with its immovable deadline necessitated its speedy completion at a vastly inflated cost. It was hardly surprising that the ultimate cost of the extension, at £3500m, was nearly twice as much as the £1900m estimate at the start of construction. The protagonists of the PPP put the escalation of costs down to the failings of public sector project management but, as this chapter shows, there are a range of reasons for the cost overrun, not all of which sustain their argument.

The idea for some sort of line stretching from north-west London into the south-east of the capital had been mooted in the study into the metropolis's rail needs in the aftermath of World War II. But, as we have seen,

London Transport was starved of capital during the post-war years, and with the project that was to become the Victoria Line always higher up the agenda, there was no prospect of the line being built during that period. The London Rail Study[1] published in 1974 jointly by the GLC and the Department of the Environment set out a series of possible new lines which included the River line, as it was then called, with a different route through Aldwych, Cannon Street and out into south-east London and Thamesmead – this was before Docklands regeneration was on the agenda. Although the study favoured another project, the Chelsea to Hackney line, which offered a higher benefit–cost ratio, the loss of patronage on the Underground and the subsequent economic recession meant that no new projects were likely to get government backing. London was, however, already getting the stub of a new line, the embryonic Fleet line which involved taking over the Stanmore branch of the Bakerloo and building a new route into central London through Bond Street and terminating at Charing Cross. This was opened in May 1979 with its new Jubilee name, after the inevitable delays during construction.

As demand on the Tube increased dramatically in the 1980s, another report into London's rail needs, the *Central London Rail Study*, again a joint effort,[2] was published. The study found that Crossrail, the scheme to link Paddington and Liverpool Street stations with a tunnel large enough to accommodate main-line trains which would then continue both eastwards and westwards on the national railway, was the best option, offering Londoners the greatest benefit, with Chelsea–Hackney also being supported. The third major new rail route, an extension to the Jubilee, was the one regarded as being the least useful in relieving congestion in the capital's transport system and was effectively kicked into touch.

But other considerations came into play. The regeneration of London's Docklands had started in the early 1980s. Originally the project had been viewed as a relatively minor development creating warehouse and back office space because its location was felt to be too far from central London. However, G. Ware Travelstead, an ambitious Texan developer, changed that by proposing a massive development involving two fifty-floor skyscrapers at Canary Wharf, right at the heart of the Docklands area. In the midst of the late 1980s boom the idea seemed a sure-fire winner but the big problem was transport. How would the 50,000 people expected to fill the jobs in this breathtakingly large development, with a planned 1 million square metres of office space, get to work? Travelstead's vision proved too big even for his Texan boots as he quickly ran out of money and the scheme was taken over by Olympia & York, controlled by the reclusive Canada-based Reichmann brothers.

From the beginning, Docklands itself had been a highly political project. It was an experiment on a grand scale, allowing the market and thus developers, rather than local councils, to determine how a run-down and near-abandoned inner city area should be regenerated. All sorts of inducements were offered to companies. Normal planning rules were suspended, with neither local people nor councillors having any say over what should be built as decisions were taken behind closed doors by a group of people appointed by the London Docklands Development Corporation, a government quango; there was an Enterprise Zone in which no rates had to be paid for ten years; and hundreds of millions of pounds of government cash were invested in the infrastructure. Initially, a light rail system, the Docklands Light Railway, was considered sufficient to meet the transport requirements, but clearly it would be inadequate for the Canary Wharf development, as the railway had originally been designed for a maximum of 30,000 daily journeys. Although the DLR was extended, Olympia & York realised it would still be inadequate in the long run as later stages of Canary Wharf were developed, and the company began pushing for a dedicated rail link between Docklands and central London. The company favoured a direct route to Waterloo via London Bridge, but even a government as business friendly as Mrs Thatcher's could not quite countenance having a whole Underground live across London for the principal benefit of one company – even though O&Y executives frequently dropped in on No. 10. Showing a North American disdain for the formalities of local culture and planning systems, O&Y drew up a plan and a parliamentary bill for a Waterloo & Greenwich railway, dubbed Canaryloo, which would cross the Thames twice to serve Canary Wharf. The company very optimistically reckoned this would cost just £300m, which it would largely fund itself. London Transport's suggestion that O&Y's aims would be better achieved by extending the line beyond Waterloo to meet with the Jubilee Line was brushed aside and the company put the proposal to government in the autumn of 1988.

In response, the government, eager to accommodate the developers of its pet major project, commissioned an additional assessment of rail needs, the East London Rail Study,[3] which had the remit of finding 'the best option for further improving rail access from central London to Docklands and East Thameside in order to accommodate the rapid pace of developments in Docklands'. There was little doubt over what answer the study would come up with: predictably, it recommended a Jubilee Line Extension, from Green Park to Stratford, adopting O&Y's idea of a Greenwich to Waterloo railway en route. Encouraged, a joint London Underground and O&Y team put forward a private bill in November 1989 which eventually, after the usual hiccups and delays, received the Royal Assent in March 1992. As one senior insider put it, 'the Reichmanns were very influential and eventually we were told to develop the railway'.[4]

So instead of getting Crossrail or the Chelsea–Hackney tube that would have regenerated a much more populated and arguably even more deprived area of the capital, Londoners got the Jubilee Line Extension whose principal beneficiary was a private developer. Both the other schemes had a much better benefit–cost ratio and the JLE was certainly not the line which was best for London's transport's needs. As Steve Norris admitted to the Commons Transport Committee: 'It is occasionally the case that schemes like the Jubilee Line are authorised for construction because although it is recognised that they do not meet the standard cover tests, there are nonetheless regeneration issues at large there which demand a call on the public purse. It is unhelpful and would be misleading solely to believe that cost benefit is the only criterion on which investment should take place.'[5] Yet, oddly, the regeneration of south-east London, through which the line was designed to pass, was not a consideration compared with ensuring that the politically prestigious Docklands project benefited from the project. It was only the intervention of Simon Hughes, the highly effective Liberal Democrat MP for Bermondsey, backed by Tunnicliffe and Southwark Council, that ensured the building of a station at Bermondsey rather than the trains simply being allowed to thunder through most of the borough in their rush to serve Docklands as the developers had originally intended. The new station has quickly proved to be a vital boost for the local economy. After some debate Westminster, rather than St James's Park or Embankment, was chosen as the next station north-west after Waterloo, a decision that must have been helped by the fact that MPs would enjoy a completely new station and a new line, although the ostensible reason was that it would make communication between government departments easier if one were relocated to Docklands. It meant that the section of the original Jubilee Line between Green Park and Charing Cross, opened merely a decade earlier, was abandoned, a staggering waste of money given the shortage of funds for the Underground.

The developers might have got their line, which was now estimated to cost around £1300m, but the government expected them to cough up a substantial amount of money to help pay for it. The sum of £400m had been agreed, spread over a quarter of a century. While O&Y executives had been haring round Whitehall pushing aggressively for the line, the Reichmanns had been confident of making a killing on the development as the economy was in the middle of a boom, but by April 1992 when the company was being asked for the first £40m instalment, O&Y was on the brink of insolvency and, indeed, the Canary Wharf scheme went bust a second time six weeks later, the company being forced into administration. Without a private sector contribution and with, as we saw in the last chapter, a difficult Spending Review, the government withdrew its support for the project, stressing that it would not proceed without any money from the developers. For a while, it seemed that the project would be killed off for good. O&Y was controlled by the notoriously risk-averse banks, and the Treasury, as ever hostile to big projects, would have been quite happy to see it founder. There was an eighteen-month delay while an alternative source of private cash was found. That delay proved to be expensive, as the scheme was put on ice, and indeed the eventual sum obtained from the private sector probably amounted to much less than the cost of that delay. Eventually, after tortuous negotiations, largely designed to save the face of the government, the European Investment Bank (EIB) came to the rescue, promising £98m for the line and a further £300m over the next twenty-five years. As ever, this commitment from the private sector was not quite as advantageous as it seemed. According to London Transport's annual report for 1998–9, LT has 'indemnified the EIB in the event of insolvent winding up of O&Y' and, moreover, 'if the extended line does not meet certain conditions, damages will be payable by the Corporation [LT]'.

Inevitably, the line's performance was below the original specification. London Underground say that some money was paid over by O&Y but the precise terms are 'commercially confidential'. And, in the 2001–2 accounts, the large sum of £89m had been set aside as a provision against a possible claim by O&Y (which is now Canary Wharf Limited) because the extension was not meeting 'certain performance conditions' specified in the contract. This little saga illustrates the difficulties faced by public sector organisations in enforcing such arrangements, a tiny taster of what is to come under the PPP.

Within hours of O&Y coming out of administration in October 1993 (strangely, within a couple of years by one of those twists of fortune in matters of high finance which are incomprehensible to the rest of us, the development would plop magically back into the hands of the Reichmann brothers), the initial contracts were signed, allowing London Underground to proceed with the construction, and within a week contracts worth £900m had been let. The cost was now estimated to be £1900m, with a total budget, to allow for contingencies, of £2.1bn.

The private sector contribution was, by now, a financial irrelevance. O&Y's original promise to contribute £400m towards a cost of £1300m had ostensibly represented almost a third of the project. Now, with the payments spread over a quarter of a century, the real value[6] to the government was estimated to be £186m, barely 10 per cent of the projected cost and, indeed, around 5 per cent of the ultimate total spent on the new line.[7] The constant reference by government ministers and press releases to the private sector contribution as £400m, which implied that it covered a much higher proportion of the cost, was unashamed spin doctoring. Norris blames the Treasury for the insistence on the private contribution: 'It was a pathetic amount of money, done by the Treasury to kill off the project. The bar was raised to the level they thought that we couldn't jump over and if they had thought we could, they would have raised it even higher. The irony now is that when you look at the line, with its ridership levels and what it has done for south London, even given the pathetically bad way it has been managed, you can see how overdue it was and how the Treasury's attitude was typical of their "price of everything, value of nothing" approach.'[8] British Gas, by then, had also thrown in £25m[9] towards a station at North Greenwich, which would later serve the Dome, to allow redevelopment of the company's site there which had been decontaminated at vast expense.

The high initial cost of the Line was partly a result of the King's Cross disaster which had led to higher standards of safety being required by the Health and Safety Executive, but the delay had also added a significant amount. Moreover, the figure was artificially depressed by the fact that the Treasury insisted that the original contract tender prices were held, even though this was totally unrealistic given that work was starting two years late. But if the politicians thought the original cost was high, then the final figure was to prove a real shock. The project was completed just in time to provide a service to the Dome on Millennium Eve, nearly two years late and at a cost of £3.5bn, two thirds more than originally estimated. The line had taken ten years to be completed, from the creation of the Jubilee Line Extension Project within London Underground in 1989 to its opening.

The large cost overrun has repeatedly been used by Labour ministers to justify their support for the PPP and to argue that such a rise during a project should never happen again. John Prescott, the transport secretary from 1997 to 2001, contrasted the experience of the JLE with that of the Docklands Light Railway Lewisham extension which 'was completed early and to budget, despite the difficulty of tunneling under the Thames. It is a public private partnership. Compare that with the Swanwick air traffic control centre which is five years late and the Jubilee Line Extension which was nearly two years late – and both 50 per cent over budget. So PPP is one distinctive feature of our policy, where the public sector does what it does best, providing services, and we get the best out of the private sector, too. PPP combines efficiency and effectiveness to provide better public transport.'[10]

Prescott repeatedly cited the Lewisham project as a successful scheme during his four years as Transport Secretary. The two schemes, however, are not really comparable. The 2.5-mile DLR Lewisham Extension cost just £267m (which incidentally was a third more than the original £200m estimate) and was a relatively simple light rail line running mostly overground. Moreover, the scheme was a Private Finance Initiative, very different in scope and scale from the massive Underground PPP (see Chapter 7 for a discussion on this). Comparing such mega projects as the Swanwick air traffic control centre – where most of the delay was caused by problems with software developed by a private company – and the JLE with a modest little scheme like Lewisham is to compare grapefruits with cherries. A fairer comparison might be with the West Coast Main Line[11] where the costs have soared from an estimated £2200m when British Rail initiated the project to at least £10bn according to latest estimates and possibly even more, despite the fact that parts of the original concept, such as 140 mph running have been all but abandoned. To the embarrassment of the government, the West Coast scheme is entirely privately managed and run, although it is being built virtually entirely with public funds.

From the start, London Underground had created a strange structure for the project which restricted its ability to control costs. London Underground recruited an in-house team to run the Jubilee Line Extension Project over which it had little day-to-day control – as one insider put it, 'we were told to ignore London Underground and just build the railway'.[12] Although a London Underground board member was supposed to supervise the work, according to an analysis of the project by Ove Arup, that person had little regular involvement with the projected team and 'was not armed with the independent expertise and the resources he needed to fulfil this responsibility'.[13] While the early stages progressed well, the JLE Project team did not have the right skills to ensure that the commissioning of the line – its development from being a big hole into a working railway – was carried out as cheaply and efficiently as possible. It was that weakness which led to the project running out of control in the latter stages.

However, right from the outset, the costings were based on optimistic assumptions. There had been a sharp recession in the construction industry and therefore the quotes from the contractors were low because there was a shortage of contracts. However, according to a leading manager of the project, 'as the scheme progressed, there was no longer a shortage of work and the economics changed. All the way through, contractors used every opportunity to get more money out of the system.'[14]

Early on, the project lost momentum and delays began to stack up because of an event totally outside the control of London Underground, the collapse of a tunnel in October 1994 during the construction of the Heathrow Express. The passageway was being built using the New Austrian Tunnelling Method, a way of spraying concrete onto the interior surface as the tunnel was dug out, and as the same system was being used on two of the contracts for the JLE at Waterloo and London Bridge stations, work had to stop on those sites, affecting progress on all the tunnelling between Green Park and London Bridge, while the Health and Safety Executive satisfied itself that the method was safe. According to insiders, this put back the project at least six months. The work was stopped voluntarily, a decision questioned by some engineers, but the HSE, which tends to take an ultra-cautious approach, would probably have ordered a halt anyway. There were problems, too, with the tunnel running under Parliament Square, as engineers warned that it might cause a minuscule movement to Big Ben and even possibly result in a small crack in the famous tower. To reduce the risk, the work on that tunnel was slowed down, which resulted in the station not being fully opened until after Millennium Day.

While these sort of problems were to be expected on such a major project, their effects were compounded by the fact that in 1997, halfway through construction, the scheme was given an immutable deadline when Labour decided to go ahead with the previous government's scheme for a Millennium Dome at Greenwich. Since the Dome was predicated on the notion that the visitors, optimistically reckoned to be up to 100,000 per day, would nearly all reach it by public transport as no car parking was being provided, completion of the JLE was no longer negotiable. Once the deadline of December 1999 had been set, the contractors had the upper hand over London Underground. They knew that they could effectively charge what they wanted and, indeed, so did the workers, who bid up their wages through a series of threats of unofficial industrial action during the final couple of years of construction. As one senior manager of the project put it, 'the contractors knew about the deadline and therefore had us over a barrel'.[15]

The project had originally been due to be completed by March 1998 but was clearly already in trouble by the time the Dome decision had been made. Although the Heathrow collapse and concerns about Big Ben had slowed progress with the tunnel, the most serious delay proved to be the fitting out, testing and engineering after the completion of the tunnelling. Here the key mistake by London Underground had been the decision by its head of engineering, Brian Mellitt, to push for a completely new and revolutionary form of signalling, 'moving block', by which trains are controlled through radio links from lineside beacons rather than by conventional colour lights. The advantage would have been much greater capacity on the line; the disadvantage was that it was new and untried technology which turned out to be a leap in the dark. It is doubtful whether such a decision would have been made by a private company that would have had to bear the risk. On the other hand, Westinghouse, which was designing the system, repeatedly assured the JLE Project managers that the system would be ready and available in time. One middle manager on the project said: 'Westinghouse kept on telling us that moving block was going to happen. But the goalposts kept moving. They would not sit down and say, "We have a problem," but instead you had to read into what they were saying.'[16] Even though the suppliers and London Underground engineers believed that moving block was deliverable, the software problems defeated them. In hindsight, Peter Ford recognises 'it was hopelessly optimistic. It was like going from a typewriter to a PC and there was not enough expertise, particularly in the Railway Inspectorate [of the Health and Safety Executive] to approve it.'[17]

Westinghouse belatedly admitted that moving block would only be installed on the new section of the railway from Green Park, and it was not until late 1998, with the opening of the Dome barely a year away, that London Underground was finally told that moving block was a non-starter for the whole line. When Westinghouse finally put its hand up, a whole new set of equipment had to be ordered for the conventional signalling system. According to one insider, 'London Underground could have sued Westinghouse and put them out of business over their failure, but it was felt that would not help us progress the new line.'[18]

The whole signalling issue had already been made more difficult by the decision to split the contracts for various aspects of the control system between companies. The signalling contracts were given to Westinghouse while the software in the control centres was the responsibility of Alcatel. The companies were rivals across the globe in bidding for signalling contracts and were reluctant to cooperate. According to a member of the management team who had to deal with the signalling: 'It was not a natural split. Westinghouse and Alcatel were competitors and were not being cooperative as neither wanted to reveal details of their equipment to their rival. Westinghouse even banned Alcatel from seeing Westinghouse's rig at

Chippenham because of fears [about] what Alcatel would learn about its technology.'[19] Originally, London Underground had intended to give the whole contract to Westinghouse, which was based in the UK, as there had been a row with Alcatel, which was run from Vancouver, over problems on the Docklands Light Railway resignalling. However, eventually Alcatel had to be given part of the contract, as it was felt that Westinghouse could not cope with the whole system, creating a fudge. The problem was that the JLE project team had contracts with both Westinghouse and Alcatel, but the two companies had no direct commercial relationship. As a signal engineer explained, 'that was fine until something went wrong and then the JLE project team had to manage the very complex interface between the two suppliers when a dispute arose. It would have been much better if that interface had been in the hands of one company.'

The bad relationship between the two signalling contractors was replicated in other parts of the project. All contractors had signed an agreement to the effect that they should cooperate with each other, but in practice there were inevitable petty rivalries. The scope for such disputes was increased by London Underground's decision to let a lot of smaller contracts. According to Ove Arup, the management processes were swamped by the sheer number of parties involved: 'This was not helped by the strategy . . . to divide all the works into discrete contract packages leaving many difficult interfaces to be managed by JLE project that would better have been handled by a lead-contractor.'[20]

The complexity of the task increased because London Underground wanted the JLE to be a world class railway, using the most up-to-date technology. Moreover, as the project was being worked up during the aftermath of the King's Cross disaster, safety was a prime consideration, leading to a belt and braces approach that added considerable cost to the bill – and, incidentally, also resulted in the airy, elegant stations with lots of built-in redundancy and space that are in such sharp contrast to the poky Victoria Line stations forced on London Transport as a result of late cost-cutting.[21] For example, the stations are pressurised so that in the event of a fire, passengers will be able to escape more easily without inhaling smoke and yet, with the much higher standards to which the stations are built following King's Cross, there is little likelihood of a serious conflagration. Virtually every cupboard and storeroom in the stations is accessed by an alarmed door: not only was this extremely costly, but the controllers are bombarded with unnecessary noise as the alarms are set off which, ultimately, may make the system less safe as operators routinely learn to ignore false warnings.

By the time Westinghouse came clean, Bechtel International had been brought in, at great expense, to ensure the line was completed in time for the New Year 2000 celebrations. Appointed in late September 1998, Bechtel, renowned for its ability to push projects through, had just fifteen months in which to finish the line. Projects rarely have such a key end date but this time it was a once in 1000 years event. Money was far less important than time. Bechtel itself, according to Ove Arup, 'underestimated the task they faced' and set deadlines which were too tight. Originally the company had hoped to have a team of thirty consultants but this quickly grew to fifty: 'They did not change much, strangely enough,' says one former London Underground project manager, 'but they did provide a lot of focus.' At great expense, of course. Moreover, the public got less for its money. One of the ways Bechtel made progress was to 'de-scope' the contract – in other words, remove many of the hi-tech bells and whistles which had added to the complexity and were delaying construction. It worked. The line was open in time, though, and at least London Underground could not be blamed for the embarrassing security delays at the Dome on New Year's Eve which attracted such bad publicity that the attraction never recovered its PR élan. Much work, however, had to be carried over into the year 2000 when it could only be done in the usual early morning shutdown which, of course, made it much more expensive.

In addition to the delays, the optimistic initial assessment of the cost at the launch of the project was a major factor behind the ultimate cost overrun of 67 per cent. There is always a tendency to underestimate such costs at the beginning of a project to try to pull the wool over the eyes of the Treasury, since once a scheme is underway, it would be too politically embarrassing to leave it half built.[22] Ove Arup suggests that a more realistic assumption of the 'estimated final cost' would have been £2500m, rather than the budget of £2141m (let alone the £1900m figure for the cost used by the government) announced at the go-ahead for the project, to take into account a 'proper level of contingencies' and to reflect 'the cost of the railway, not the project alone'.[23]

So the real cost overrun is in the order of £1bn, rather than the figure of over £1.5bn used by ministers. The combined effects of insisting on leading-edge technology, having an immutable completion date, the near-paranoia about safety and the collapse of the Heathrow Express tunnel was a heady mix which would have pushed any project off the rails. The list of these factors, added to others mentioned above and a host of other minor issues, provides London Underground management with a reasonable, but by no means complete, defence to the torrent of criticisms it has faced over the project. For example, Steve Norris is probably right to argue that the signalling fiasco was largely down to London Underground management: 'They bought the idea of moving block signalling even though there was not a single example in the world where it was working in practice. They wanted twenty-eight trains per hour, but in fact Moscow gets forty trains per hour using fixed block. This is a classic example of where the private sector would have subjected the issue to much more rigorous examination.'[24] Except that Mellitt promptly went into the private sector, where, at Railtrack, he made the same mistake, persuading the company to adopt moving block signalling for the West Coast Main Line modernisation project on Britain's busiest railway, only for it to be abandoned in favour of a conventional control system after his departure because of the technical difficulties.

However, an analysis of any major project would reveal similar problems, and the extent to which the cost overrun was down to incompetence by London Underground management as opposed to a variety of external and structural factors is a matter of debate and suggests that the experience of the JLE construction offers little to the debate over the PPP. One irony, as pointed out by Jay Walder, the finance director of Transport for London, is that 'much of the overrun is blamed on contract management which is a function that London Underground will retain under PPP'.[25] One operations manager – who still works for London Underground – is convinced that blaming the public sector project management is far too simplistic: 'Oddly enough, it is not so much that the public sector were involved too much, it is the other way around. We were always getting information off the contractors far too late, as they did not liase with us and that meant a lot of the designs were wrong and there had to be expensive late changes. There were always communication difficulties, as I was not allowed to talk to subcontractors directly but only through contractors.' Interestingly, he feels such problems will be replicated with the PPP, as there will not be enough honest communication between the various parties: 'There is a reluctance for contractors to be open about any difficulties they are experiencing and there is likely to be the same problem about schemes being drawn up without sufficient consultation with the operations side.'[26]

In fact, given the special circumstances, the extent of the JLE overrun was nothing exceptional. Peter Ford, the chairman until 1998, reckons: 'If you look at the figures, and net out the effect of the Heathrow collapse and the fact that the Treasury stripped out most of the contingency before work started, then the cost overrun was more like 40 per cent rather than the near 70 per cent they use.'[27] There is no doubt, too, that the cost of digging out the initial tunnels was greatly underestimated because no significant scheme had been built in London since the Victoria Line. Tunnicliffe describes how 'it is unbelievably expensive to dig through the first two metres of the surface in London. You dig your hole and if you look up the sky is black with water pipes, electricity, telephones, etc. In Bermondsey there were 8ft reinforced boxes that really needed atom bombs to shift.'[28]

If the actual overrun was 40 per cent, it was commonplace for transport schemes. Steve Norris reckons that the JLE was typical but that its problems proved very influential: 'the average cost overrun in the Department of Transport's road schemes is 40 per cent, so whenever you said a project was going to cost £20m, you knew it actually meant £28m. The JLE convinced crypto-Tories like Blair, who had always suspected that this was the case, that the public sector could not manage big projects and that in future they were going to have to get the private sector in.'

Given the deadline imposed by the Labour government – and the delayed start caused by the Tory government – a massive overrun was inevitable. Even if the contract had been a PPP, the risk of the government coming in halfway through and imposing a deadline would never have been transferred to the private sector. The Government would have borne the extra cost. Big projects are particularly prone to such cost increases precisely because they are such rare birds that the expertise of managing them is lost as people are never involved in one more than once. In a rational world, London would have a series of continuous projects to improve its railway network – the JLE should have been followed by Crossrail and then

Chelsea–Hackney, which has now been dubbed Crossrail 2, and so on. According to Tunnicliffe, such a rolling programme would cut costs to the public sector of these projects by a third. Martin Callaghan, the project director for the London Underground PPP, says that this is a good reason for having the PPP: 'People in LU only ever work on one line upgrade because they come along so infrequently that everyone has to learn how to do them. One of the things the private sector will bring is people who are doing major engineering projects all over the world, all the time.' However, it will be difficult for the public sector to capture any savings made by using such expertise, as the companies involved will be in a very strong position during the bidding process. Moreover, new lines are not within the remit of the PPP but will be subject to additional contracts.

Indeed, there is a particularly big hole in the government's use of the failings of the JLE project to give credence to back its support for the PPP. When Ernst & Young compiled the final value for money report for the Government,[29] it specifically excluded comparison between the JLE and the PPP. As Stephen Glaister puts it, '[since] the experience with the JLE was excluded [from the Ernst & Young analysis] as that project was judged not similar to those within the PPP contracts . . . it is surprising to hear ministers citing the JLE in support of a proposition that the public sector has shown itself to be prone to cost overruns in the past.'[30]

Moreover, the true cost was not really £3.5bn. Because the project started in the middle of a recession, it is credited with creating 50,000 jobs and the Treasury was able to claw back 47 per cent of the final cost in corporation tax, national insurance and income tax, and unemployment benefits that did not need to be paid out.[31]

London Underground was punished harshly for the cost overrun of the JLE, as money which was earmarked for routine investment had to be channelled into the new link in the budget for 1996–7 and the two subsequent years. All the cost of the overrun had to come out of the Department of Transport's budget and while part of the extra cost – the £130m or so resulting from the postponement of work after the Heathrow tunnel collapse – came out of contingency funds, Steve Norris reckons that most came from the pot that would have otherwise been spent on routine investment in the Underground: 'the overrun meant that around £600m which would have gone into the existing railway was, instead, used to pay for the

JLE'.[32] This punitive attitude by the government greatly strengthened the hands of those within London Underground who were desperate to ensure that investment should never again be dependent on such Treasury-imposed whims.

Despite all the problems, London got a superb new Tube line built to very high standards of design – in a few years' time, who will give a damn about the cost? For example, who quibbles about the wonderful British Library today, which caused such a controversy during its construction? Even Ove Arup was complimentary about the high standards of 'infrastructure planning and design'.[33] And the benefit to Londoners has been immeasurable, much greater than the cost. So, far from being seen as a failure, the JLE should be celebrated, despite its difficult birth and early operational difficulties, but instead, because of political expediency, ministers have tended to paint the project in a poor light.

Indeed, the most disappointing aspect of this tale is that despite the clear benefits to London, and in fact the whole UK economy, of such lines, there is no prospect of any new addition to London's rail system for at least a decade. The Crossrail project – which has received £154m in October 2001 for a preliminary study after being abandoned in 1996 when a similar sum had already been spent – will not be completed until at least 2010 and that depends on an early decision for funding, which is unlikely to be made.

Yet there is unequivocal evidence that such lines bring benefits far higher than the initial cost and that, ultimately, a few hundred million here or there during construction are an irrelevance. A study by the Centre for Land Studies[34] showed the enormous scale of the benefits. The problem is that these benefits are gained by local landowners who have not contributed to the cost of the scheme. The author, Don Riley, calculated that for the £3.5bn cost of the JLE, there was an increase in the value of the land of £13bn. He suggests that the way of funding such schemes would be through a tax on the added land value gained as a result of a development. On the basis of a 10 per cent annual return, this is worth about £1.3bn a year to landlords. A tax of 25 per cent on this revenue stream would have led to an annual flow to London Underground of £325m, which would have repaid the cost of the extension over twenty years while leaving a surplus for other services.

Instead, we have got the PPP, a child of the JLE.

CHAPTER SEVEN

Enter the PPP, son of PFI

The preceding three chapters have built up only part of the reasoning behind the creation of the PPP: the lack of confidence of ministers in London Transport's management, the recognition that annual funding of major infrastructure schemes was nonsensical, and the experience of the cost overruns during the construction of the JLE. But there was more. It took a particularly strange set of political circumstances and battles, together with a new-found fad in the Treasury, the Private Finance Initiative, for the PPP to emerge as the government's sole solution for future investment in the London Underground. History is full of debates about whether such an episode was a result of conspiracy or cock-up. The events described in this chapter suggest strongly that those seeking an explanation for the PPP should look to the latter.

In the dying days of the Tory government in the winter of 1996–7, when ministers well knew that they were on the way out, the transport secretary Sir George Young had suggested, without much conviction, that the Tube might be privatised. It was not an idea which gained much support, even within the Tory party, but the notion found itself in the Tories' 1997 manifesto without ever having been properly worked out. Since rail privatisation had been done on the hoof by the Tories following the 1992 election, this was no obstacle to the implementation of the policy had the party won in 1997.

Labour countered with a last-minute addition in its manifesto,[1] rejecting 'the Conservative plan for the wholesale privatisation' – though note the weasel word, 'wholesale' – and saying there would be a 'new public/private partnership [the term had not developed capital Ps at that stage] to improve the Underground, safeguard its commitment to the public interest and guarantee value for money to taxpayers'. But what did it mean? Nobody quite knew. PPP was the invention of John Prescott, who expected to take over the transport brief after the election, and the origins of the idea are as opaque as his syntax. Prescott had long supported the notion of the private sector investing in the railways, and as far back as the previous election hustings, he had suggested that rolling stock could be financed in that way. But that was a conventional Public Finance Initiative concept which Labour, in opposition, had argued against and therefore Prescott had to come up with a new idea – thus the PPP was born.

The difference between the two concepts, PFI and PPP, is therefore hazy. In some ways, the only difference is that the PFI was used by the Tories and PPP is its newer Labour equivalent, which sounds friendlier because of the word 'public' and the omission of 'finance', definitely a word associated with the Conservatives. Even government documents use the terms interchangeably, struggling to disentangle the ideas. For example, a briefing[2] to MPs from the Department of the Environment, Transport and the Regions (as it then was) in May 2001 completely mixes up the two concepts. It says that 'PFIs since 1995/6 have and are delivering new Northern Line trains and new power, communications and ticketing systems for the Underground' but then says in the next paragraph, 'PPPs are essential to the Government to renew Britain's infrastructure, with more investment, at predictable levels, for the long term'. The briefing continues: 'PPPs have delivered efficiency savings of 17 per cent compared with the public sector alternative' and goes on to state that projects involving thirty-five hospitals and 373 schools 'are underway'. It mentions the Underground PPP and says that 'a forerunner of the PPP is already working on the Northern Line, where trains are far more reliable thanks to a new maintenance regime operated jointly by LU and its private sector partners'. That is a reference to the PFI arrangement through which the Northern Line trains were obtained from Alstom, described in the first chapter. Under the deal 106 trains, which cost around £400m to build, were leased to London Underground by the manufacturer. However, the contract was not to provide a set number of trains, but to fulfil the timetable required by London Underground which necessitated having ninety-six trains in service every day. Provided the trains were available for service, London Underground paid the contract price in full – a commercially confidential figure estimated to be £40m to £45m per year[3] – and a bonus; but every time services have to be cancelled because no train is available, Alstom has to pay a penalty. This is classic PFI: it involves a large capital asset for use by a public sector organisation but built and maintained, in the long term, by a private company, selected through a competitive bid process, *which takes some of the risk* of the financial consequences of failure. However, as mentioned in Chapter 1, the penalties to Alstom were capped and thus there was little real risk transfer.

The PPP, therefore, grew out of the PFI, though as we shall see in the next chapter, the London Underground PPP is not a PFI writ large, but, contrary to the suggestion in the briefing quoted above, is a completely different animal because of its size and complexity. Indeed, Bob Kiley recounts how when he met Tony Blair, the Prime Minister had copies of the Northern Line trains contract and the PPP documents on his desk and said to the Transport Commissioner: 'These are not the same at all.'[4]

Nevertheless, the PPP is about the private funding of public projects and risk transfer, both concepts that first emerged with the PFI, which means the history of the PFI is crucial to an understanding of the story of the Tube PPP. The PFI first emerged as an idea within the Treasury when Norman Lamont was Chancellor of the Exchequer before the 1992 election. The strategy was that private money would be used to finance government projects, such as new hospitals or transport infrastructure. Hitherto, such 'unconventional finance', as it was called, had been banned by the Treasury which simply prevented it by insisting that it would count as government spending and had to be value for money. Since private finance always costs more than government borrowing, that effectively prevented such schemes. A breach in the ban had emerged in the late 1980s when it became accepted that privately built road or bridge schemes which were funded by tolls would not count against government spending.[5]

However, the key was to get the other routine types of capital spending off the government's balance sheet so that they did not count as part of the all important Public Sector Borrowing Requirement, which the Treasury was always anxious to keep as low as possible in order to keep interest rates down. Therefore, it was not a simple matter of the government borrowing money from private banks to build these projects. Instead, there had to be an element of risk for the private sector so that if things went pear-shaped, the private consortium got paid less. The concept had been developed by Steve Robson who, as head of the Privatisation Unit in the Treasury, had been responsible for devising the Tories' privatisation programme, and Stephen Dorrell, then the Financial Secretary to the Treasury.

The PFI can be seen as the logical extension of two other policies the Tories had implemented to enable the private sector to provide public services. The first was the privatisation programme of the 1980s which had progressively grown to encompass all the utilities and, eventually, even British Rail. Running in parallel was the legislation forcing local authorities to offer services for competitive tender by the private sector. As a result, the private sector began providing services which had hitherto been a public monopoly, such as refuse collection, leisure centre management and park maintenance. PFI incorporates elements of both privatisation and competitive tendering. As the booklet outlining the advantages of the PPP approach puts it, 'Contracts are awarded to private sector suppliers for a long service contract, that also typically involves provision of assets and therefore a commitment of capital. *The responsibility for core services provision continues to be retained by the public sector*'[6] (my italics).

Essentially, the government is in the position of a man who wants to buy a car but does not want to ask his bank manager for an overdraft. So he arranges a hire purchase agreement which allows him to pay for it over a period of years. Of course, it will cost him more because he has to pay interest (and, indeed, the bank manager who knows him might well have given him a cheaper deal, just as the government can borrow more cheaply than anyone else) and the hire purchase company has to make a profit, but at least his bank account will stay in the black. The difference is that if things go badly and the driver fails to keep up his payments, then the hire purchase company will repossess the car. But if the government has built, say, a new hospital using the PFI, then it cannot simply decide at a later date that it cannot afford to keep up the payments; in other words, the PFI may keep the Public Sector Borrowing Requirement (now called Public Sector Net Borrowing) low, but only at the cost of committing the government's cash flow for decades ahead.

Lamont made an announcement launching the PFI project in the 1992 Autumn Statement. He relaxed the rules governing the Treasury's rules on public projects in order to open the way for private financing of projects. Hitherto, the rules had made it virtually impossible for 'unconventional financing', to be used for capital expenditure, however desperate the need.

At first, nothing materialised and the idea, which would soon revolutionise the way that public projects are financed, attracted little attention. After the 1992 election, Lamont's successor Ken Clarke relaunched the concept creating a PFI panel, a group largely drawn from the private sector but with some civil servants and headed by Sir Alastair Morton, a former chairman of Eurotunnel, to try to initiate schemes.

For those who, like Sir Alastair, had long toiled at the interface between the public and private sectors, the PFI offered several attractions. First, it was perceived as an additional source of finance with which to fund projects. The drawback is that the private sector cannot borrow money as cheaply as government, which is always able to command the lowest interest rates because the markets know that the state never reneges on its debts. Sir Alastair argues that the point about the private sector having to pay higher interest rates is an irrelevance: 'Public sector money is available until the point at which the Treasury turns off the tap in that direction in that particular year. From the moment the tap switches off, the cost of public money is infinite because it is unavailable.'[7]

The second reason for the development of PFI was the sheer scale of the task of modernising Britain's infrastructure after years of neglect, typified by the railways and the Tube, but also apparent in every other facet of the public sector, such as health, education and housing. PFI was intended to provide extra, otherwise unavailable, resources for investment. As government spending was perceived as unavailable, the PFI was the only way forward. Indeed, it later became widely known as 'the only game in town'. From the Treasury's point of view, the advantage was that investment through PFI schemes kept the spending outside the Public Sector Borrowing Requirement. So the PFI was Treasury heaven. As long as sufficient risk was taken by the private sector, then the investment from PFI schemes would not count as part of the PSBR, which meant that there was no control over how much could be spent.

Well, that is not entirely true. It was, of course, not free money. The investment may indeed no longer have counted as government spending, but it still had to be serviced with payments to cover interest, costs and profits to the private contractor. As an analysis of the PFI for hospitals puts it, 'The argument over whether PFI permits more investment than conventional Exchequer funding is a red herring. The taxpayer will eventually pay, either way. Given the Government's current tests of fiscal prudence [i.e. that it should only borrow for investment and not for current spending] there appear to be no macroeconomic reasons for preferring PFI to Exchequer financing, or for regarding one approach as any more affordable than the other.'[8] The author of the analysis gives the following example:

> If the NHS manager can find room in his budget this year to pay a £1m charge to a PFI consortium, but does not have the £10m available in the capital budget to buy the same asset up front (i.e. conventionally-financed), then the PFI is 'permitting' an investment that would otherwise not take place. However, this is simply a consequence of the government applying a tight cash limit on the capital value of assets purchase if they are paid for by borrowing from the Exchequer but not if they are financed by private sector lending. The same resource, broadly speaking, will be used in building the asset, however it is financed, and the taxpayer will eventually pay for it either way.[9]

In other words, the government is no more getting a free hospital than a homeowner who takes out a mortgage to buy a new house is getting it free; and like the homeowner, it is committing itself to regular payments over a period of many years.

There is an added advantage of the PFI. Under the old Treasury rules, there was no distinction between investment and current expenditure. If a new train line were built over the space of, say, five years and cost £1bn, that would be shown in the accounts for each of those years as costing £200m. This has always been a daft convention, as a private company, of course, spreads the load on its balance sheet across the life of the asset, but as anyone who had dealt with the Treasury will confirm, 'rules is rules'. The PFI, therefore, theoretically gets round both the problems of annuality and additionality. To the spending department, it seems like extra spending that is spread over the lifetime of the asset.

Oddly, bonds never get mentioned by the government as a possible solution to this problem. In many European countries, organisations such as the state-owned railways or energy companies are allowed to raise money through issuing bonds which do not count as being part of those countries' equivalent of the PSBR. Ken Livingstone and his transport commissioner, Bob Kiley, have never tired of pointing out that were they allowed to raise money through such bonds to fund the upgrading of the Tube system, the whole rationale for the PPP would collapse. The Treasury has refused to consider the idea, even though, as we saw in Chapter 2, this was the way that London Transport was financed in its 1930s heyday and, as we see later in this chapter, bonds were used to rescue the Channel Tunnel Rail Link from collapse.

This brief analysis confirms that the government – both Conservative and Labour – skewed the choice for the way that capital spending is made in the public sector. In the NHS, which was an early testing ground for PFI because of the need for new hospital buildings – and, indeed, transport – the public organisation purchasing the infrastructure is being forced by the government to obtain it through PFI because the Treasury limits the amount of capital expenditure it will pay for in any given year but is more relaxed about funding the long-term spending entailed by borrowing in the private sector through PFI schemes. Therefore, there is no choice and this explains the basic reason why London Underground has ended up with the PPP. It is not so much that the PFI expenditure is additional; it is, as Sir Alastair Morton stressed above, the only option because the Treasury will simply not fund these projects in any other way.

The third justification for the PFI is, of course, the notion that private management will be better and therefore considerable efficiency savings can be made. Indeed, this is the core argument for PFI because it is only through the added efficiency which the private sector can harness that the added cost of capital – since governments can borrow more cheaply than private companies – and the profit margin for the PFI contractor can be offset. There is a fierce controversy over two aspects of this assumption. First, are private companies *necessarily* more efficient than the public sector and, secondly, how much more? If any single issue could be said to be at the core of the row over the PPP, it is this one.

Here, too, there is enormous and wide-ranging controversy. The World Bank has few doubts that the private sector is unequivocally more efficient. In 1992 the bank published a booklet[10] which argued that the very act of transferring state industries and services to the private ownership *in itself* improves economic performance. Brendan Martin, the author of a book on the experience of privatisation across the world, points out that prior to this the Bank had been more circumspect about the issue, arguing that ownership had nothing to do with efficiency. The booklet, he says, marked 'an important departure not only from the Bank's previously declared position but also from the conclusions of other major studies of the effects of privatisation'.[11] Martin cites numerous other studies which suggest that the World Bank's confidence is based more on political assumptions than on economic facts. Moreover, he points out that the Bank's argument is based on purely 'economic-financial performance', which is not a fair basis for comparison given that other criteria, such as social benefit and the impact on employment, should be taken into account in an overall assessment of the effects of privatisation. In assessing the PPP, we will return to all these considerations (see Chapter 12).

There is, too, a fundamental ambiguity about whether the PFI/PPP programme does allow public investment without the pain of the spending counting against the Public Sector Borrowing Requirement, or its successor, Public Sector Net Borrowing, which is a slightly more sophisticated measure that does not include, for example, receipts of privatisations. There is an element of smoke and mirrors when talking to Treasury officials and government ministers about the benefits of the programme. As the author of the booklet on the NHS PFI programme puts it, 'The macroeconomic management and accounting treatment arguments are bound together and have something of the character of an over-elaborate and ultimately disappointing conjuring trick.'[12] Given that the Tube PPP programme is several orders of magnitude more complex than the most elaborate PFI programme, that argument applies in spades to what is happening on the London Underground.

The PFI programme had quickly gained tremendous momentum, with the Treasury rules being completely turned on their head within the space of a couple of years. From the position of a total virtual ban on such funding, in November 1994 at the instigation of the Chancellor, Ken Clarke, the position was completely reversed with government departments seeking cash for major capital schemes now being required by the Treasury to show that PFI options had been tested before seeking public funding. Only if private finance were not available at a reasonable cost would Exchequer funding be available. Despite the Conservative government's clear support for PFI, few schemes had been signed – a couple of prisons were the biggest ones during the Tory years – before the 1997 election because there was still widespread scepticism among civil servants about the idea. In particular, according to members of the PFI panel, many senior people in the Treasury were reluctant to sanction spending under PFI schemes.

It was not until Labour took office in May 1997 that the PFI ball really got rolling. The party's hostility to the concept while in opposition rapidly turned 180 degrees into much greater and concerted support than the Tories had ever demonstrated. The Chancellor, Gordon Brown, embraced the idea wholeheartedly: 'Through the Private Finance Initiative, the private sector is able to bring a wide range of managerial, commercial and creative skills to the provision of public services, offering potentially huge benefits for the Government.'[13] In the early 1990s the secret agenda behind the PFI had been the notion of the government's appearing to reduce borrowing without cutting public investment. Labour decided to use it for rather different purposes, to fund its renovation and expansion of public services on the never-never.

The take-off of PFI has been astonishing. According to the 2002 Budget Report,[14] 'projects with a combined capital value of around £18bn have been approved since May 1997 in such diverse areas as schools, colleges, hospitals, local authorities, defence IT and property management.' Over the following three financial years, the report said, a further £25.5bn of new investment was expected as a result of PPP and PFI.

It has proved a fantastic bonanza for the consultants, lawyers, bankers and financial advisers who have developed the concept, particularly those who were in on it early. PFI deals are by their very nature complex, far more so than the ordinary provision of services through contracts. They are invariably bid for by consortia who must have all the usual team of advisers, consultants and bankers. Peter Hendy, a former executive of FirstGroup and now Transport for London Managing Director of Surface Transport, who was involved in the development of the Croydon Tramlink which opened in May 2000, explains how the fees for even such a relatively small scheme begin to represent a substantial percentage of the total cost: 'The system cost a total of £225m to build, of which £135m was public money, but the process to obtain that private component is extremely expensive. But the rules of the game were that the deal had to be a PFI, so there was no alternative.'

Hendy explains that all the bidders have to create consortia and there are only a limited number of advisers who have experience of the concept: 'You had to be in a consortium and obviously each one had to have an operator, a construction company, a tram manufacturer and financial backers, together with legal, financial and other consultants, but you can't necessarily get the best people in every respect because they may not be available and may even be in a rival consortium. There's a limited number of legal advisers with PFI experience, for example. So you have to select them and enormous sums of money are then spent bidding.' Moreover, most of these companies just want to be involved in the part of the work where they have expertise. As Hendy puts it, 'Why is a construction company interested in a 99-year concession to run trams in Croydon? The answer is that they are not. They are interested in building it, which is a £150m job, and getting out. But the PFI forces them into a consortium of parties with nothing in common with one another.' The final signing of the deal shows just how many highly expensive people are involved. Hendy reckons that on the night the deal was complete, 'there were around a hundred legal agreements to be signed, and there must have been eighty people in the room, all night, most of whom were lawyers and consultants'.[15] A conservative estimate must be that this kind of jamboree was costing taxpayers £20,000 per hour.

Interestingly, the Croydon Tramlink is a great transport success but a financial failure. Although numbers of passengers have been above predicted levels, revenues are below expectation because of the way that the income in the contract was calculated. At the time of writing, the contractor, a consortium of Bombardier Eurorail, CentreWest (part of FirstGroup), Sir Robert McAlpine, Amey Construction and Royal Bank of Scotland, was trying to negotiate a reformulation of the deal, but Transport for London has proved unwilling to accept a change.

PFI has become a huge industry. According to a table compiled by the newsletter covering the PFI industry,[16] fifteen organisations have each been involved in contracts totalling over £5bn, for which they are routinely paid both commission and success fees. In a survey of signed deals in April 2001, for example, the lawyers Allen & Overy (thirty-nine projects) and

Clifford Chance (forty-seven) had both handled schemes worth over £10bn; the top financial advisers were Price Waterhouse with £8.7bn spread over a remarkable ninety-five deals; the top bank was the Dai-Ichi Kangyo Bank with £7.6bn on just twenty-one projects; while the top 'contractor/consultant' was Halcrow Transportation Infrastructure with £8.4bn covering twenty-six schemes. (In July 1998 Price Waterhouse, which had merged with Coopers & Lybrand, started using the name PricewaterhouseCoopers, PwC, but for the sake of clarity it has been called Price Waterhouse throughout this chapter.) There are of course advisers and lawyers on both sides, so there is some double counting, but the total worth of PFI at that time was estimated to be around £20bn. Amazingly, the Tube PPP is now reckoned to be worth that same amount, £20bn, over thirty years, which shows its vast scale, equivalent to all the other PFI deals signed up to the spring of 2001.

So back to Mr Prescott who duly obtained the transport brief after the 1997 election. Indeed, he was given a whole mega ministry to suit his ego and his position as Deputy Prime Minister: the Department of the Environment, Transport and the Regions, a huge department that was virtually unmanageable, as demonstrated by the fact that it was split up again by the summer of 2002. It did not take a minister in tune with New Labour thinking like John Prescott long to realise that the PFI represented his one hope of obtaining large amounts of money for any pet transport schemes. And the biggest, given that the railways were already privatised and supposedly funding themselves, was the London Underground. Like other ministers, Prescott was working under the constraints imposed by Tony Blair and Gordon Brown in the run-up to the 2001 election which had been designed to prove that Labour was a responsible party capable of prudent management of the economy. The key commitment was that the Tory spending plans, which had been cunningly reduced in the run-up to the election to make the Conservatives look responsible, should be adhered to for the first two years of a Labour government. Prescott, a strong supporter of public transport and, in particular, the railways, was desperate to try to solve the problems of the London Underground where the scale of underinvestment was obvious to any passenger and which, under the Tory regime, had been scheduled for a 50 per cent cut in grant during those two years. It was, of course, only after the election that Prescott had ministerial cars at his disposal, so he knew at first hand how desperate the situation was on the Tube.

Prescott realised quickly that to get any money for the Tube, he had to play the game. It was fruitless going cap in hand to the Treasury, now dominated by PFI zealots, and asking for lots of cash through the conventional borrowing route. He had, in any case, as we have seen, long advocated the use of private finance for public sector schemes and, indeed, fancied himself as a bit of an expert on the subject. He had no ideological hang-ups about the concept which he saw as a way of boosting the public sector with private companies footing the bill.

Prescott had also been clever enough to ingratiate himself with Gordon Brown before the election. The two were not natural allies. Indeed, Brown, a man who sees himself as an intellectual heavyweight, was rather contemptuous of the structurally inarticulate Prescott. Before the election, he had even tried to persuade Blair not to allow Prescott to take over a spending department, but clearly, given that Prescott was Deputy Prime Minister, this plea was always likely to fall on deaf ears. During 1996, relations between Prescott and Brown had been stretched to breaking point. Brown made a speech on 1 May that year which suggested that the Treasury would be a super ministry, encompassing both finance and 'long-term economic and social renewal'.[17] Prescott was deeply opposed to that idea, as such a dominant ministry would turn other senior ministers, like himself, into powerless ciphers. Moreover, he had already fallen out with Brown over the policy on Railtrack, which was being floated on the Stock Exchange at the time. Prescott was pushing for Labour to commit itself to renationalisation (which, ironically, has effectively happened), but Brown, backed by the shadow transport secretary, Clare Short, blocked the move.

Within a couple of weeks, Prescott responded at an obscure conference in Bournemouth, by slamming into the Treasury: 'Too often in the past, the dead hand of the Treasury has stifled initiative and motivation, in the public and private sector with a rigid inflexibility in the interpretation of Treasury rules.'[18] This was beginning to look like war in a shadow cabinet already riven with feuds before its members even had a whiff of power.

Brown decided to offer an olive branch. According to Colin Brown, Prescott's semi-official biographer, Brown sent Prescott a ticket for the crucial England–Scotland soccer match at Wembley in the European championships in June: 'Prescott and Brown sat together at the match, and Prescott began to come to terms with the dynamics of the Shadow Cabinet: he was never going to be able to prize Blair away from Brown; it would be better to work with him.'[19]

The two remained sceptical of each other despite the warming of relations, but after the election they began to work together, which turned out to be easier than either expected. Although there was never complete trust, the fact that these two big hitters of the Blair government were prepared to talk turkey was to prove crucial for the genesis of the PPP. As a confidant of Prescott put it, 'Prescott decided he was going to try to make things easier with Gordon Brown rather than go to war with him. I don't think Brown really believed him when it first happened, but in government they had to work together because it [the Department of the Environment, Transport and the Regions] was such a big department.'

The Tube was high on Prescott's agenda because very early in office he had been presented by his civil servants with a graph of the expected future government grant over the following three years and the amount, therefore, that London Underground could invest. And it was a mess, with the sum available for investment yo-yoing in the customary way explained in Chapter 5. Prescott knew enough about transport to realise that his aim must be to try to establish a steady and stable level of investment for the Tube, but the financial constraints imposed by the commitment to stick to Tory spending levels seemed to make this impossible. Denis Tunnicliffe, who was a known Labour sympathiser, was also emphasising to Prescott the need for such long-term stability. In the style that quickly became the norm for New Labour, Prescott commissioned a study into the future funding of the London Underground.

In fact there were two studies. The Department asked Price Waterhouse to undertake research on its behalf and London Underground embarked on its own study, using KPMG and Lazards as advisers, but liasing with Price Waterhouse. The two came to very different conclusions. Price Waterhouse's preferred option was for a 51 per cent sale of the Tube, but this was always going to be politically unacceptable to Prescott, especially as it seemed to breach the no privatisation commitment in the manifesto. Knowing this, Price Waterhouse also offered a series of other options, stressing the one involving the separation between operations and the infrastructure, on the basis that since it was the latter which required the major injection of cash for investment, the best way to ensure that money could be channelled there would be to separate it off.

Moreover, Price Waterhouse gave a hostage to fortune on behalf of all supporters of the PPP when it suggested that the whole deal could be self-funded by the private sector and would require no subsidy. In other words, the infrastructure companies would be able to raise money and pay for all the investment on the basis of what was being collected in the fare box.

London Underground was opposed to the Price Waterhouse approach. Indeed, its own report,[20] which continues to haunt the supporters of the PPP because it is always quoted by its opponents, found that the option closest to the PPP concept came 15th out of 16 in an analysis of the benefits of the various approaches. The report argued that there

> are powerful arguments against splitting up the Underground. Subdivided structures would create more boundaries, which impose higher set-up and transaction costs. They will make it more difficult to achieve co-ordination between technical and operational elements of the system and reduce the seamlessness of the network from the customers' point of view. They will also increase the risk of things going wrong at interfaces, which could affect service performance and safety.[21]

The LU report looked at a series of options ranging from the existing structure to outright privatisation of the whole system or groups of lines, splitting operations from infrastructure as well as the current PPP option which it called 'structured PFI'. There was only tepid enthusiasm for the private sector: 'The private sector may achieve greater efficiencies, because of the greater financial incentives . . . . There is evidence from other utilities, however, that these effects are as much due to the creation of competition as from private ownership *per se*.'[22] And competition, of course, as the report admitted, is virtually impossible to achieve on the Underground. Only 15 per cent of passengers have any choice of line and, in any case, it proved virtually impossible to create competition between operators in the privatisation of the national railway, a much more extensive network than the Underground.

As for safety, the wording was surprisingly strong: 'Subdivision creates greater concerns on the Underground than on the national railway. It is more highly interconnected, so problems on one line have an immediate knock-on effect elsewhere. It is more highly integrated technologically, especially between signalling and trains. The intensity of service and usage are such that the consequences of safety failure are much more significant.'[23]

The various options were compared in an analysis assessing the benefits over periods of fifteen, twenty-five and forty years, and on each one the PPP type option came near the bottom. Moreover, in the conclusion, the report makes a telling point that is one of the key arguments of those opposed to the PPP: 'The Underground is too important to experiment with. It is essential that the Underground is not driven down the path of difficult and uncertain change simply by a failure to challenge a series of conventions and assumptions. It is convention which excludes the possibility of committed grant, direct borrowing or hypothecated revenue. The assumption that the private sector will be more effective needs challenging.'[24]

Yet, despite the forcefulness of the findings in the report that was published in September 1997 with the endorsement of the London Transport board who had unanimously argued against splitting the infrastructure from the operations, within three months the decision had been made to do precisely that. The London Underground report was never likely to cut much ice with ministers considering their dim view of its management.

The exact genesis of the PPP is, inevitably, a story as murky as the average Tube tunnel, and the history is bound to be tailored according to what happens with the PPP. As Denis Tunnicliffe put it, 'if the PPP is a failure, I will be the sole parent. If it is a success, at least a dozen people will claim ownership.'[25] The crucial time was a few weeks over the turn of the year during the winter of 1997–8 when Prescott was keen to go ahead in order to ensure that the matter was sorted out before the creation of the London Mayor and the Greater London Assembly, ensuring that the money for the renewal of the Underground would be available as soon as the two years of spending controls were at an end. It all looked so simple. Create some kind of public private partnership in line with the manifesto and push the button. If only.

Following a couple of meetings between the London Transport management and Prescott, the fundamental principle of the PPP, the separation of London Underground into infrastructure companies and an operator, as set out by Price Waterhouse in its report, had been agreed as the *only* way forward. And London Underground fully acquiesced in the decision. Denis Tunnicliffe had been against the idea, as had Martin Callaghan, who later became the PPP director, yet both were to play a key role in its development. So what happened to make London Underground's best and finest change their minds?

In his meetings with London Transport, Prescott gave its report, on the options facing the Underground, short shrift. Prescott let it be known at the second meeting, in February 1998, that he wanted London Underground to create an infrastructure company and an operator.

According to Peter Ford, the then chairman, when, at the second meeting in February 1998, he asked Prescott whether he had read the report, the Deputy Prime Minister responded with his characteristic gruffness: 'I've sort of looked at it.' Ford, who actually favoured outright privatisation, was brave enough to point out that the option being suggested by Prescott had come out last but one on the list. He was met with silence and, as he puts it, 'clearly I realised my days were numbered'.[26]

Between the production of the London Transport report on options and Prescott's decision announced in March 1998 to go for a PPP for the Tube, there had been a frenetic round of behind the scenes negotiations. The key player was Geoffrey Robinson, who was the Paymaster General in the Treasury under Gordon Brown, and who had a private sector background, having run Jaguar Cars. Brown and Prescott's relationship was too fragile for serious face-to-face negotiations and therefore Robinson acted as a go-between to broker a deal. Basically, two entrenched positions emerged. Prescott's bottom line was his opposition to outright privatisation. He was adamant that the Tube would remain in the public sector, but he was equally keen to ensure that money was available for investment. Robinson's position was that the London Underground management could not be given responsibility for refurbishing the system: 'We could not possibly give the money to the London Underground as it was too badly managed. The money is a bit more expensive in the private sector, but that does not matter if you save it on efficiency.'[27] The Treasury was still enthusiastic about rail privatisation, which had, so far, not run into the problems that would emerge in the second half of the first Blair government after the Hatfield accident in October 2000.

Brown and Robinson really wanted to see a part privatisation, the sale of 51 per cent of the Tube, which had been Price Waterhouse's favoured option, so that investment would be spread across the private and public sectors; but Prescott was completely opposed. He did not trust Price Waterhouse's findings and in order to allay his concerns, Robinson, with the blessing of both Brown and Tony Blair, appointed a group of four men in late 1997 to examine the options for the Tube. It was, according to an insider, 'a compromise to break the deadlock'. But the choice of the members of this little group predetermined its conclusions since all were businessmen with experience of similar deals. The groupuscule, chaired by Sir Malcolm Bates, who had a long-term interest in PFI and later became chairman of London Transport, comprised: John Roques, an accountant and former senior partner with Deloitte & Touche; Sir Graham Hearne, chairman of Enterprise Oil; and Ed Wallace, chairman of PowerGen. Robinson revealed the existence of this group to Parliament nearly five years later, explaining: 'We had to find a way forward. We could skin the cat in so many ways and there were many different options available. Number Ten had its view, the advisers to Number Ten had their view, the then Department of the Environment, Transport and the Regions had its view. I had my view, the Treasury had a view – and the Deputy Prime Minister had very strong views.' So, oddly, it was left to the four businessmen, handpicked by Robinson, to break this deadlock that seemed to have paralysed the whole political establishment: 'With the Deputy Prime Minister's agreement, I convened a group of four business men with experience of both the public and private sectors to make a recommendation to us. Essentially, that recommendation is what we have today: a split at a point that can logically be defended and can, from a business point of view, be implemented at least as easily as the proposal to leave it to the present London Underground management to continue on their own.'[28]

The negotiations between Prescott and Brown's bagman had become even more complicated with wheeling and dealing over a series of other transport issues. There was no formal deal, no signing of a peace treaty between Brown and Prescott, but, instead, a stand-off that included a series of 'understandings' over a range of issues which affected the two. Brown wanted the privatisation of National Air Traffic Services to go ahead, Prescott wanted councils to be able to keep revenue from congestion charges so that they could reinvest it in improving public transport. The issue of local authority-owned airports being able to borrow money to invest in expansion without the money counting against the Public Sector Borrowing Requirement also became part of the series of trade-offs between the Deputy Prime Minister and Brown. On those side issues, which actually were potentially very important, Prescott obtained key concessions. Local authorities were allowed to keep the money from congestion charges, though ironically, by 2002 the only area with a well-developed scheme to begin charging was London, run by mayor Ken Livingstone, Brown's political enemy; airports got the right to borrow money; Brown was able to flog off NATS, though the private component, 46 per cent, went to a consortium of airlines which promptly had to be bailed out with extra government cash after 11 September; and London got the PPP and an extra £365m grant to London Transport over the next two years in order to enable it to keep investing until the PPP kicked in, which was supposed to be by 2000, in time for it to be handed to what would then be the newly created Transport for London.

Prescott later gained another concession from Brown, which was that the money from any above inflation rises in petrol prices, the fuel tax escalator, would go direct to the transport budget, but this proved only a theoretical victory since the escalator was scrapped immediately afterwards and cannot now be revived because of the fuel protestors' widely supported demonstrations of autumn 2000. Nevertheless, that showed that Brown thought he owed Prescott for agreeing to the PPP for the Tube, despite the latter's misgivings about the extent of privatisation which it entailed.

The key transport issue that ended up being interwoven with the Tube PPP was the funding for the Channel Tunnel Rail Link. The Tory government had given the concession to build the 68-mile link between the mouth of the tunnel and a new terminus at St Pancras to London & Continental Railway, a consortium of eight companies including Virgin, National Express, Bechtel and Ove Arup. The consortium had been given a £1.8bn grant, the trains and a stake in the Eurostar service and, in return, were expected to fund the construction of the link estimated to cost around £4bn. However, early in 1998 the consortium announced it needed extra money from the government because its forecasts of passenger numbers on the Eurostar had been wildly optimistic and therefore it could not afford to build the new line.

Prescott faced a dilemma. He did not want to hand over more money to the private consortium. Yet his boss, Tony Blair, was keen to see the project through, as it would cut half an hour off journeys to Paris and Brussels, and the fact that trains had to trundle through Kent where they were frequently held up by commuter trains was a source of great embarrassment to the European-leaning leader. Prescott refused to bail out LC&R directly, but instead entered into a lengthy set of negotiations with the company and, of course, the Treasury. The details of the ultimate deal announced in June 1998[29] need not detain us except for one key facet which has greatly affected the debate on the PPP. The small print of the press release of the announcement showed that, remarkably, Prescott had managed to persuade the Treasury that the deal should be underwritten by the government through £3.8bn worth of debt and bonds which, remarkably, would not count against the Public Sector Borrowing Requirement. Prescott had been helped by the fact that the Treasury was faced with a stark alternative: if the deal had not gone through, then the government would have had to continue funding the loss making Eurostar service. Prescott would have been happy with that, as he would have been able to boast to his Labour colleagues that he had renationalised the service with the Treasury supporting the losses.

According to a Prescott ally, 'We got the deal through because the Treasury reckoned that there was less than a 5 per cent chance of the bond having to be called upon. If it had been 6 per cent, then we would have had to put the full amount into that year's government spending.'[30] This bending of the rules would come to haunt the protagonists of the PPP. After all, if bonds could be used to back the Channel Tunnel Rail Link, why not the Tube? Bonds are the cheapest form of obtaining finance since they are government-backed, but the Treasury always vetoed the idea because it saw them as giving carte blanche to other government departments to spend its money. The CTRL was an exceptional case, argued the Treasury without quite explaining exactly why. Interestingly, the CTRL has been built by the private sector with public sector money underwritten by a government guarantee and yet, at the time of writing, is both on budget and on time, with the first stage due to open in the autumn of 2003.

The key part of the PPP structure to which Prescott acquiesced was the break-up of the Underground into four parts – an operator and three infrastructure companies (infracos) – and, crucially, the privatisation of the latter on thirty-year contracts. Prescott had resisted all attempts to privatise the operator principally because it employed the vast majority of the employees. They were strongly unionised and their unions, with whom Prescott had well-established links stretching back to the 1960s when he worked for the seamen's union that was later incorporated into the RMT, were fiercely opposed to privatisation. Moreover, he managed to negotiate very good terms for those 5000 employees who were going to transfer over; better than the statutory protection under the TUPE[31] rules, as they retained full pension rights which was not usually the case for workers whose company was being privatised. A close ally of Prescott's accepts that the motivation was to protect the 11,000 operational staff but that this decision was not related specifically to the RMT: 'He did not want to privatise the people and he fought very hard to make sure they were not threatened. But it was nothing to do with the RMT. He had seen other privatisations in which people got less well treated and he did not think TUPE was quite strong enough. He did the same with the air traffic controllers. Both times it was contrary to the advice of the Treasury which thought it would deter investors.'

For Prescott, the compromise of what was a part-privatisation, even though notionally the infrastructure returns to the public sector at the end of the contracts, was a price worth paying for ensuring the whole thing was not privatised and that most of the employees remained in the public sector. However, as we shall see, there is little logic to it. The other ostensible reason for the manner of the split was the one argued by Price Waterhouse: since it was the infrastructure which needed the money and as the cash had to come from the private sector, the logic must be to privatise that part of the Underground system. However, keeping the operations in the public sector did not seem to fit into a coherent policy on what functions are best carried out under public or private control, particularly in the light of what was happening simultaneously on the national railways. There, the Labour government has shown no interest in taking back the rail franchises even though many of them run out in 2003–4, which would therefore present an opportunity to rethink the structure. Instead, during Labour's first term the Strategic Rail Authority was under instructions to refranchise out the network on longer contracts, up to twenty years, and to give two-year extensions where this was not possible. And the equivalent of the Tube infrastructure companies, Railtrack, was effectively renationalised when in October 2002 it was re-created into Network Rail, a not-for-profit company backed to the tune of £9bn by borrowing supported by the Strategic Rail Authority, a government organisation.

In truth, there was a bigger political imperative at play. The whole thrust of the approach of Blair and Brown towards the public sector was not to allow it any great freedom in which to make what they would see as further cock-ups, and to place great store in what the private sector could offer. It is quite probable that even without the Jubilee Line Extension overrun, and all the other historical reasons which resulted in the development of the PPP for the Tube, the sheer momentum of New Labour's approach would have led down that path anyway.

Prescott, therefore, announced in Parliament on 20 March 1998 that there was to be a 'first class Tube for everyone'[32] with £7bn worth of investment over fifteen years and 'one, two or three' contractors for the infrastructure: 'It is not nationalisation, nor privatisation, but a radical new third way.' There was precious little detail in the announcement or in the subsequent debate. Prescott confirmed that London Underground would get an extra £365m grant on top of the Tories' spending plans, sufficient to enable it to spend £1bn on investment in the following two years with the PPP then kicking in. He was, though, vague about where the money was coming from and about the details of the scheme, which was hardly surprising since they had not been worked out. On money, Prescott said: 'by adopting this private sector initiative, we will be able to use the assets and the income stream from London Transport operations to guarantee payments for long-term investment'. This statement suggests that Prescott did not quite understand what he was talking about, as he seemed to be thinking of a model that is not part of the PPP but one in which the future income stream of London Underground would be 'securitised' – i.e. a large sum would be borrowed against it and used to refurbish the system. It is an idea which, in fact, has been rejected by the government but which many opponents of the PPP suggest as one of the best ways forward.

Prescott stressed that 'public accountability will mean just that, and public ownership means that we shall have a stronger sanction in making sure that the contracts work'. Private companies, he added, were queuing up to bid for the contracts, ensuring there would be healthy competition, though he did not explain how that could be when the concept was still in embryonic form.

There was precious little opposition from either side of the House to the announcement which, oddly, had been made on a Friday when the House is usually empty and debates are generally confined to private members' bills. There was merely a hint of scepticism from the Tories about the cost of the scheme. As Sir Norman Fowler, Prescott's opposite number, put it, 'Is there not a danger that the system announced today will prove to be the most expensive means of attracting private investment into the system?'

On the Labour side, even the left-winger and Ken Livingstone acolyte John McDonnell broadly welcomed the announcement. One London Labour MP, who is now a fervent behind the scenes opponent of the scheme, reckons that the reason Prescott's announcement seemed so uncontroversial at the time was because 'there was no sense when the statement was made that this was a nightmare in the making. People were not thinking that this was a completely new type of contract procurement. Instead, it was presented as a way of levering in huge amounts of cash that we would not otherwise have. It was PPP with the emphasis on the "public" bit.'

But, as we shall see, what Prescott signed up to and announced in March 1998 was a very different PPP to the one that has eventually emerged. For a start, the contracts are now for thirty years and the sum of money being talked about is £13bn rather than £7bn. The contracts were supposed to start in April 2000, before the mayor was elected, so that the newly created Transport for London would be presented with a fait accompli. Transport for London is the transport arm of the mayor which took over the buses and main roads on its creation in July 2000 but because of the delays to the PPP will not take over the Underground until the contracts for the PPP deal are finally signed, now expected to be in 2003.

The most significant change is, of course, the fact that far from being self-financing, the PPP will require over £1bn to be paid annually in contract charges by Transport for London, and as London Underground is no longer making a profit, that will have to come from government coffers or London council-tax payers. As a former member of Prescott's office team put it, 'John had been sceptical of PPP but suddenly he thought it was wonderful. I think he was sold a pup. He thought all the £7bn would come from the private sector and that the extra grant would keep investment flowing until then.' It is, as the next chapter shows, rather more complicated than that.

CHAPTER EIGHT

So what is the PPP?

Before moving ahead to cover the battle over the PPP, it is necessary to try to explain it. That is not an easy task in a book aimed at a non-specialist audience because it is almost as if the designers of the PPP do not want anyone to be able to understand it. The documentation itself stretches to 135 volumes with an estimated 2800 pages and two million words and, at the time of writing, the summer of 2002, it is growing all the time as further complexities and issues of potential contention emerge.

To explain the full details of the contracts would take up the whole of this book and ensure that no one would read it. This outline, in order not to bore readers rigid, is therefore a somewhat cursory *tour d'horizon* of something so complex that even those with an intimate knowledge of it cannot provide a detailed explanation of its scope and intent in less than a couple of hours. We are in uncharted waters. No one has tried to explain the PPP in any detail in layperson's language. Nor is this the place for a critique. This chapter largely sticks to the explanation given by London Underground in both interviews and published material. The analysis comes later (see Chapter 12).

The PPP is a contract between the operator, London Underground, which will eventually be transferred to Transport for London, and the infrastructure companies – infracos as they have become known. There are three infrastructure contracts. Two, the sub-surface lines (SSL) and the Jubilee, Northern and Piccadilly lines (JNP), were won by Metronet, and the other, for the Bakerloo, Central and Victoria lines (BCV) by Tube Lines. (The bidding process and the details of these consortia are covered in Chapter 11.)

While the endless stream of very thick and extremely dry documents produced by London Underground give all the facts and the reasoning behind the PPP, there is a need for a guiding hand and there is only one person in London Underground qualified to provide it. Martin Callaghan is London Underground's PPP director, its Mr PPP who now has a mission to sell it. For many months, years even, London Underground's executives were not allowed to discuss the policy because of the political controversy but now they have been allowed off the leash. It is, according to the chief press officer who gives me a stern little lecture before I am allowed in to see Callaghan, a great privilege to have been allocated an hour with the master. 'Martin Callaghan's time is our most precious commodity,' he whispers with reverence, especially given that it is May 2002, the height of the final negotiations over the PPP. Callaghan is a gaunt nervous fellow whose formidable intellect is not in question. He talks like a father whose adored baby has been kept in quarantine; now that he is free to show it off, he is eager to seize any opportunity to do so. On a sunny summer day, in his sparse office enlivened only by a joke fish bowl on his meeting table whose plastic occupant seems to be in perpetual and frictionless motion, a metaphor far too obvious to mention, it takes not one hour, but two and a half for Callaghan to outline the scheme. The proceedings are only interrupted by his PA occasionally popping her head round the door with news of urgent calls, most of them from Price Waterhouse, all of which Callaghan says can wait.

The baby analogy is not entirely fatuous. Callaghan has worked on the PPP since its creation and there is a lot of personal investment in it. The hostility which the PPP has engendered is clearly personally hurtful and he is genuinely bemused by it. While giving an emotionally charged lecture to 200 rail executives at the Railway Forum in July 2002, Callaghan was quite visibly upset about what had happened over the PPP. The delegates were astonished at the tone of his remarks which seemed to suggest that what he had done had been thoroughly developed but that the message had not been conveyed to the public:

> Maybe we thought that it was all too complicated for people to understand, or we just wanted a quiet life, or maybe we just rather naively thought that because it was government policy, it would inevitably happen . . . The PPP is a hugely well thought through, imaginative, rational, well-tested response to the challenge given to us by Government, which is to find a value for money and safe way of getting the best you can for customers out of a billion pounds a year of public expenditure.

Yet, according to Callaghan, the 'public debate has provided not much illumination about what this PPP thing is'. It is almost as if he were blaming the public for the failure of the protagonists of the PPP to get their message across.

In outlining the history to me, Callaghan covers the creation of the PPP in great detail; but as the elaborate explanations come out, so do the questions, and clearly the exercise, which started at 10 a.m., could have continued well into the night. Callaghan has been with London Underground for a dozen years, but most of that time has been spent as a freelance consultant. It was only recently that he joined the staff to take the organisation through to the PPP. After a lengthy education with an economics degree from Cambridge and a PhD in business systems from Aston, he spent a few years with Dunlop and as a consultant, but he sees himself as a long-term Underground man employed for much of his time, to his delight, as Denis Tunnicliffe's extra brain with the task of fleshing out his boss's stream of ideas.

His explanation of the PPP makes it sound like a journey, an exceedingly long one, and is peppered with expressions like 'the view we took' and 'in order to do that'.[1] Every solution involves opening up new issues which, in turn, must be solved. It was what the management consultants call an 'iterative process', one which started as a relatively simple idea and which built up gradually as the need to cover more and more eventualities became apparent. The best metaphor is probably that favourite school science experiment, the copper sulphate grain left hanging in a strong solution which grows into a complex crystalline structure as the water evaporates. Except that no one would suggest the PPP is beautiful.

The first question about the PPP is why the particular solution of splitting the Underground into four was chosen, especially in the light of the fact that, as we saw in the previous chapter, the 1997 options paper produced by London Underground so firmly rejected the idea. Callaghan admits that they were wrong at the time in 1997. Tunnicliffe had set up a system of management for each line which incorporated the basic maintenance, creating an integrated structure that led to an improved performance because it gave managers a clear area of responsibility. The idea was that one manager, or at least the same management team, would be in charge of making sure both that a train was available and that there was someone to drive it.

The London Underground options paper argued for the retention of such an integrated structure but Callaghan says this logic missed an important point over the way LU used its engineers. He sets out this reasoning, on what seems a relatively arcane point, at great length: 'By the end of the 1990s, we realised there was a significant issue around the long-term future of our engineering activities. Increasingly in the industry, people were coming to buy major assets on a "design, build and maintain" basis with the idea of ensuring the designer had the long-term maintenance costs in mind, rather than simply doing the lowest cost job which would then be more expensive to maintain.'

As more and more of London Underground's assets would be run on that basis, Callaghan was concerned that it would become increasingly difficult to find engineers: 'It makes perfect sense to obtain long-term assets on a "design, build, maintain" basis but the consequence is that all the knowledge of modern assets is outsourced. What you are saying to graduate engineers who you are trying to recruit is effectively that "we have a heap of old assets and we want you to come along and look after a dwindling portfolio of these assets, recognising that by the time these assets are being looked after by the private sector, you've got no job and you know nothing about these new assets, and therefore you will become unemployable". If you were a graduate engineer, you would not think that is an exciting proposition.'

Therefore, Callaghan and his team needed to devise a way of ensuring that engineers would still want to work for London Underground: 'One of the things the PPP does, and one of the things that we did not give enough weight to in 1997, is that it creates a portfolio of old and new assets, and that the engineers who have to look after the assets are also keeping their skills current as they are looking after the new assets, maintaining their position in the labour market. It seems to me inevitable that eventually we would come to realise that bundling these assets up into portfolios of old and new and having them looked after in a way that allowed people on both was something that was going to end up happening.'

Clearly, the problem over continued employment of engineers, on which Callaghan dwells for a long time, was not the only reason for the decision to split the infrastructure from the operations. Callaghan went on to say: 'What drove the decision was a perfectly reasonable piece of analysis –

which is the thing about accessing private finance and private sector engineering skills. The bit of the railway which needed the money was the infrastructure and not the operations which is a people business. So is it not obvious that the infrastructure is what you package up to try to get the money – and not the operations?'

The key question was where to have the separation between the infrastructure and the services. On the national railway, the infrastructure was privatised as Railtrack, while the passenger services were split between twenty-five operating companies who were responsible for light train maintenance, although the stock is leased from rolling stock companies. This split between rail and wheel created maintenance problems, as it was realised, especially after the Hatfield train crash in October 2000, that it was vital to have that interface managed by one organisation. So, instead, in the London Underground model, the maintenance on both trains and track is carried out by the infraco and the interface is a time one: the trains are handed over to the operator every morning and handed back at night when the service is terminated. Thus the trains are the responsibility of the infraco overnight, but the operators are in charge of them during the day.

Once the decision to split the infrastructure off from operations had been made, as we saw in the last chapter, in early 1998, London Transport began to develop the model, with help from consultants and advisers: PricewaterhouseCoopers, as it had now become, which was strange given that its research had contradicted London Underground's own 'options' report – 'though we disagreed with everything they said, we thought they had approached the problems in a sensible way and had listened', according to Callaghan – Freshfields, London Underground's lawyers and Ove Arup as engineering adviser, as well as various teams of its own managers.

According to Callaghan, 'the structure had to fit parameters fairly well defined by us' and the key one was 'we don't care how it is done but it is going to have a performance regime which aligns the interests of the infracos – though they were not called that at the time – with the interests of the travellers'. In other words, and this is the very centrepiece of the whole concept of the PPP, if the infracos manage to reduce delays, they must be rewarded for it, and if they make them worse, they must be penalised.

Indeed, the most fundamental point to understand about the PPP is that the value of the contract is not based on fixed monetary transactions but is highly dependent on the performance of the infracos. That performance is measured not through the positive achievements of the infracos but through their ability to minimise 'lost customer hours', which broadly means delays to the service. There are three other factors making up the measurement of performance, which are outlined below, but by far the most important in terms of the conception of the PPP and the daily running of the Tube is this notion of 'lost customer hours'.

Just a digression, leaving Callaghan in mid flow for a moment, to stress the uniqueness of this idea. There is no other contract in the world which has attempted to measure the output and, therefore, the payment levels through such an indirect concept as 'lost customer hours'. Of course Private Finance Initiative contracts have all sorts of odd measured outputs, such as the availability of hospital beds or classrooms, but none has attempted to use such an abstract construct as 'lost customer hours' on which to base a billion pound per year contract that involves the management and renewal of a vast swathe of existing assets as well as major enhancements to a highly complex metro system.

Callaghan says that they looked at the performance regime created for the railways as part of privatisation, which attributes every minute of delay between Railtrack (now Network Rail) and the train operators who, consequently, have to pay each other penalties when time is lost as a result of their actions. However, the system was crude – it did not sufficiently reward good performance by Railtrack and, crucially, there was no incentive in the structure to encourage Railtrack to invest in increasing capacity on the network. Therefore, the Tube PPP takes the concept much further by measuring each delay in terms of the number of passengers affected. So a signal failure on the outer reaches of the system such as Mill Hill East or Ickenham will have a much smaller 'abatement' – the word 'penalty', according to Callaghan, is banned: 'penalties have a particular legal meaning and they are not penalties but abatements' – than one at Piccadilly Circus or Embankment. The time of day will also be taken into account, with delays during rush hours generating much higher abatements. In the jargon, 'the main requirement on a day to day basis is that infracos should make the railway infrastructure available and in a fit and proper condition. The PPP therefore provides financial incentives for infracos to minimise asset-related delays measured in terms of "lost customer hours".'[2]

Callaghan is confident that the information is available in London Underground to calculate delays for every eventuality. Whether it is three minutes to a Piccadilly Line train at Earls Court at 5 p.m. or an hour to a Central Line train at Mile End at 2 p.m., there will be information estimating how many passengers are likely to be affected: 'It is based on the failures and delays system which was already in existence when I first arrived at London Underground in the late 1980s. All we have done is improve the precision and built a computer system which records all the failures and multiplies it by lost customer hours.' The information is transformed from time into cash through a simple formula, as London Underground calculates that time lost is worth, on average, £6 per hour to passengers. In the other direction, if performance improves, the infracos will receive only £3 extra per notionally saved customer hour. There is, too, a kind of 'unacceptable' level of performance below which the infraco will have to pay £9 per hour.

There is a complicated rationale behind the difference between the level of abatements and the reward for improvement. London Underground do not want to 'incentivise' the infracos to make too many improvements. As Callaghan points out, 'the public sector would not invest in a one-to-one benefit–cost ratio'. In other words, unless £1m of investment could bring in, say, £2m of benefits, as calculated at £6 per hour, then the improvement will not be carried out. The performance regime has to be calibrated 'in such a way that the infracos spend a sensible amount of money to get a sensible level of benefit'. Therefore, there has to be a performance regime which 'optimises the way we spend taxpayers' money. We don't want to offer too much money because then we are spending taxpayers' money that would be better spent elsewhere in the public sector, and we don't want them to underinvest because otherwise we are not optimising what transport delivers to London's transport users.'

The concept of lost customer hours is, of course, highly dependent on the benchmark used as the basis from which payments and abatements will be calculated. The benchmarks relate to the average performance in a sixty-four-week period between September 2000 and November 2001 but were set at 5 per cent below the performance during that period. This was set according to the *Final Assessment Report*, the document produced by London Underground giving details of the PPP for the public, at this level because 'LUL considered it would not offer value for money to have bidders price this risk in full'.[3] That is a very revealing sentence, as it suggests that the risk for the performance regime rests with London Underground since the bidders will have incorporated that risk into the pricing of their bids. In other words, London Underground is actually bearing the risk of the infracos failing to meet the performance regime since the companies have, effectively, built the cost of anything short of catastrophic failure (which itself is capped as we see below) into the pricing of their bids.

Although the benchmark is 5 per cent below existing levels of service, London Underground argues that to obtain bonuses, the infraco would have to do better than current performance. That is because the targets are calculated in four-week periods and, by the simple law of averages, vary. Since the bonuses for good performance are half the abatements for bad performance, such random variation around the same level of performance would lead to a net payment by the infraco.

Originally the idea was that there would be a cap which limited the extra payments if performance improved by 35 per cent, but this was scrapped during shadow running. The explanation is interesting. According to the *Final Assessment Report*, the cap was originally imposed because it was felt that the infracos would try to improve performance beyond what was economically worthwhile to the public purse, but during shadow running it was realised that the extra costs of improved performance were not that great. The potential liability for London Underground, and Transport for London when it eventually takes over the management of the Tube, is, consequently, higher – though, of course, the ultimate cap to bonus payments is when performance reaches 100 per cent which, realistically, is not achievable. When asked, London Underground was unwilling to provide estimates of the potential amount of money which a highly efficient infraco could obtain annually through improved performance, but Transport for London has commissioned research on this from Deloitte & Touche (see below).

To Callaghan, the changes in the contract concerning the cap demonstrate the care which has been taken in devising the PPP. To its opponents, this episode shows that the calibration is so difficult that the PPP is likely to lead to perverse outcomes as the contractors work out the best way to play the system rather than what is best for Londoners.

In order to show how a relatively simple concept such as lost customer hours quickly becomes enmeshed in daunting complexities, consider the way the regime treats temporary speed restrictions (TSRs). These are imposed on the railway when something is amiss that is not serious enough to stop all services but, for safety reasons, requires trains to operate at less than the normal line speed, often 10 mph. This, of course, slows down services and may well reduce the number of trains through cancellations. So how should this be reflected in the regime? That was clearly something of a struggle for the designers of the PPP because temporary speed restrictions were a significant part of the availability score on a line. 'Availability' is, in a way, the converse of 'lost customer hours', as when availability goes down, the number of delays will inevitably rise. Clearly, the better the availability, the fewer lost customer hours.

The first problem encountered with shadow running was that TSRs were not being recorded consistently, so this was remedied. According to London Underground, after that 'it became apparent that TSRs could represent a significant part of the total availability score in any period, and the TSR availability score was far more volatile than that for non-TSR availability'.[4] In other words, temporary speed restrictions could, to a large extent, determine whether an infraco was achieving the required performance level to avoid paying abatements or to obtain premium payments under the contract. Since TSRs can be large, unpredictable events with huge consequences on the amounts of money flowing to the contractors, LU decided to separate the availability score for TSR from the rest of the formula. LU also felt that because of the uneven nature of the imposition of TSRs, an even longer period than sixty-four weeks was required to be used as the benchmark – November 1999 to July 2000, eighty-four weeks.

OK, so far so good. We have the benchmark. But the infracos are due to improve the track over the first 7.5-year period, and TSRs, which are usually due to a track defect, are unlikely to occur on these renewed stretches of line. Therefore, the benchmark target must become more demanding as the years of the contract unfold. The contracts assume that 30 per cent of the track will be renewed in that first period and 'the benchmark calculation assumes that infracos will replace sections of track in the order which reduces the level of temporary speed restrictions most quickly, having regard to how often there have been TSRs on any section in the past and the number of lost customer hours which would accrue if there were one in future'.[5] Therefore the benchmark will be adjusted accordingly.

Still with me? We are almost there, but there is a bit more. Speed restrictions may have to remain in force for longer than originally envisaged. For example, if a whole section of line is due to be replaced in six months' time, it would be a waste of money to patch up a faulty track in the interim. Therefore, temporary speed restrictions which have been in place for more than twelve weeks are 'closed out' and no longer deemed to result in 'lost customer hours'. Instead, they are included as a reduction of the 'capability' score, explained below.

The importance of the concept of the 'lost customer hours' at the heart of the PPP cannot be overestimated. As we have seen from the example of the way that temporary speed restrictions are dealt with, they are used as the mechanism through which the interests of the infraco and the public are aligned. In answer to the question, 'So what you are saying is that the concept of lost customer hours is the core of the whole PPP and has driven it?', Callaghan's answer is simple: 'Absolutely.'

And the proof is in the tasting, according to Callaghan. Since September 1999, the system has been tested with London Underground being separated into three infracos and a sole operator. Of course, it is only 'shadow running' because no real money changes hands, but Callaghan is delighted that it has led to major improvements in the management of the infrastructure. Callaghan argues that the key is the way that this regime will impact on the contractors, aligning the incentives between passengers and the infrastructure: 'If we, as the client, were merely able to tell them that they had cost passengers 30,000 hours, they would not know if that is a lot or a little. But if you can say, do you realise that signal failure at Oxford Circus cost £250,000, they can engage with that. If you are the managing director of a company that is seeing £5m every month go out because you are not fixing faults, you make sure that the people who are responsible for it do the work.' And he reckons this has worked in shadow running. He points to the improvements in performance by the shadow infracos since September 1999: 'The shadow infracos have started thinking quite differently about how they can make sure that things don't fail. They ask things like "how can we redeploy people, where is the best place to put a train technician so that if something goes wrong, they can get there as quickly as possible?"' Moreover, according to Callaghan, the process of shadow running has meant that many mistakes have been spotted, allowing London Underground to fine-tune the contracts, which have changed substantially since they were first written. The first year of shadow running involved a testing programme where every aspect of the contract was examined to see which parts worked well and which did not. There were all kinds of arguments between the shadow infracos and the operator, London Underground, over the meaning of words in the contract such as what is understood by a 'minor closure'. As Jon Smith, London Underground's director of contract services, put it, 'when did a minor closure start and when did it end? So that you make sure you don't start running down the service halfway through Friday and so that you can close it on Sunday'. According to Smith, there were a myriad such issues that have been cleared up during shadow running.

One difficulty on the national railway was developing ways of attributing faults between Railtrack and the various train operators, and a whole panoply of clerks have been employed to allocate every minute of delay on the system. The system in the Underground is simpler since there are only four organisations involved, rather than the thirty on the national network, but nevertheless there are around a thousand service disruptions every week which will need allocating between infracos and the operator. London Underground reckon that this has been relatively successful under shadow running with only 9 per cent requiring 'review at middle management level' and only 1 per cent at levels beyond that. Most of the payments will be from the infracos to the operator but there is one major exception. If the infraco has organised work on the line and the operator has failed to provide access – normally because services have been running later into the early morning than timetabled – it will receive compensation, something like £100,000 for a routine job, say a small section of track replacement.

Apart from lost customer hours, there are three other elements which make up the structure of the contract. They are less important in terms of day-to-day operation but are still all designed to 'incentivise' the infracos. They are: ambience, service points and, the most complex, capability – not to be confused with availability. In terms of the amount of money at risk, capability is by far the most important.

Capability is a measure of the potential performance of each line which is designed to ensure that the infracos invest in improvements in the line. However, rather than specify clear outputs, such as 'you shall refurbish the Piccadilly Line by 2010' and 'you will provide *x* new trains' as with conventional contracts, the investment is measured by what it achieves. Therefore, for example, the capability target will be to reduce the time taken by trains between two stations by a certain number of minutes and/or increase the number of people able to make that journey.

This could be done in several ways: the trains could be made longer or the signalling improved so that they could be run closer together; or at a much more micro level, the time that doors take to open and shut could be reduced or the acceleration of the rolling stock could be improved. The key point here is that the infracos have an incentive to improve the capability but they are not instructed as to how to do it – it is their decision as to which of these investments are made. The higher the capability, the lower the average potential journey time on that line can be.

Once the investment has been made, the infraco will be rewarded. The basic payments to the infracos will, therefore, increase during the length of the contract as they are expected to complete work to improve the speed of journeys and, as Callaghan put it, 'there will be a big increase. As with lost customer hours, infracos will be rewarded with bonuses for performance better than benchmark and vice versa.'

The calibration of the capability concept is even more complex and difficult than 'lost customer hours'. Here is Callaghan's explanation of how the calculation is made: 'We had to find a way to incentivise investment in new equipment to increase capacity. In order to do that, we had to find a way of defining increased capacity. What you get out of a line upgrade is that the "average generalised cost" of a journey in terms of the time taken, the crowding, whether you have a seat – this stuff is weighted so that a minute on the platform or on a train or on a crowded train are all calculated differently – is reduced. So we set targets to reduce the average generalised cost of a journey and developed this concept called capability, setting a capability target for each line, which all require a step change from where we are now.' The bidders for the contract were presented with this information, enabling them to draw up schemes to make long-term improvements on the system.

The idea was worked out by giving a value to the journey time – broadly, again, £6 per hour – and therefore any reduction can be counted as a benefit. So, crudely, if there are 300,000 users of a section of line every day, and their journey is cut by three minutes, that gives a daily saving of 900,000 minutes, or 15,000 hours, which, at £6 per hour (5p per minute), is worth £90,000. Annually, that is worth about £33m (although there is a complication about whether you count weekends as the same, but we will leave that aside). That benefit of £33m annually can be translated through a process called Net Present Value to a fixed amount. Again, crudely, let us say, with interest rates at 6 per cent and the benefit expected to last in perpetuity, the Net Present Value would be worth around seventeen times the annual amount, which gives us £550m. It is rather more complicated because the £6 per hour is not standard throughout, as time in a crowded train rates more than time on a platform, but we will ignore that. So, in theory, within the PPP, it should be made worthwhile for the infraco to spend £550m or less on an investment that will cut three minutes off the journey time on that section of track. The example given in the Invitation to Tender document is that a two minute improvement on the Victoria Line would generate £12m per annum (10p, i.e. 5p per minute each, for 120 million passengers). Originally, the Invitation to Tender had suggested that a 15–20 per cent improvement in capability could be 'achievable on most lines' within the first 7.5 year period of the contract, but this aspiration has subsequently been greatly reduced (see Chapter 12).

This type of measurement, a cost benefit analysis, is used widely in assessing whether a scheme should go ahead, but the PPP takes it further by rewarding the contractors directly for the benefits in terms of reduced journey times, rather than paying a set amount for work carried out. The contractors will use this methodology to assess whether it is worthwhile undertaking a particular improvement.

Callaghan is absolutely certain that the capability benchmarks have been set to ensure that the infracos will have to invest and they cannot get away with merely cosmetic improvements: 'We have calculated a level of change that can only be delivered by renewing the trains or the signalling. We said to the infracos, "You cannot do this simply by better maintenance; you have got to use new technology."' However, it is up to the infracos how they deliver this improvement, choosing between new trains, renovated signalling, seating arrangements and so on. For example, according to Rod Hoare, chief executive of Metronet, the successful bidder for two of the three infracos: 'London Underground had suggested a heavy engineering solution to boost the Circle Line, involving flyovers and underpasses. We have worked out that the improvements can be achieved with signalling that will allow us to have a much more controlled flow at the four junctions – South Ken, Edgware Road, Baker Street and Aldgate. That has probably saved them £1bn.'[6]

This is the key and controversial aspect of the whole PPP. Payments are not governed by work that is done but by what that spending achieves, which is designed to overcome the tendency of the public sector, highlighted by the construction of the Jubilee Line Extension, to change requirements during the procurement process. As London Underground puts it, 'through the use of output specifications, PPPs can help Government to focus more clearly on what people want and help shift the focus from input to outcomes'.[7] The aim is to 'increase the scope for innovation and flexibility in the management and delivery of the services' and 'ensure that potential service providers are assessed on their ability to achieve results'.

But the approach of using outcomes inevitably begs the question of how to measure them. Even the simple calculation of the benchmark for 'journey time capability' is not straightforward. How do you work out exactly how long it takes a train to get from High Barnet to Morden under normal circumstances? Under what conditions do you run a train? Do you put your best train, which has the greatest acceleration, or an average one? And do you choose your most capable driver? The possibilities are endless and shadow running revealed these complexities. Therefore, it was decided to measure journey time capability. According to London Underground, the contracts had to be redrafted in order to provide a suitable benchmark, as the mechanism for carrying out tests proved unsatisfactory because of the complexities of how to assess the journey time. During the negotiations, for example, the infracos were given the right to preclude 40 per cent of the trains – the fastest ones – from being used for test running by London Underground to set the base time. Moreover, now 'the contract allows for the substitution of some of the physical train tests with alternative methods of survey, modelling or simulation to eliminate problems encountered during shadow running'.[8] In other words, the benchmark will not necessarily be measured by actual train times, but by a model designed to incorporate relevant information – a theoretical, rather than a real, time will be the basis of this aspect of the contract which is, in fact, potentially the one where the bigger bonuses can be earned by the infracos.

The third and fourth measurements under the PPP are relatively simpler and involve smaller amounts of money: ambience and service points. The 'ambience' measure is designed to ensure that the infracos improve . . . well, the 'ambience' of the stations. Callaghan explains that for many years London Underground has measured aspects of the ambience, such as cleanliness and lighting, and the PPP is designed to 'incentivise the contractor to improve ambience'. Therefore measurement will be partly through the 'mystery shopper' surveys which involve people from a market research company checking on cleanliness, graffiti, litter and even staff helpfulness. As with other measures, payments depend on performance relative to a benchmark which, in this case, has been set higher than recent average performance because the London Underground view is that 'current levels of litter and cleanliness are considered unacceptable'.

The fourth criterion of measuring performance of the infracos under the PPP, service points, is actually – like abatements – another euphemism and effectively means penalties for failing to carry out repairs. Callaghan explains, sounding rather like a social worker obsessed with political correctness, that 'typically in contracts like this they are called deficiencies but one of the things that we decided we wanted to do was not use language that sounded like it was penalising. Instead, we invented this word, service points, to get away from the concept of deficiency but it is the same thing.' The infracos are given an allocation of service points and if they exceed that number, they are charged £50 for each one. Service points, therefore, are one of the tools used to measure the ambience. On some assets, the infracos are given a set amount of time to fix faults and only after that do they begin to accrue service points, while on others they have to start paying penalties straight away. The latter includes such equipment as platform indicators showing when the next train is due, the help points for seeking information, CCTV cameras and public address systems. For these, ten service points – £500 – are charged to the infraco for every day that the item is not working. On the other hand, infracos can earn service point credits for meeting urgent requests by LUL to fix faults sooner than the standard clearance time. For these, according to Callaghan, the 'message is that it is worth investing money in preventative maintenance to make sure they do not fail'. The others, which are aspects of the system not seen by passengers, such as staff toilets, or those which do not have much bearing on the service, such as a broken window, must be fixed within a set time, such as three days, from which time service points begin to be accrued. In order to reflect the fact that London Underground wants to see the Tube improve over the period of the PPP, the service point regime gets harder with the benchmark, which starts at a level reflecting existing performance, being raised annually to 'reflect the rate of improvement judged to be achievable through better resourcing and incident response management'.

Interestingly, the original intention had been to apply ambience and service point measures on trains as well as stations but both ideas, according to London Underground, proved unworkable. In the case of ambience, the idea was to measure aspects such as public address audibility, quality of ride, noise and lighting but 'this has proved more difficult to do than expected' and 'is still to be resolved'.[9] Service points, too, have proved to be impossible to apply to trains. This is because while infracos are required to attend to faults on trains, 'the system for reporting these is much less well-developed and raises a number of logistical problems which have yet to be satisfactorily resolved'.[10] Therefore, that too has been left out of the PPP contract, demonstrating that some things have proved too complex even for the architects of the scheme.

These concepts of ambience and service points are, as mentioned above, relatively minor, accounting for a mere 1 per cent of the possible bonuses which could potentially be earned by the infracos. Indeed, of the four measures outlined above, the one with by far the greatest impact on the level of payment under the contract is capability. According to research carried out by Deloitte & Touche for Transport for London,[11] the maximum annual theoretical amount that could be gained by the three infracos would be £273m for capability compared with £49m for availability and £24m for ambience. Of course these figures are notional maxima which cannot be achieved in practice because of the sheer amount of investment that would be needed. A more realistic calculation, made by Deloitte & Touche, was that if the infracos reached halfway to the overall thirty-year capability target within the first 7.5 year period, they would earn an extra £100m per year on average during that period. The way the performance regime could affect the finances of the Transport for London, which fears that Londoners would be paying very highly for the improvement in their Underground system, is considered in the critique of the PPP in Chapter 12.

The architects of the PPP recognised that not everything can be measured in terms of performance and therefore some parts of the contract involve the conventional purchase of improvements. As London Underground put it, 'certain works would cost more to do than they would earn in incremental payments under the performance regime. For example, modernising a station improves ambience but not enough for the ambience regime to provide an adequate incentive. The same applies to train refurbishment.'[12] Therefore, such works are treated conventionally, with London Underground paying for them when they are carried out under a defined programme of work set out in the contract. Failure to carry out the work on schedule will result in financial 'abatements' having to be paid by the infraco.

Let us just look at one final complex area, the way that assets are treated over time. One of the watchwords of the PPP is 'whole life asset management', the notion that an organisation looks after its assets in such a way that they cost the least over their whole life. Therefore, it may be worth paying more for something at the beginning because maintenance will be cheaper, rather than buying an inexpensive equivalent that requires more care over its life. Similarly, it is likely to be worth carrying out regular preventative maintenance to ensure that the asset does not fail, resulting in delays, rather than waiting for things to go wrong. However, since the contracts are for thirty years, divided by three breakpoints at 7.5 year intervals, how can London Underground ensure that the infracos will leave the assets in a good condition, rather than running them down so that they all begin to fail soon after the contract ends? In the ponderous language of London Underground, this problem has been considered: 'it is of key importance to the PPP that Infracos take decisions about the balance between upgrade, renewal and maintenance of assets on a whole-life basis, regardless of when in the contract period such decisions are made'.[13] A really canny infraco, for example, could ensure that just enough is spent when replacing assets to ensure they last until the end of the contract, which is unlikely to be in the best interests of passengers.

Therefore, to avoid such shenanigans by an infraco, 'asset condition or residual life targets (whichever is more appropriate)' are set for each periodic review date and the contract end date. The condition of the assets has been categorised from A to E, where A and B are OK, while C and D need improvement and E is unacceptable. The targets involve ensuring that a set percentage of assets are in each category with the aim of improving their condition over time. The basis of measurement, however, has been hampered by the fact that London Underground, remarkably, has no asset register, though it does know the condition of many of its assets and one of the first tasks of the infracos under PPP will be to establish the condition of the assets. Infracos are given a financial incentive to meet these targets (called milestones), but some of this money will be withheld if they are not met.

Although the contracts are for thirty years, as we have seen there are breakpoints every 7.5 years. As with virtually every aspect of the PPP, the precise role of these are the subject of a fierce row between the protagonists. The supporters argue that they merely provide an opportunity to reassess the price of the contracts and to ensure that they still offer value for money, since there will be an arbiter to determine the cost and to ensure that both parties are treated fairly. To the opponents, the break effectively means a complete rewriting of the contract, an issue that is discussed in Chapter 12.

The arbiter will face a difficult task, to become quickly familiar with prices and charges in the industry before making a decision on the very large amounts to be paid under the contracts. There is, too, the expectation that a lot of routine disputes will emerge under the PPP contracts but these will be subject to a different procedure, a complex resolution process with, in difficult cases, up to ten stages. London Underground hopes that the vast majority of cases will be resolved amicably through what it calls the spirit of 'partnership', but unresolved cases will go to an arbitrator – but, just to make things more confusing, that will be a different person from the arbiter mentioned above.

The breakpoints are important, too, in that the contractors are supposed to be responsible for cost overruns. However, this liability has been capped at £50m for each period, with the exception of the first period for Tube Lines where it is £200m,[14] provided that the infraco has been 'economic and efficient', a concept that appears self-evident but is in practice difficult to define. Cost overruns beyond that point by an 'economic and efficient' infraco will be the responsibility of London Underground and this, therefore, represents a restriction on the amount of risk being transferred.

The financial structure of the PPP is that the infracos will borrow huge sums in the early stages of the contract to pay for the backlog of work. The government is now committed to putting in around £1bn per year as subsidy during the first period, which will represent about 45 per cent of the cost of the PPP. Another 30 per cent will come from revenue, leaving 25 per cent to be raised by the private sector. This will be paid back through the increased revenues generated by the improved Tube in the latter part of the contract.

According to London Underground, even in shadow form the infracos have responded to these incentives (although the capability measure has not kicked in yet because the investment has not yet begun). According to Callaghan, 'The thing that was really dramatic was on fault rectification where the level of abatements has fallen. In 1999, before shadow running, nobody ever fixed the faults and you could report faults till you were blue in the face. There were howls of anguish from the infracos we created saying that this is costing us millions per month. And we said, "It is easy, guys," and eventually they got themselves organised and completely changed the way they reported faults, so they now have computer systems. You ring up and report a fault and it is dealt with.'

Yet overall performance since shadow running has not been good and indeed, as we saw in Chapter 1, has deteriorated. According to Callaghan, this is explained by the failure of the operator to respond to the improvement in asset maintenance: 'Even if the infracos were 100 per cent perfect, the operations side could still mess up the service by not having the staff in the right place, or by making poor management decisions when things go wrong. When the infrastructure started working better but the service did not improve, this forced us to start looking for the cause somewhere else and we identified the fact that our process for recruiting and allocating drivers was not very good.' This implies that the operations have been deteriorating at a faster rate than the infrastructure has been improving. But Callaghan is confident that things will improve as the operations side, which of course remains in the public sector, gets better.

One exception to the deteriorating performance has been the Northern Line, where the PFI contract for the trains has worked remarkably well and has resulted in almost 100 per cent train availability. Again, this is subject to differing interpretations: supporters of the PPP argue that this is why private sector should be involved; its critics argue that the PPP is so completely different from the PFI that it is not a relevant example.

Of course, there are many other aspects to the PPP which have been omitted from this short description and this has merely been an attempt to give the flavour of how it was developed and how it works. Those who have managed to read so far in this chapter deserve a break and a return to the narrative of the book and, specifically, the political battle over the PPP.

CHAPTER NINE

Monte Carlo – or is it bust?

With hindsight, it is remarkable how little fuss was provoked by the PPP during the passage through Parliament of the bill which legislated for it. The main purpose of the Greater London Authority Act was to create the London mayoralty and the related assembly, a kind of scrutiny body, but the PPP was tacked on since it required primary legislation. Yet it was not until the mayoral elections and the decision of Ken Livingstone to quit the Labour Party in March 2000 in order to stand as an independent that the PPP really became a controversial issue.

The most cogent explanation is that no one really understood what it meant. As was mentioned at the end of Chapter 7, the announcement of the PPP was greeted with relative equanimity by Labour MPs, of both Left and Right, because it was felt not to be a privatisation but merely a way of harnessing some private capital to what would remain a public service. The Tories, still smarting from their election defeat, were unable to mount a coherent response to the PPP. There was so much relief among Labour backbenchers that the Tube was not going to be privatised that they did not notice what was being done by their own government. Moreover, the notion that the whole scheme would be self-financing and would take London Underground investment off the public books was particularly seductive, given Labour's adoption of the Tory spending plans and the knowledge that any new money, when it eventually came through, would inevitably be concentrated on health and education.

Karen Buck, the chairwoman of the London Labour MPs group, adds that the absence of concern about the PPP was also the result of the contempt in which London Underground's management was generally held: 'Partly it was that the political implications were not spotted, but also it was felt amongst our side that London Underground managers were a bunch of muppets. If you asked people, they would say, OK, do you have faith in this new intelligent dynamic Labour government bringing in new solutions. Or do we have faith in London Underground's managers. Remember, too, that this was at the time when the mounting cost overruns of the Jubilee Line Extension project were emerging.'[1]

The other problem was the difficulty, during the early stages of the development of the PPP in 1998, of opposing something that was still so ill-defined. In giving evidence to the transport select committee in April of that year, Denis Tunnicliffe and his fellow London Underground executives were unable to provide much detail of the contracts. Indeed, Tunnicliffe suggested that the length would probably be between fifteen and twenty-five years,[2] rather than the eventual thirty, and there was still uncertainty over whether there would be one, two or three infrastructure companies. That decision was not made until July when the Treasury view, which was always that there must be competition and preferably that there should be three players,[3] prevailed over the preference of John Prescott and London Transport for a single infrastructure company. At the time, the deadline for the contracts to be signed was envisaged to be April 2000, in time for the creation of the Greater London Authority and the mayor.

However, it soon became apparent that this target was unattainable. Doubts about the timetable had been expressed by potential bidders as early as October 1998. An article by the well-informed business editor of the *Independent*, Michael Harrison, said: 'The Government is likely to miss its deadline of part privatising the London Underground by April 2000, business leaders warned yesterday.'[4] Two months later, at a big meeting of ministers and civil servants in December 1998, when the final shape of the PPP was determined before the process of putting it out to tender began, PricewaterhouseCoopers estimated that the earliest possible completion date would be September 2000 and, more likely, the end of that financial year, i.e. April 2001. This raised a sticky issue that was to prove politically damaging to the protagonists of the PPP. The notion that the PPP would be signed off by the time the mayor took office in July 2000, as originally envisaged, was just about politically sellable to the public. Once it became certain that the preferred timing could no longer be achieved, the scheme inevitably looked like a crude political fix by ministers – which, of course, it was. Indeed, the December meeting of ministers, civil servants and advisers included two junior ministers, Glenda Jackson and Nick Raynsford, who later became potential mayoral candidates. They had realised that the election might be won by someone hostile to the PPP – not necessarily Ken Livingstone, who had barely expressed any thoughts on the matter at the time, but more likely a Tory such as Lord Archer who was in favour of outright privatisation of the Tube. They insisted, therefore, that the legislation should ensure that the PPP would be signed before London Underground was handed over to Transport for London, the new body which was part of the mayoral structure due to be created in the summer of 2000.

This was the argument that ministers used in Labour Party circles to ensure that the Greater London Authority Bill, an Act of unprecedented complexity with a staggering 277 clauses, the longest piece of legislation since the Government of India Act in the 1930s, contained the legislation for the PPP. The government had refused to reveal the financial modelling on which the contracts were being based on the standard grounds of 'commercial confidentiality', a coyness for which the authors of a critique of the process could 'see no justification'.[5] The timing problem created a bizarre scenario that was to cause endless hassle for Labour. London Underground would remain directly controlled by the Department of the Environment, Transport and the Regions until the contracts for the PPP were signed.[6] In other words, a third party, central government, would negotiate the deal between Transport for London and the PPP contractors, and then pass the results of its efforts on to the new devolved body. The Tory spokesman on London, Richard Ottaway, was one of those who spotted that Transport for London, and indeed Londoners, were having an agreement foisted on them: 'My understanding of a contract is that it is something that is agreed by two parties. If they are not of the same mind, there is not an agreement. If a party enters into a contract and the mayor then wants to vary the contract but the contractor does not agree, there is not a meeting of minds. Therefore, there is not a contractual relationship.'[7]

The decision to have the PPP signed before handing it over was such a naked piece of control freakery from the centre that it inevitably led to trouble, subsequently compounded by the fact that the negotiations and rows over the PPP eventually resulted in a delay not of a few months, but of over two years, by which time the mayor was more than halfway through his first term. Right from the start, the decision was a recipe for conflict, especially once opinion polls began to make clear that no New Labour poodle would ever win the mayoral election.

Because of the vagueness of the legislation and the absence of any information on the details of the contracts, the PPP provoked remarkably little debate in committee, given what a major controversy the issue would later become. The Tories did express some concerns about the exact nature of the scheme and called into question its financing, and the Liberal Democrats (helped by the fact that one of their members, Ed Davey, was a former management consultant who worked on privatisation schemes) made a bit of a fuss, but Labour members were voting fodder who largely sat on their hands. Livingstone, though on the committee which spent twenty-six sittings on the complex bill, was mute throughout on the subject of the PPP. Speaking in 2002, he explained: 'I am not opposed to public private partnership. If the Underground had been passed to me and Bob [Kiley, the transport commissioner] in 2000, you would have seen exactly the same firms modernising the Underground but they would have been much smaller defined contracts that were manageable for the same sort of money – well, probably less. When Prescott first launched it, he was talking about £7bn and I remember saying to Simon Fletcher, my researcher, given that the mayor's budget is £3bn, you can't ignore an input that is twice your annual sum. So when I produced my 1998 prospectus on why I wanted to stand as mayor, there was no rejection of PPP. I did not vote against it in committee as I only became alarmed about it when you had the rail crash [Ladbroke Grove, October 1999]. In 1998 I thought the deal was a way of levering in billions of pounds to modernise the Underground, which needed it. I had no idea at this stage that it would be a particularly wasteful way of doing it or that the fragmentation would have the same problems as with the privatisation of BR. My opposition is not ideological, it is purely empirical.'[8]

Some of his colleagues on the committee are rather more sceptical of his reasons. As one put it, 'He did not attend much and when he did he was more concerned about smoking in cabs which he had a row with Glenda [Jackson] about. He is a lazy bugger but I also think his parliamentary experience was so awful – partly his fault, partly not as he was consistently treated badly by the hierarchy – that playing a constructive part in a dialogue with ministers did not occur to him. By 1999, he was so far out on a limb that maybe no one would have listened to him anyway.'

The most remarkable aspect of the committee hearings on the bill was that the government persisted in believing that the PPP would be self-financing. This had been implied by the government's spending review plans of the time, which showed no contribution going to London Underground for the financial years 2000–2001 and 2001–02. Glenda Jackson, the minister for London transport, confirmed the notion when she told the committee: 'The modelling suggests that TfL will be able to fund PPP. That is not to say TfL will not need grant for its other transport activities, but the modelling suggests that grant should not be necessary to fund the Underground.'[9] The model involved a 1 per cent above inflation fare rise in 2000 and 2001 but apart from that the PPP would be self-financing. A couple of days later in the committee, when pressed on this point, she accepted that it might be necessary to pay a grant eventually to meet London Underground's payments to the PPP contractor but that the scheme would only go ahead if enough of the bids represented value for money. This implied that only small payments might be necessary, nothing like the £1bn per year which it is now going to cost. Another Tory member of the committee, John Wilkinson, was prescient in spotting the problems to come if government money were needed: 'However, once the principle of supplying grants to make up the difference is conceded, obtaining them will become an annual event. Operating companies will go cap in hand to the mayoralty, to the government and to all and sundry who can be lobbied.' In other words, he was suggesting it would be back to annuality. Moreover, the government was proceeding with a policy whose key rationale – self-financing – had been removed. Ironically, as my previous book, *Broken Rails*,[10] shows, the rationale for the privatisation of the railways – on-rail competition between different companies – had also been shown to be impossible long before the railways were sold off. It is part of a phenomenon that British governments suffer from perennially: the inability to do a U-turn even when keeping to the course ahead is demonstrably futile.

Within a month of Jackson's statement in the Commons, in March

1999, doubts were emerging about whether the PPP could really be self-financing, with the Department admitting in a 'progress report'[11] published by the Underground that government money might be necessary to help fund the scheme, which it was now calculated would bring in £8.1bn of investment, compared with Prescott's estimate of £7bn a year previously, the start of a continuous 'PPP inflation' process. The report set out, for the first time, the shape of the contracts, which would be for thirty years with review points every 7.5 years, which would enable an independent arbiter[12] to determine whether payments should be increased if more spending were needed or reduced if costs had been cut through improved efficiency.

Although opposition to the concept of the PPP remained muted, partly because the specifics of the scheme as presented publicly – notably rapid improvements in services at no cost to the taxpayer – made the plan almost irresistible, there were influential voices beginning to suggest that it was not quite as good as it seemed. The most thorough critique came from the Greater London Group of the London School of Economics in a pamphlet written by Stephen Glaister, an academic and former board member of London Transport, Tony Travers, a local government finance expert, and Rosemary Scanlon, an American urban affairs expert. In a pamphlet[13] brought out during the passage of the Bill, they argued for amendments to give the mayor the right to choose the method of financing the investment in the Tube which, as they put it, all parties agreed was essential. The PPP, they suggested, was 'flawed in principle and impracticable'. The group had spotted that the notion of a self-financing PPP was quickly unravelling and that this changed the whole dynamic of the enterprise. In particular, the scheme seemed to be based on a high level of operating profit being generated by the Underground.[14] Even though, thanks to a decade of above inflation fare rises and a booming economy, this had reached £265m in 1997–8, the operating surplus still fell well short of what would be required if the need for a government grant were to be avoided. (In fact, as we see in Chapter 12, the Underground profits rapidly declined over subsequent years, putting further pressure on the economics of the PPP.)

In the event, given the delay to the start of the PPP, a short-term rescue plan for the Tube was inevitable. The Treasury was forced to bail out London Underground which would clearly not be able to cope with the 'no grant after April 2000' scenario set out in the spending plans. The settlement was not ungenerous, as ministers feared a rapid deterioration in the Underground for which they would be blamed. In July 1999 Prescott announced that an extra £517m would be given to the Underground to boost investment which, he said, brought average payments to over £500m per year for each of the four years between 1997–8 and 2000–2001. It was, indeed, by historic standards a good settlement, especially given that, at the time, the Underground was making a considerable contribution to its investment needs out of the operating profit.

Like John Wilkinson, the LSE authors noted that once the PPP was no longer self-funded, its potential advantages were greatly reduced. Moreover, the PPP would place an intolerable burden on its eventual owners, Transport for London: 'The PPP offers what is basically a one-shot, up-front infusion of cash investment, which requires a payback period that will stretch out for thirty years. As such, the investment programme will be directed towards those needs identified for the earliest stages of the plan. Combined with the absence of funding provision for extensions or new lines, and the inherent pressures to produce large profits for payback each year, the PPP proposal poses as many financial constraints as solutions for the problems arising from the need to expand capacity on the Underground.'[15]

The group also outlined possible alternative ways of financing the investment programme, which was at the core of the controversy. They noted that the solution which Prescott had adopted for the Channel Tunnel Rail Link was ideally suited to the London Underground. As we saw in Chapter 7, Prescott had rescued the Channel Tunnel Rail Link project in the summer of 1998 through the mechanism of government-backed commercial borrowing while not including anything in the public accounts on the basis that the chances of a call being made on the guarantee were very low. The bonds received the highest credit rating, AAA, which meant that the interest rate payable on them was low – just 4.5 per cent – as they were effectively regarded as the same as government borrowing. As the pamphlet put it, 'this is a striking example of how commercial debt can be used to finance a commercially non-viable piece of infrastructure, given the appropriate support from the state'.[16]

The LSE authors therefore recommended that London Underground's investment should be paid for in the same way, by allowing the Greater London Authority to issue bonds as had happened in the 1930s (see Chapter 2). With fortuitous prescience – since at the time Bob Kiley was not on the horizon, though one of the authors, Scanlon, had recently worked for New York state – they cited the example of the New York Metropolitan Transportation Authority (MTA) which had funded $14bn of investment since 1981 for the transit authority through bond finance.

The warnings from Glaister and his pals seemed, however, to be falling on deaf ears. The momentum behind the PPP gained strength as the doubts over its viability grew. There seemed to be a force pushing it through that made the process unstoppable. As the Bill finally received its Royal Assent in November 1999, the opposition was at last being vociferously articulated. The public was treated to the bizarre spectacle of the right-wing press attacking a supposedly left of centre government, in alliance with Ken Livingstone, an avowed old-fashioned socialist, over a scheme that seemed, on the face of it, to fit in with the Conservative agenda of privatising as many public services as possible.

The Economist, for example, was bemused but seemed to have cottoned on to the faulty economics at the heart of the scheme: 'Almost every urban transport system in the world from Paris and Rome to New York and Washington received public subsidy. It is strange, therefore, that a left of centre government, committed to promoting public transport and reducing car use, assumes that London's Underground can run successfully without subsidy.'[17] It went on to describe the PPP as a 'tortuous solution' and a 'messy political compromise' and, citing the CTRL, concluded that 'there is no reason why the rules cannot be similarly bent for the capital's impoverished transport system. Financing a monopoly business like London Underground in this way would make a great deal of sense.'

Not, however, to Prescott. Given he has a fuse as short as those on old penny bangers, he could not resist occasionally responding to the growing media opposition to the scheme, particularly over the funding. In a revealing letter to the *Financial Times*,[18] he disputed the suggestion made by the paper's transport correspondent that the type of system used to finance the Lewisham extension of the Docklands Light Railway could be used for the London Underground: 'It would be entirely legitimate for a private sector partner in the London Underground PPP to raise money by bonds. The critical issue is that the bond would not be backed by government, but the private sector would carry the risk. London Underground raising a bond is an entirely different matter. Backed by the government, this would obviously be just a form of government borrowing with taxpayers and Londoners in line to pick up the costs.' Quite apart from the obvious point that taxpayers and Londoners pay for the borrowing anyway, this type of bond financing is precisely the deal he arranged for the Channel Tunnel Rail Link.

The funding issue united City experts with left-wing politicians and left New Labour stranded in a minefield of its own creation. Even Tony Blair was bloodied when he entered the fray, implying in an interview in November 1999 that New York had gone bankrupt because of problems with bond finance. In fact, Rosemary Scanlon, in response, pointed out that the Prime Minister had told 'an utter untruth' – the city's financial crisis was in the 1970s, five years before the MTA began to use bonds to finance investment 'which was a major success story'.[19] The episode caused acute embarrassment to companies in the US bond markets (whose stability was being questioned) and something of a minor diplomatic incident. Blair kept mum about bonds thereafter but the incident may have been a little bit of the ill-advised New Labour spinning for which, later, Bob Kiley was to be a regular target.

Lord Archer, installed on 1 October 1999 as the Tory candidate for the mayoral election, was soon on the warpath against the PPP. In a speech at the Tory Party conference in Blackpool a few days later, Archer, who favoured outright privatisation, said that as mayor he would not sign up to the Prescott plan and warned the bidders: 'If you're looking for payment, look to the member for Hull East [Prescott], because Londoners aren't going to shell out for this half-baked scheme.'[20] The prospect of a titanic battle between Archer and Prescott over the PPP was, however, ended when a few weeks later Archer had to resign his candidacy after it emerged that he had lied in a libel case over his alleged liaison in 1986 with a Mayfair prostitute. He was replaced by Steve Norris who had a far more emollient attitude towards the PPP, as demonstrated by the fact that he later joined the board of Jarvis, a member of one of the successful consortia for the PPP contract. Archer, meanwhile, ended up with a four-year jail sentence.

Livingstone had, by now, woken up to the implications of the PPP and had started using his opposition to it as the central plank of his campaign for the Labour nomination for the mayoralty, so much so that it almost precluded him from becoming a contender. Livingstone and the other candidates, who included No. 10's favourite, the former Health Secretary Frank Dobson, and Glenda Jackson, had to appear before an interviewing panel on 16 November 1999. Livingstone's chances of being shortlisted for the candidacy rested on whether he would agree to go along with the PPP which was obviously now party policy. The session eventually extended over two days as the panel, chaired by the veteran Labour MP Clive Soley, adjourned the meeting to consider the issue and discuss the matter with the party hierarchy. Livingstone says that they desperately tried to find a compromise: 'On the second day we met, they passed a piece of paper over which said, "I accept the PPP." I refused to sign it, so they asked me to leave the room and think about it. So over the next couple of hours, they tried various formulae but it did not work. So when I went back in, there were three things on the piece of paper: I agree to be bound by Labour's manifesto, I accept the rules of the party and I accept the government's plans for a PPP. So I put a line through the third one and handed it back. So they allowed me to stand without ever having signed it.'[21] In other words, he refused to say he would abide by the – as yet unwritten – party manifesto which was, to say the least, strange for a potential candidate. It was a highly intricate game of cat and mouse as both sides had a lot to lose. Livingstone clearly wanted to stay in the Labour Party but it was widely expected he would stand as an independent should he be barred from standing, and the party hierarchy knew that his defection might well lead to defeat in the eventual election. Livingstone was emboldened by the fact that he was convinced Tony Blair did not want him barred and, moreover, even his rival, Frank Dobson, warned he would stand down if a ban were imposed: 'I went in there knowing that the PM had decided that I would be allowed to stand. I knew I did not have to compromise over the PPP.'[22] Livingstone was particularly vociferous about Railtrack's potential involvement in the PPP since the company's failings over safety had been highlighted by its role in the Paddington train crash that had killed thirty-one people just a month previously: 'My objection to the PPP was fuelled by the Paddington crash, where there seemed that something had gone wrong with the way the railways were maintained after privatisation.'[23]

In the event, all these shenanigans were irrelevant. Livingstone lost the contest for the Labour nomination by a whisker to Dobson because the electoral college had been gerrymandered specifically to prevent him winning it: MPs and MEPs had been given a third of the votes, and unions, which represented another third of the votes, had not been required to ballot their members while those that did all came out strongly in favour of Livingstone. After a few days' tortured soul-searching, Livingstone, who was leading by a mile in the opinion polls, declared in March 2000 that he would stand as an independent, with opposition to the PPP as the focus of his campaign – as he put it, the mayoral election was 'transformed into a referendum on the future of London'.[24]

The outcome of the election, while not quite a walkover, was never in doubt. Livingstone led throughout in the polls, and in the final count, between him and the Tory runner-up, Steve Norris, he obtained 58 per cent of the vote, a comprehensive if not totally convincing victory, given his much larger lead in the polls. Along the way, his relationship with the Labour hierarchy was severely damaged. Livingstone had not exactly endeared himself to the leaders of the Labour Party during his term as MP for Brent East. Although there had been behind the scenes moves to offer him a ministerial post in 1997, it never materialised. Moreover, he had managed the rare feat of antagonising both Tony Blair and Gordon Brown: the latter because he had written articles in his column in the *Independent* calling for the Chancellor's sacking for being too prudent. This has led many commentators to suggest that it is the antagonism between Brown and Livingstone that is at the heart of the government's insistence on the PPP for the London Underground in the face of overwhelming opposition, but as we shall see (Chapter 12), Livingstone denies this, arguing instead that the fault lies with a few Treasury officials and the British political system.

After his election victory on 4 May 2000, Livingstone thus took office in an unique constitutional position. Not only was the whole concept of a directly elected mayor with a scrutinising assembly new, but he was also in the weird position of not having control over what was London's most important transport service until it was handed over to him, by which time it would have been committed to an agreement that he had just been given a political mandate to oppose. Here, the government, indeed Tony

Blair in particular, missed its first chance of a compromise. When Blair rang the new mayor on the Saturday morning after the election, Livingstone told him: 'There is an honourable way out. Londoners had clearly rejected PPP, blah blah blah.' But according to Livingstone, Blair did not take the bait and merely told him to talk to Prescott.

While Livingstone refused to back down and took every opportunity to criticise the PPP, the issue bubbled over quietly in the background rather than exploding onto the front pages. Not only was it arcane and complicated, but there was the expectation that it would be resolved one way or another quite quickly. After all, Livingstone had been given a strong mandate by the electorate, and the government's counter-argument, that the PPP had been mentioned in its 1997 election manifesto, was pretty feeble given the vague nature of the concept at the time. As a bidder put it, 'Can the government afford to ignore the wishes of the London electorate? I believe Livingstone and Prescott will have to reach a compromise.'[25]

Yet there were no signs of government compromise. Indeed, Livingstone was told that the PPP would be a done deal within a few months of his achieving office: 'After my election, the transition team of civil servants told me at my first briefing that "You would be able to have the Underground by the autumn".'[25] Livingstone reckons that this timetable was never feasible and this briefing was part of a pattern of deception by officials over both the timetable and the content of the PPP.

By the end of 2000, the debate was, at last, hotting up. But then, another excuse for avoiding a proper debate began to be espoused. Labour supporters, even some who were lukewarm about the concept, began to argue that since three years had passed after Labour's election victory, it was better to proceed with the PPP, even if it were flawed, than to begin the whole process again. Several commentators, bored with the seemingly sterile positions of both sides, took this view too, and the 'let's get on with it' line of argument was to gain increasing momentum throughout the next two years.

But not everywhere. In particular, the Commons Transport Committee became one of the sources of dissent. It was chaired by the redoubtable Gwyneth Dunwoody, one of those old right-wing Labour politicians who have watched aghast as the rest of their party has flowed so fast past them that, having merely stood still, they find themselves, much to their consternation, on its extreme Left. She was no fan of rail privatisation or the

PPP and ensured that her committee scrutinised the funding of London Underground regularly. Its second report[27] on the subject, published in July 2000, was the first real in-depth summary of the pros and cons of the PPP, and its conclusions expressed scepticism about the government's uncritical endorsement of the concept. The report highlighted the convoluted nature of the arguments and the difficulty the wider public would have in making an informed decision, given the contrasting views of the 'experts'. Thus, the committee was presented with widely differing financial scenarios. The government, citing figures from PricewaterhouseCoopers, argued that the PPP would save £4.5bn over fifteen years compared with a bond issue. This argument was backed by Lord Currie, a Labour peer and professor of Economics at the London Business School, who suggested that funding the Underground's investment programme through the PPP would save around 20 per cent – £2.3bn – compared with bond finance.

But Glaister and his colleagues, Travers and Scanlon, gave evidence which argued the opposite case. They told the committee that, over the thirty-year life of the PPP, the Underground would require an annual grant of between £95m and £262m whereas the bond option would require a top-up of only £16m to £182m. In the event, of course, these figures proved to be gross underestimates as the Tube is to receive government funding of £1bn annually for the first few years of the PPP. A fourth analysis, by a trio of academics which included Professor Allyson Pollock of the School of Public Policy at University College, London, a long-time critic of PFI, suggested that both bond finance and PPP were 'simply unaffordable' and that the existing structure should be retained with investment being made through conventional contracts.

The contrasting results from these calculations carried out by this warring band of experts are, of course, a result of the assumptions underlying them, particularly over the relative efficiencies of the private and public sectors. Despite the precision of the numbers which are expressed rather fancifully to the nearest £1m, the modelling is more art than science.

While Chapter 12 assesses the general arguments of the two sides over the PPP, a digression to consider just one aspect of these calculations shows the difficulties. One of the fundamental debates is over the assumptions of how the public sector would respond should it retain control of the Underground and therefore a calculation is made to produce a 'public sector comparator'. This is crucial for the value for money test which the government always argued had to be passed to allow it to proceed with the PPP. Therefore the preparation of the Public Sector Comparator is at the heart of all the arguments over the PPP and, indeed, other PFI schemes.

The National Audit Office, which decided, prompted by a recommendation from the Commons Select Committee, to take a look at the PPP before its introduction, an unusual move as it generally only looks at such issues after the event, examined the issue of the public sector comparator in some depth in a report published at the end of 2000. The NAO report spotted a series of flaws in the way that the comparator had been calculated. The report accepted that London Underground had followed 'a thorough and comprehensive bid evaluation strategy to identify which bidder has submitted the most economically advantageous bid'.[28]

However, the NAO stressed that there were 'limits, which London Underground recognises, to the weight that can be put on the figures emerging from the comparators exercise'.[29] In particular, there were problem areas: the obvious one being that there is uncertainty in modelling costs over thirty years; moreover, the financial models could only give a partial picture of the likely costs in a publicly run Tube over that time, with various assumptions resulting in differences of several billion pounds; and the assumed costs of public operation were influenced by how the Tube would be financed – with big differences if, say, a public sector organisation were allowed to issue bonds as opposed to being forced to continue bidding for Treasury grants with the rest coming from the fare box, which would lead to much higher costs because of the uncertainty generated by such a system, as shown in Chapter 5.

Reading between the lines of the conventional language used by the NAO, it was clear that there was a strong suspicion that London Underground was guessing. Take, as an example, this paragraph: 'The model depends on fixed inputs of base costs, which are multiplied by inputs of plausible ranges for risk and efficiency factors. These input ranges are used to generate *several hundred possible values* for the comparators'[30][my italics]. As a result, the NAO criticises London Underground for using too many variables, as 'in such circumstances it is difficult to be sure that there has been no double-counting of uncertainty in different factors'.

So, the NAO analysis concluded, 'as a result of these issues, we and London Underground have concluded that the modelling provides some useful information about the upper and lower bounds of public sector costs over the next thirty years but cannot reliably be taken to produce a single expected value within those boundaries'.[31] The comptroller, Sir John Bourn, went further in the press release which accompanied the report, saying, 'the financial analysis carried out for the London Underground PPP cannot, on its own, be expected to show clearly which public or private sector option for managing and funding the Tube will provide better value for money.'

The assumptions behind the calculations of the comparator demonstrate the difficulty of obtaining a precise figure, or, for that matter, a ball park one. In calculating the assumed costs of future investment in the system, London Underground looked at 242 previous projects, with an average overrun of 20 per cent. Some were omitted because the overruns were a result of exceptional circumstances and some because they were irrelevant, including the Jubilee Line Extension tunnelling, since the PPP envisages no such work – a point that strongly backs the argument set out in Chapter 7. Moreover, while the costs are presented in very precise numbers, the estimates were obtained through a series of workshops with London Underground management to produce adjustments based on their judgement. It may look like science but it sounds more like art. To analyse the data, London Underground used a sophisticated technique to calculate the comparator called, believe it or not, the Monte Carlo simulation. It was criticised by the NAO because it relies on the assumption that the cost overruns taken from the schemes would follow a symmetrical pattern, an assumption not borne out in practice. As a result, London Underground tried another technique, arising out of a workshop in November 2001, called 'key driver analysis', which examines the various components of potential cost overruns. The independent review of these techniques concluded that whichever way it was done, 'the process of assessing the breadth of range of uncertainty is subjective and ultimately derived from the views of experienced staff making informed judgements supported by a body of knowledge of *variable relevance and accuracy*'[32] [my italics].

The biggest way in which the comparator was weighted against retaining the system in the public sector was through a calculation of the likely performance of the Tube under the two possible regimes. London

Underground assumed that, since it had not met performance targets in the past, it would not do so in the future. Using its standard cost benefit techniques – basically £6 per customer hour as explained in Chapter 8 – London Underground added the cost of this *assumed future* failure to the public sector comparator on the basis that the private sector would definitely meet the performance targets since it was 'incentivised' to do so. The difference between the two resulting figures – £1.35bn – is very large, 15 per cent of the total cost of the PPP over thirty years, and is sufficient to tip the balance in favour of the PPP scheme as offering the best value for money. Remember, though, this is not an assumption involving real money, hard cash that will be saved by the council-tax payer or the government. It is, instead, an assumed social benefit which will not happen should the Tube stay in the public sector and remain as inefficiently run as it is at the moment. Just to ram this point home: there is no actual saving of money for those who pay for the Tube – the passenger, the council-tax payer and the government; what is being quantified is merely notional time saved by people travelling on the Tube in the future.

Another questionable assumption was the notion that management costs would be the same whether the PPP went ahead or not. But the Underground had been restructured into a system which required an operator and three infracos, and was clearly much more expensive than the old simple unified management. Yet no account was taken of this. The management costs were assumed to be the same even if LU remained entirely in the private sector. As TfL put it, 'these costs would represent a very significant increase over the current internal costs of managing the infracos'[33] and, indeed, represent some 15 per cent of the total value of the public sector comparator.

All these counter-arguments were being gathered by Transport for London largely through the use of its own financial advisers who, not surprisingly, came up with conclusions which largely backed Livingstone's contention that the public sector comparator was a fiddle. Much later in the process, in 2002, but worth mentioning here for the sake of clarity before returning to the main narrative, Deloitte & Touche was commissioned by TfL to assess the value for money analysis which the government had used as the basis for proceeding with the PPP.

Consultants do not like being too rude about their rivals because it is a small world in which they all know each other, but Deloitte's went a long way to question the very basis on which the figures for the comparator had been produced by London Underground and its advisers.

The key aspect identified by Deloitte & Touche was the fact that the public sector comparator kept on growing like weeds every time London Underground issued a new set of figures for the PPP. The unstated suggestion is that London Underground had to do this in order to ensure that the PPP remained value for money in comparison with the public sector. Deloitte analysed the increase in the public sector comparator, which had risen from an estimated thirty-year cost of £14.7bn in March 2000 to £18.3bn two years later. The stated reasons were principally that the costs had originally been underestimated and required changing at a late stage, which Deloitte called 'unusual', and an assumption that the inflation rate would be higher than first calculated.

In particular, TfL, on the basis of Deloitte's work, wondered how it was that the public sector comparator kept on growing while the amount of investment being required of the bidders was being reduced: 'It is difficult to understand how the PSC can have increased dramatically while the work scope that is purportedly priced in the private bids has been significantly reduced'.[34] LU's response, in its answer to the contributions to the consultation process from Transport for London, was rather feeble, arguing that the 'descoping' of the PPP meant the postponement of projects to future years, and not their cancellation. However, TfL responded that since the contracts are effectively renegotiable after 7.5 years, any projects in the latter three-quarters of the PPP should not be included. And we leave them there, an irreconcilable dialogue of the dead as we are beginning to chart such profound depths of the PPP that any future nuggets of understanding are likely to be few and far between. And note that this is merely the exploration of one aspect of a scheme – partial at that, as the question of the assumed interest rate, an issue where a slight variation in predictions can lead to massively different results, has not been considered – in which there are at least half a dozen other aspects of similar complexity, some of which are examined in the conclusion in Chapter 12.

As a final point, it is worth pointing out as an aside that London Underground obtained 'independent assurance' on the validity of the public sector comparator from a host of advisers including Ove Arup, PricewaterhouseCoopers and KPMG who are, of course, all involved in a host of PFI schemes and who all concluded that the way the public sector comparator had been assessed was fair. It is not being only slightly cynical to suggest that these companies rarely come up with the suggestion of 'leave well alone' or 'you would be better off doing this yourselves'. The PPP is merely an extension of a trend of using consultants and outside expertise that started in the 1960s and has been expanding ever since. I have even heard of consultants themselves confessing, privately, that their recommendations can, at times, be self-serving. It is also noticeable that different analyses come up with different answers, generally favourable to the client. Hence, London Underground's advisers broadly endorse its approach, TfL's criticise it and Ernst & Young, appointed by the government but with a balanced remit, stays largely neutral and couches many of its findings in vague language allowing the report to be interpreted by all the parties as being favourable to them. Ernst & Young's final judgement of all this work is a lukewarm endorsement, one which might satisfy the legal test of a civil court – on the balance of probabilities – but never the criminal one – beyond all reasonable doubt: 'it is our view that London Underground has produced a reasonable assessment of the likely cost to the public sector of meeting the PPP contract requirements. However, the PSC contains significant subjective assumptions and the comparators should be used in this context.'[35] Ernst & Young made explicit the fact that they had not questioned the assumptions behind the reasoning over the comparator, but merely checked the arithmetic which followed on from them. And as a barbed little aside, the conclusion ends with the point that 'the performance adjustments should be presented as non-cash amounts' – in other words, London Underground should not have slung in the extra £1.35bn of costs on the public sector comparator.

This digression into the debate over the Public Sector Comparator shows, if nothing else, the extent to which the case for the PPP is unproven. A prudent government, driven by a genuine concern for what was the best way forward, might have hesitated at the point at which the NAO expressed doubts over London Underground's analysis. Instead, it pressed forward regardless, as if stuck on a runaway train.

With the strong feelings being expressed by the all-party Commons committee, the detailed doubts being outlined by many experts and public opinion clearly behind him, Livingstone was convinced the battle over PPP could be won and, as mayor, he had a powerful position to use in what was fast becoming a propaganda war. On his side, he had virtually everyone other than the government and its civil servants, the bidders and some, but by no means all, City commentators. The *Evening Standard*, though a traditionally Tory paper, had rather taken to the left-leaning Livingstone and, of course, was happy to join in with his opposition to the PPP since it involved bashing New Labour. The Tory group on the assembly also came out against the PPP. But, more impressively for Livingstone, so did a whole range of independent experts who joined Glaister in criticising what they saw as a complex and expensive scheme.

Livingstone himself commissioned Will Hutton, the head of the Industrial Society and a former editor of the *Observer*, to carry out an investigation into the PPP scheme. Hutton's findings published[36] in September 2000 were probably a bit more equivocal than Livingstone would have liked, but nevertheless the report contained several damning criticisms of the PPP. The report found that the potential rates of return for the infracos were unusually generous, a criticism that would later be repeated many times by Transport for London. Hutton seemed quite impressed with the ability of the PPP to tackle the backlog of investment in the Underground system but was concerned about its complexity and whether it was flexible enough to cope with changing demands. Like Deloitte, Hutton was most concerned with the way that the public sector comparator had been calculated. He questioned the assumption that the public sector would not improve its efficiency despite what he described as, 'the step change that might be expected in a bond regime that was coupled with delegated private sector programme management of investment'.[37] Hutton, therefore, found it unfair that in the value for money test, the potential efficiency gains of the PPP were assumed to be certain, while the public sector was expected to be as inefficient as in the past. Note, though, that he was working on the assumption that the alternative to the PPP would be bond finance raised by Transport for London – something which the Treasury, throughout this whole affair, never even hinted might be possible. Therefore the report suggested the scheme should only go ahead provided it passed a modified test in relation to the public sector comparator: 'The PPP should not proceed unless it passes the re-specified PSC we have outlined. In other words, the PPP should go forward only if it meets much more rigorous safety and value for money criteria and if it is substantially amended to protect against the risk that the contracts are incomplete and overgenerous.'[38]

Helped by such independent support, Livingstone was winning the propaganda so easily that many commentators felt the government would have to buckle. When even old-fashioned Tories like Simon Jenkins, the former *Times* editor, joined in the fray, it seemed that the PPP had no friends at all apart from the people paid to support it. Jenkins was equally surprised to find himself in this position and wrote: 'It seems absurd to have to argue the virtue of public sector values with a Labour government. I am an enthusiast for most forms of privatisation, but this one makes no sense. Further fragmenting ownership and investment in mass transit is stupid.'[39]

Livingstone was quick to play the safety card, helped by the fact that the Health and Safety Executive was examining the scheme, which it was legally required to do. Right from the beginning Livingstone warned of the dangers of splitting the track from the trains, repeating his concerns which had been raised by the Paddington crash.

The PPP's supporters, including the government, stressed that the structures of the national rail network and the model envisaged for the PPP were very different because, as explained above, on the Tube, there will be just one operator, which remains in the public sector and provides the service, and three privatised (for thirty years) infrastructure providers, whereas on the national rail there are thirty passenger and freight operators running trains on infrastructure all owned by Railtrack (now Network Rail).

That did not satisfy Livingstone and the trade unions, which had been equally vociferous about safety, and the issues they raised were given credence by a leak in August 2000. For a major change in operating procedures, such as the PPP, London Underground had to submit a safety case – an assessment of all the potential risks of the system and an outline of how they would be mitigated – to the body which oversees safety, the Health and Safety Executive. A leaked letter[40] from its inspector, Stanley Hart, to the London Underground management warned of a 'growing concern' about safety under the scheme. In particular, Hart accused London Underground of a 'breakdown in local management control' in the new structure that had been created with the start of shadow running in September 1999 with three infracos and one operator, albeit all still publicly owned and run. There was, he said, 'either no proof that the systems work or proof that they are not working'. Livingstone, of course, jumped on this, saying that the letter would 'confirm Londoners' worst fears about the government's public private partnership scheme and highlights the risk of a Paddington-style crash underground. The partial sell-off is a threat to Londoners' lives.' It was a theme to which Livingstone and, when he arrived, Bob Kiley would return time and again over the ensuing months. Indeed, Livingstone's point about safety was reinforced by the Hatfield crash in October 2000 that killed four people and was caused by a broken rail that had been allowed to deteriorate because of a failure of communication between Railtrack and its contractor, Balfour Beatty.[41]

The Industrial Society report, too, raised the safety issue, especially the use of subcontractors. As its author Will Hutton put it, 'Hatfield showed that if maintenance is left to reams of sub-contractors, you get problems. PPP repeats this difficulty.'[41] There were a series of further leaks about safety over the following months, and the unions called a number of one-day strikes on the issue, but eventually the Health and Safety Executive approved London Underground's safety case in the summer of 2002.

But throughout all this – the warnings about safety, the doubts about the feasibility of the structure, the ever growing complexity of the scheme and the deteriorating finances of a plan that had originally been sold as self-financing – government ministers appeared completely unmoved. Indeed, if there was ever an opportunity for a blatant U-turn, the circumstances of the Hatfield crash seemed almost perfect, a clear warning that meddling with the structure of the Tube could have dire consequences. Even when the press, both broadsheet and tabloid, quickly pointed out the analogy, warning that Hatfield could be a precursor to similar disasters on the Tube, Prescott did not flinch. It was not until the arrival of Bob Kiley as Transport Commissioner (see next chapter) that some behind the scenes moves were made to try to avert the public row.

At this stage, during 2000, the government's Achilles heel was that there were growing doubts over whether the private sector would express any interest given the highly politically charged situation. So, much of the government's effort was devoted to trying to drum up interest among potential bidders. The search for private sector partners had been launched in earnest at a government organised 'market sounding' conference in July 1998 attended by 400 people representing every type of company that might have a potential role in the PPP, addressed by Tunnicliffe and, interestingly, Geoffrey Robinson, the Paymaster General. There was the customary optimism from the government suggesting that large numbers of groups would be interested – it was suggested that a hundred groups had expressed an interest – but in fact very few companies and consortia were in a position to bid because of the sheer scale of the contracts. There was, too, the usual positioning by companies trying to influence the shape of the contracts. For example, Amey, a large engineering company, said it wanted the infrastructure to be hived off to a separate business which would then raise money by a stock market listing, and Railtrack, which at the time was a favourite to obtain one or all of the contracts, was seeking a 99 year concession.[43]

The structure of the PPP had become clear by the time that London Underground asked bidders to prequalify by 27 July 1999 with three sets of lines on offer – sub-surface lines, JNP (Jubilee Northern Piccadilly) and BCV (Bakerloo Central Victoria). In a bizarre and ill-fated strategy, Railtrack was barred from bidding for the two deep tube schemes but granted the handsome compensation of being accorded exclusive rights to bid for the infracos for the five sub-surface lines – Metropolitan, Hammersmith & City, District, Circle and East London. Prescott's argument was that Railtrack, at the time riding high in the Stock Exchange FTSE-100 with a buoyant share price and an aggressive and confident management, 'can raise money cheaper than anyone in the private sector', but he insisted that the company should contract out its project management, in the same way it had for the Channel Tunnel Rail Link, as already its troubles with the West Coast Main Line project, one of the major causes in its subsequent demise, were beginning to emerge.

The idea was that main-line trains would be able to use the section of the Metropolitan and Circle lines between Paddington and Liverpool Street to provide a cheap alternative to Crossrail, the scheme for a new tunnel linking the rail networks of east and west London. That always seemed a fanciful idea because this section is the most crowded part of the Circle Line with junctions at both Edgware Road and Baker Street that involve trains crossing each other's paths. Anyone with even a cursory knowledge of the Underground system knew that the scheme was impractical, but in any case, the Ladbroke Grove disaster in October 1999 did for Railtrack. The crash, a head-on collision between a Thames commuter train heading out of London whose inexperienced driver missed a red signal and a First Great Western high-speed train from Cheltenham, killed thirty-one people and had a devastating effect on confidence in the privatised rail system. Although the signal in question, SN 109, had been passed at red eight times in the previous six years, Railtrack had ignored the recommendations produced by inquiries into these incidents and failed to convene meetings on improving the sighting of the signal.[44]

Railtrack was clearly in the dock over the accident and, barely six weeks after the disaster, John Prescott suddenly announced that London Transport and Railtrack were not proceeding with discussions over Railtrack taking over the upgrading and maintenance of the sub-surface Underground lines. Instead, Prescott said, there would be a competition for bidders for the sub-surface lines in the same way as for the two deep tube contracts, and some bidders heaved a sigh of relief because they felt that Railtrack would have prevented the creation of a level playing field. Prescott denied that the accident had anything to do with his decision, merely putting out the official line that it had been impossible 'to identify schemes that would deliver integration between the London Underground and the national railway network in the way envisaged',[45] although he did admit that 'the tragic accident at Ladbroke Grove highlighted current issues relating to capacity in the Paddington approaches'. Moreover, a consultant's report had suggested the costs of improving the infrastructure to cope with through running were in the billions. However, with Labour MPs siding with Livingstone over Railtrack's involvement, the announcement was clearly politically motivated. As the Lex column in the *Financial Times* put it, 'it seems odd it has taken so long to realise integration is problematic'.[46] In one of the many ironies of this tale, given that Railtrack went bust in October 2001 and effectively reverted to the public sector through its phoenix, Network Rail, the sub-surface lines of the Underground might well have remained unprivatised had Prescott not been forced to bow to the political pressure from opponents of the PPP.

While this gave the various consortia another contract to bid for, several of the companies which had now examined the Invitation to Tender and assessed the political climate that was hotting up over the election of the mayor decided that the PPP was not worth the hassle to submit bids. Already, some companies had declined to participate in the process because of concerns about the political process which had thrown up two PPP opponents, Lord Archer and Ken Livingstone, as the frontrunners for the mayoralty. A spokesman for Bouygues, the French multinational, said at the time of the prequalification process in July 1999: 'we are interested in the project, but the extreme-left and extreme-right views of the prospective mayoral candidates who will take over the Tube mean that there is too much uncertainty for us over the deal at the moment. It is a view shared by a lot of contractors we have spoken to. I cannot believe LU has come up with the final solution.'[47]

Nevertheless, there was still a strong field when the short list was announced in October 1999. About a dozen consortia had sought to prequalify, of whom five – Linc, Metronet, NewMetro, TubeRail and Tube Lines – succeeded in being shortlisted for the two deep tube contracts, with each contract having four bidders. Three of them – Metronet, Linc and Tube Lines – were later, in March 2000, shortlisted for the sub-surface lines. Despite absentees such as Bouygues, the membership of the consortia still read like a *Who's Who* of heavy engineering, with most major companies in the business, particularly the British ones, being represented. Balfour Beatty, Mott MacDonald, Brown & Root, Bechtel, Halcrow, Carillion and a dozen others were all in there. The bids were due in by the end of March 2000 but during the run-up to that deadline there was a series of high profile drop-outs which greatly weakened the list and threatened to undermine the credibility of the scheme. Taylor Woodrow was the first to go, just a couple of days after Railtrack had been booted out of the scheme, and within a month its NewMetro consortium, which included Siemens and Mott MacDonald, pulled out completely, leaving just three bidders for the BCV contract.

There was a further difficulty later in 2000 when Adtranz, which was the train builder in the Metronet consortium, was taken over by Bombardier who had the equivalent role in Linc, which meant the two parts of the same company were bidding against each other. Chinese walls will suffice to keep the bidding details of each consortia secret, intimated a company source with just, perhaps, a slight lack of conviction.

The climate of uncertainty which had deterred Bouygues was clearly troubling some bidders. Peter Mason, the chief executive of Amec, the construction group which was part of TubeRail, said at the unveiling of its annual figures in March 2000 that the whole scheme might collapse: 'We have long been concerned about the political impact on the PPP of the mayoral election. There's now doubt over whether it will go ahead. Even if it does, it will be very difficult to work under a mayor who is opposed to the PPP. I'd be surprised if other companies felt differently.'[48] TubeRail, led by Brown & Root project managers, had already pulled out of bidding for the sub-surface lines arguing it would be too onerous to bid for all three simultaneously, and blamed the government for not delaying the sub-surface contest until after the deep tube lines process had ended – but clearly ministers were trying to push through the whole controversial issue as quickly as possible, particularly with a general election likely in 2001. Eventually TubeRail failed to win any of the contracts, possibly because the uncertainty made the consortium bid too conservatively. Similar doubts had been expressed during the same week in March 2000 by Mike Welton, the chief executive of BICC, part of the Metronet consortium, when he said: 'This is a very unsatisfactory situation, there are so many political pressures and differences of opinion.' The concerns of the bidders over the political situation increased, with Livingstone warning them, at a conference of business people, that 'they should give up and go home'[49] because he would seek a judicial review should he become mayor, and even Frank Dobson, the Labour candidate, expressed doubts over whether the PPP should go ahead. The consortia's worries about the political situation suggested that they were going to put in conservatively priced bids because of the risk. However, they were likely to be playing a canny game, too, as anything they uttered publicly once the bidding process had got under way must be viewed as potential positioning in the negotiations.

Unabashed by doubts among the bidders and by Railtrack's demise, the government and London Underground pressed ahead with the process of appointing contractors. The shortlisting process had been followed by the publication of the Invitation to Tender and the submission of the bids. Prescott had already foretold a delay by saying in December 1998 that he did not want a rigid deadline set for the PPP as this would weaken the hand of London Underground in the negotiation process. The process, though, was being delayed at each stage, partly by the uncertainties over the politics but also because of the sheer complexity of the scheme, which had to be worked out in detail, and because of Treasury interference.

This was no problem for the consultants, who have been the first beneficiaries of the PPP. The issue first came to prominence when, in April 2000, Prescott admitted to the House of Commons Transport Committee, which was investigating the Tube deal, that consultants had already been paid over £40m and, according to the *Daily Telegraph*[50] at the time, this was set to reach £100m. Since at that stage no discussions with the shortlisted candidates had even started and the final deal was not to be signed off until over two years later, that is a conservative estimate. By the end of the year Keith Hill, the junior transport minister, admitted that the total had reached £69.4m, and would reach at least £92m.[51]

An insight into the numbers of professionals employed in such complex schemes was provided by an article in the *Lawyer*[52] which explained that London Underground had tendered out through a bidding process the bulk of its legal work to Freshfields. The firm, which had long been London Transport's principal external legal firm, had, in addition to the thirty-strong in-house complement, a team of twenty-four advising London Transport and the Department of Transport on the deal. In addition, every bidder had a team of lawyers and the individual members of the consortia also required their own legal advice. Since most of these costs (see next chapter) were eventually paid by the government, many tens of millions of pounds of taxpayers' money will have been used up before a single pound of investment is made. Indeed, as we see in Chapter 12, the estimate for the total cost of drawing up the contracts was revealed at the Judicial Review in July 2002 to be an amazing £400m.

Once the short lists had been drawn up, the contracting process largely went quiet as the consortia prepared their bids, but Livingstone kept on fighting against the scheme with continued public support. And then he made one of the canniest moves of his political career by forging an unlikely alliance with a former CIA man whom he appointed as Transport Commissioner. While the bidders worked away in the background trying to make sense of the huge contracts and to pitch reasonable bids against them, the real public battle was about to begin; for Livingstone's new man, Bob Kiley, was to prove to be even more of a political operator than his boss.

CHAPTER TEN

An American in London

It was pure happenstance that resulted in Bob Kiley arriving in London in the autumn of 2000 to take on the job as the capital's first ever Transport Commissioner, by coincidence a very American-sounding title. Kiley, who had run the New York transport system in the eight years up to 1991, had heard about developments in London and had even been the key speaker at a 1999 weekend seminar about devolution organised by the government. His speech, arguing that there could not be effective devolution unless tax-raising powers were given to the new local organisations, had so shocked the No. 10 Policy Unit people that he was invited the next day to talk to them. In a conversation that was to be repeated many times over the next couple of years, Kiley told them: 'What on earth made you think devolution could work unless the regional government is given the ability to raise taxes? In the US, 65 per cent of taxes are raised at the local level.'[1] His interlocutors were clearly embarrassed, as the London mayor had been given only a very limited ability to raise taxes in the Greater London Authority Act 1999.

While he had followed events in the UK from across the pond in New York and his name had been mentioned by those looking for a transport commissioner, Kiley had not thought to apply for the job, and in London it was thought he would never be persuaded, at the age of sixty-five, to take on such a responsibility. But when a woman working for the headhunters, PricewaterhouseCoopers, called from London requesting a reference check on someone who was a candidate for a job at, as Kiley puts it, 'something called Transport for London', he was intrigued: 'I said I was happy to give the reference although I did not know the person very well, but I was kind of curious and asked for a pack of information to be faxed to me.' He read the information and the PwC woman called again saying its 'head of search and executive selection', Hamish Davidson, wanted to speak to him. Davidson told him they were looking for seven people – a commissioner and six second-tier managers, which Kiley thought was a strange way of going about creating a new organisation since the commissioner would want to choose their own managers. When Davidson asked him if he would be interested, Kiley said, 'I don't think so,' but agreed to consider it overnight: 'In fact, I was getting a little restless in my job [with a business community association in New York somewhat similar to London First] and I talked to my wife [Rona] who was so enthusiastic about living in London that she was packing our bags before we got five sentences into the conversation and she encouraged me to pursue it.'

From then on, Kiley's appointment was a shoo-in. A series of teleconferences ensued and then within a fortnight of the headhunter's first call, Kiley was on a plane to meet the board of Transport for London and, in particular, Ken Livingstone who had taken on its chairmanship.

Livingstone and Kiley – Ken and Kiley as they have become universally known in London – were not obvious soulmates: 'Ken started by saying he never thought he would be trying to recruit someone who worked for the CIA and I said I never thought I would be talking to an unreconstructed Trotskyite.' They hit it off straight away. Kiley says: 'There had to be a chemical reaction that worked, and there was.' Livingstone reckons that Kiley 'is one of only three public officials who I have been really close to and thought of as friends who shared policy objectives. The first was Harry Simpson who was housing director at Lambeth [when Livingstone was vice-chairman of housing there in the early 1970s] and also trained John Major, by the way, and the other was Maurice Stonefrost [the director general] at the GLC.'

Kiley had, indeed, been at the CIA for much of the 1960s and even worked at the heart of the organisation, as executive assistant to the director of central intelligence, Richard Helms, the man who tried to overthrow Castro, at 'the nadir of the Vietnam war'. He had been a student leader himself, as the president of the National Student Association, and was recruited by a couple of predecessors who were in the CIA: 'It was they who contacted me and said, guess what? And if you tell anyone, you are dead meat.' His work was to channel funding into national student, youth, women and labour organisations. This was a time of decolonisation and a Cold War battle was raging in many countries between US and Soviet funded local organisations. For example, for students, there tended to be a 'free world' organisation, backed by the CIA-funded international student conference, Cosec, and a Soviet one, supported by the Prague-based International Union of Students.

Even though Kiley is a lifelong Democrat and probably not that distant politically from Livingstone, whose left-wing edges have been blunted by the reality of having to balance conflicting interests as mayor of a very diverse city, he is quite happy with his involvement with the number one target of hatred for the Left: 'This was the McCarthy period with the Committee of Unamerican Activities in full flow, so it was very difficult to do this sort of thing overtly as the CIA money was going into left-wing activities, at least by the standards of those days. Sure I had mixed emotions because it was good to know there were resources available but a lot of worry about secret relationships and where the control really lay. But in my experience, control was always with the local organisations.' He says that by the time he was thirty, he had visited eighty-seven countries to 'promote the cause of democracy'. Officially he worked for the Agency for International Development, but the ID he carried was fake.

After a series of interesting and mostly public sector jobs, largely concerned with city management, particularly policing and transport, Kiley ran unsuccessfully for mayor of Boston and then in 1983 went to New York at the request of the governor, Mario Cuomo, to run the Metropolitan Transportation Authority.

Kiley was something of a legend for having turned around the New York metro system. There were several attempts during the PPP controversy by both politicians and civil servants to question both the extent of the success in New York and Kiley's role in it. His detractors argue that much of the money was in place anyway and that, in any case, the New York system is not so wonderful even today and is, moreover, much less complex than the London Underground network. Kiley accepts some of these arguments, agreeing that some extra money had been won for the system by his predecessors, but says he found the organisation in a mess:

'The place was a disaster from an operating point of view, much worse than the Underground is today. I did have some pump priming money, but I spent a lot of time raising money to get us through the next ten years.'

Kiley's account of his initial management meeting in New York, and his explanation of how he got rid of graffiti on the system, suggest that whatever his critics may say, he has a proven record of achievement and, moreover, that he has a deep-rooted scepticism of the value of consultants who, of course, have been almost entirely responsible for drawing up the PPP: 'The MTA had got into such a mess because it had brought in a whole bunch of consultants. One of the first things I did was to get all the one hundred MTA top managers and the consultants into a really large room. I said I wanted a clear answer to one question: "Who here is in charge?" Nobody responded and I said, that's it. For the consultants, it was all over. The meeting lasted just ten minutes.'

Kiley set about changing the whole top level of management but also employing a lot more managers: 'When I arrived, there were just a few hundred people to run this huge organisation with a budget of around $7bn in today's dollars. We got about 3500, a lot from outside, working on performance incentive based contracts which is what we are going to do here, as well. The running of the bus depots, train depots and the maintenance of the track, all of it was in the hands of consultants and we just rationalised the organisation and returned to a more conventional structure. They had simply lost their way and there is an uncanny similarity of circumstance twenty years later in London.'

Kiley's most public triumph was the victory over graffiti. It was a problem that seemed intractable, as it had become such an entrenched part of the New York system that it was seen as a feature of the Big Apple like the Empire State building or the illuminated advertisements in Times Square. The *New York Times* had even argued it was part of the culture, suggesting that some of it was good art: 'There wasn't a human being in New York who bought that line,' says Kiley. 'Our view was that the fact graffiti could not be controlled was effectively saying to the public, no one is in control, proceed at your own peril. Crime was very high – though actually less on the subway than elsewhere – and so we decided to take graffiti on. The system was completely covered with graffiti – 6200 train carriages, 480 stations, the depots, the shops. It was a kind of leprosy.'

Kiley did two things. First, every time a train set was refurbished or renewed, the rule was that any carriage with marks or graffiti that could not be immediately removed would be taken out of service, just as if it had a mechanical failure. He also redeployed 3000 cleaners, and put them on subway platforms, concentrating on the late afternoons when the kids come out of school, as graffiti can be washed off very easily if it is still wet. The police were given orders to arrest culprits and this concerted action meant the system was free of graffiti within four years.

Kiley also addressed the issue of performance. The trains kept on breaking down at an alarming rate. The mean distance between failures, the standard measurement for train fleets, was around 2500 miles, a 'miserable performance'. By the time Kiley left, in 1991, it was 40,000, 'which was a big improvement but not great', and now it is over 100,000 miles. The London Underground was 7000 miles, the last I looked.' He says the key is ensuring that the train fleet is always in a good condition and refurbishing the trains in mid-life, around twelve to seventeen years: 'You also have to replace the fleet when it is needed, doing it systematically as you don't want to replace it in spurts because later on that becomes a maintenance nightmare. The long-term spending cycle is eternal, it never stops. But you do not go for a great technological leap, you just take advantage of the technology that works. The government is right to say there should be a thirty-year plan.' Kiley changed the perception of the New York subway system – it became usable again for the middle-class New Yorkers who had shunned it. Ridership is now 5 million daily, compared with 3 million when he took over, with no extra lines.

The most telling criticism of Kiley is that he is a politician rather than a public official, a distinction that is much more blurred in the US, where elected people bring in whole coteries of acolytes whose job prospects are exactly the same as those of their boss. Kiley quickly plunged into the deep end on the PPP. Martin Callaghan, London Underground's PPP director, recalls his first meeting with the American and expresses surprise that he had so quickly adopted the same position over the PPP as Livingstone: 'The first time I met him was in September 2000. We were in Derek Smith's office [who was then London Underground's managing director] and I said, "Bob, there is one basic decision you have to make, whether to accept the fundamental structure of the PPP and your focus is going to be on dealing with your reservations within that framework, or you are simply going to oppose it." And he replied, "Yes, I have got that choice, I am going to oppose it." So he came in not knowing anything about it, having decided it was wrong. He could not have known anything about it as the only thing in the public domain at the time was an eight-page description.'[2]

Kiley, who – as with Callaghan – says he likes the other man, replies that he did know quite a lot about the scheme and pressed Callaghan at that first meeting about it: 'I knew enough to be extremely sceptical and I had read a fair amount of the government's case, which was thin at the time and has grown thinner since. I could have been persuaded then, but approached it with real scepticism. I did not make a definite conclusion at that stage.'

Moreover, Kiley had already talked about the scheme with Steve Polan, a US lawyer who specialises in transport schemes across the world and who was to become one of Transport for London's legal advisers on the PPP. Polan had been to a lunch when John Prescott had come to New York in the summer of 2000 on a fact-finding mission about how New York raised the money to pay for investment on its transport system. Polan recalls: 'I was there with half a dozen other people and Prescott gave a talk about the PPP. I was just there to listen, not to represent anyone, and I said to Prescott, this is insane. We talked about it and I felt he was honestly searching to see if this [the PPP] was necessary to raise private finance. The aim was to get money but I told him you could do something else to get money.'[3]

Polan was very clear straight away about what was wrong with the PPP and told Kiley before the latter went over to the UK. His objection is one of the most succinct criticisms of the PPP and nothing that has happened subsequently has changed Polan's view. Indeed, quite the opposite: 'What I thought was crazy was the idea that one could define with precision what one wanted in terms of an improvement programme for such a long period of time and then hand over the decision making to private companies with really minimal public control on how they would execute the work.'

Kiley was quick to try to wrest the initiative. He hit London running. Throughout the autumn he commuted half a dozen times to London while fulfilling his commitments to his New York job and in December he issued his alternative plan. He criticised the PPP, arguing that the contracts were weak, and his scheme was to raise £10bn of financing for investment for fifteen years with £6bn coming from operating surpluses and the rest from securitising future income (basically a bit like a mortgage, borrowing money against expected future income, which on the Tube is a very predictable flow of cash). Kiley's initiative was widely welcomed by both business and the media, and the government started making conciliatory noises about the possibility of a deal. Prescott and his transport minister, Lord Macdonald, met Kiley twice in the run-up to Christmas. Livingstone, too, tried to cool the temperature by saying he might back off from making a legal challenge. Kiley immediately made a powerful impact. He spoke to the London Labour MPs and according to Karen Buck, 'he was a wow. He just said I have no political axe to grind, but here's my record, and I can give you private sector procurement, delivery, the money and so on and the meeting just roared with approval. We came out thinking we have seen the future and it is called Bob Kiley.'[4] Kiley's PR skills and charisma, his laid-back American delivery combined with profound knowledge, proved a hit everywhere he spoke. And he appeared amenable to talking through the issues.

Therefore, despite Kiley's publicly stated misgivings and his immediate publication of an alternative plan, ministers and London Underground's bosses thought they could negotiate with him. Kiley, demonstrating that he still might be prepared to compromise, went along with them. It seemed that a deal was imminent, with the political spinning leading to headlines such as 'Ministers may back down on Tube plan' in the *Guardian* on 15 December and the *Daily Telegraph* going even further with 'Victory for Ken as Blair yields on Tube' on the following day. Although Livingstone crowed in his *Independent* column that 'Mr Prescott is coming round to my way of thinking about the Tube',[5] the fact that all the press ran similar stories in the ten days before Christmas demonstrates that both sides were making genuine efforts to reach a solution. Prescott was spurred on by the fact that the initial bids for the PPP contracts turned out far higher than expected. The final offers had been submitted in November 2000 and it had been expected that the preferred bidders would be announced in January 2001, but the Treasury decided that they were too expensive and the bidders were asked to resubmit on a reduced specification.

It was to be the first of a whole series of false dawns over the coming year. In the New Year, the tone changed dramatically with the government appearing to backtrack. Instead of a deal, there were talks. Lots of them, an extraordinary sequence, spanning three months and over a hundred meetings which began as soon as Kiley took up his post full time in the New Year. According to one participant with just a bit of hyperbole, 'it was hand-to-hand combat, trench style, and we went right over the entrails of the deal'. It was the nearest that the two sides ever came to a deal during the whole five-year controversy over the PPP and, inevitably, the various participants have differing views as to why, at the eleventh hour, the negotiations collapsed.

Indeed, the recollections of those who attended the meetings vary so widely that the accuracy of the following account of the tortuous process, patched together from a series of personal accounts, is bound to be challenged by one side or the other, especially as there was a steady stream of leaked – but not always accurate – stories in the press. History is, in a way, what people want it to be.

The negotiations started with a presentation of the contracts to Kiley and his team, which consisted entirely of Americans: the lawyer Steve Polan, TfL's finance chief Jay Walder, David Gunn, the man who would have run the Tube had a deal been successful, and a couple of others – 'not an Englishman among them' as one of the other side put it sniffily, but all fearsomely clever and all with experience of running metro systems. The Brits batting for the PPP also fielded a bunch of brains: the key man was Adrian Montague, a patrician Treasury man who was now deputy chairman of Partnerships UK, the quango created to develop PFI schemes, and as both a lawyer and a banker had helped to create the PPP; David Rowlands, the rail chief at the Department, the title of which has changed twice during this tale and is now simply the Department for Transport; Tony Poulter from PricewaterhouseCoopers; and from the Treasury, John Gieve, the head of finance, and Shriti Vadera a special adviser to Gordon Brown; Richard Phillips of Freshfields, the lawyers; and Martin Callaghan of LU. 'Not an operator among them,' says Kiley dismissively – and, moreover, to confirm his suspicions about who was driving the PPP scheme, two of them from the Treasury, plus a third, Montague, who though not representing the Treasury had strong links with it (athough, according to one participant, 'Montague was representing Prescott rather than the Treasury').

The cultural difference proved to be a hidden barrier between the British and Americans as there were nuances in the levels of meetings, those little distinctions so beloved of the British bureaucracy, which the Americans may not have fully understood. Thus Montague and Poulter tended to take on the 'working level' meetings, but Rowlands joined in those denoted 'official working level', while the more senior meetings were attended by Vadera whose status as a Treasury special adviser – a political appointee – gave her direct access to the Chancellor, Gordon Brown.

The personnel varied, with deputies sometimes attending the meetings which were held variously on the territories of the players. The endless string of meetings dominated the lives of the participants, with one exhausted player recalling: 'They took up half of my working hours from January to March, either attending them or writing notes.' As most of these people were on City rates of £250 per hour or more, the whole fruitless exercise could also have bought a new Tube train or two. The meetings overran into Saturdays and Sundays, and some were even held at Kiley's famous £2m town house in Belgravia, rented for him by TfL.

Kiley's position was summarised by one of the Brits: 'His prescription was chuck the PPP, give me a bond issue and control, trust me and fly me, I'm Kiley.' The government side began to make concessions over his demands. He wanted less focus on stations and more on trains; he did not like the payment for ambience and 'we were prepared to kick it out', although it only makes up a tiny slice of the performance regime; he wanted open-book subcontracting – i.e. the contractors would have to provide clear accounts of how much they were making on the deal – and that was agreed to; he fought for the right to have more control over the investment programme and 'we were ready to find a way around that'; he wanted observer directors on the infracos; and so on.

The other side thought they were in a play: 'The meetings were endless and there were points when it felt scripted. David and Adrian on one side, us on the other, and everything was scripted.' Gradually, information was released by London Underground and the government representatives, 'so one of the advantages was that we were getting more knowledge of what was going on'.

By the end of January 2001, 'we were discussing a one-page summary of changes'. The Treasury was being 'reluctantly dragged along' according to one side, 'not moving' according to the other. But a draft press release had been prepared and a deal seemed imminent. Again there was much spinning and counter-spinning. On 29 January Kiley told the *Evening Standard*, 'I don't want to give the impression that I've completely given up hope but right now we are talking to people who don't seem to be in a position to deliver a deal. They are not really authorised to make a deal and it's not clear to whom they would go.'

Yet, four days later, it appeared to be just a matter of dotting the 'i's and crossing the 't's. On 2 February *The Times*' transport correspondent, Ben Webster, confidently predicted: 'Prescott expected to agree Tube deal today'. While the PPP would not be scrapped, Kiley would get the 'unified management' which was his sticking point throughout the whole process. That day, the *Evening Standard* splashed on 'Kiley victory on Tube plan', but in fact there was little substantial progress. In the statement issued by Kiley but approved by Prescott, there was merely an agreement to work 'together' on modifications to the scheme and produce a 'son' of the PPP with 'mutually acceptable changes'. The contractors were still to have long leases but they would work to specifications and timescales set by Kiley at Transport for London. Prescott and Kiley were pictured smiling together. Despite running the story prominently, the *Standard*'s long-standing and canny transport correspondent Dick Murray got it right when he added: 'Within minutes of the announcement, there were clear signs of government gears crunching into reverse with a Downing Street spokesman describing Mr Kiley as "extremely effective" and a "serious player".'

There was a spate of such positive stories over the next few days but already the bidders were expressing concern over the possible changes to the contracts and unhelpfully joined in the spinning. They were worried that they would have to re-tender on a different basis. One commented: 'The uncertainty is ridiculous. It is a farce that the Government is now considering the unified management that Bob Kiley wants. Unified management was not envisaged under the PPP as tendered.'[6] There were threats of a legal challenge to recover the costs of bidding, which could amount to £30m according to Linc, which was furious at the prospect of 'having Kiley as our managing director'.

Indeed, there seemed to be a practical impasse. Either Kiley had control and the Tube remained in the public sector, with the consequences for the government's balance sheet, or he did not, in which case he would have no further truck with it. As one commentator put it, 'to suggest, as Prescott did, that the PFI can be tinkered with to fit the new order is either a statement of breathtaking cynicism or a tragic example of how little he understands the private sector'.[7] Not surprisingly, over the next few days, there was no further announcement. Inside the negotiations, the atmosphere began to sour with the Brits beginning to think that Kiley would never sign on the dotted line. Although they all recall his charisma and charm, they now express doubts about his sincerity, albeit in polite language: 'Kiley was very nervous about committing to a deal. His strategy was the Jericho strategy, blowing his trumpet so that the walls would fall down. He was not really negotiating on detail, so that one could drive towards a consensus. He was standing back, blowing his trumpet, at which he is extremely good.' Then it gets personal: 'I have tended to believe in life that people do not actively pursue conspiracy theories, that there is general good faith [long pause] . . . I came close to questioning that with Kiley.' He was like a flirtatious girl – 'every time we got close to him, he danced back'.

At one stage Montague even went round to Kiley's house on a Sunday afternoon with a paper he had written to try to unblock the process. Callaghan, too, became a visitor. Kiley recalls: 'Martin was the most flexible of the group. His favourite gambit was to come over to my house and say I've got some ideas, why don't *you* write them down on a piece of paper, because I am not going to get anywhere with them. I tried this a couple of times but it never worked. The first roadblock he had to get around was David Rowlands but the ultimate one was the Treasury and when Shriti Vadera joined the conversation, it became impassable.'

Indeed, for Kiley, Vadera, described in a newspaper profile as 'abrasive and aggressive' and very confident in her opinions, became Kiley's *bête noire*. She had had a very successful career with Warburg, the merchant bank, before becoming one of Gordon Brown's four special advisers early in 1999, concentrating on Third World debt. Throughout the negotiations, she was particularly adamant about ensuring that control of Tube investment should not remain in the public sector, and Kiley felt she was there to veto any scheme that left any vestiges of control with London Underground.

The *New Statesman*, in one of the few contemporaneous accounts of the talks, said she and Kiley represented two wholly contrasting cultures, with the wily old transport operator being pitted against Treasury officials with glittering academic careers but no practical experience: 'Kiley was suspicious of her sitting there, taking notes, maintaining strong eye contact and choosing her moments to signal the Treasury's will.'[8] Vadera's role is played down by the other side, who point out that Gieve, as director of finance, was the Treasury's top man round the table, but Kiley dismisses this: 'So she had nothing else to do and decided to drop in? She was the watchdog of the Treasury, an institutional representative.'

While Kiley was sounding off publicly about Vadera and about Gordon Brown's refusal to meet him to anyone who would listen, the Treasury was not averse to a bit of its own mischief making – but in private, as is the British way. When Kiley did an 'Is there anyone here who has authority to make a decision?' tirade at one of the meetings, in a reprise of his New York MTA performance, the Treasury took revenge by briefing against him with a story in the *Sunday Times*, questioning whether he understood the British way of doing things: 'It's like the Americans coming over and saying, "gee, you drive on the left, that's wrong, you must drive on the right".' As mentioned above, there were regular hints in shady briefings that his performance in New York had not been as triumphant as had been made out.

Despite all this, somehow, after the early February hopes had been dashed, the whole merry-go-round started again, this time with many more issues on the agenda. Montague had now got a seventeen-page paper setting out seventy-five points, with a detailed set of changes that the government would make to accommodate Kiley. One participant explained: 'There was a paper written by Adrian and Tony [Poulter] which put maintenance back with TfL but by March, on our side, we increasingly thought that Kiley's views were so extreme in this regard that either he had not thought through what he meant, or he did not want to compromise. He was somewhere on that spectrum and there are a lot of civil servants who think his intentions were so tactical that you could not meet them or he was untrustworthy.' Again, a climax seemed tantalisingly close but was never reached. It was like blowing up balloons which always burst before reaching their full size. According to one participant: 'We got him back on board but then he backed off again.'

Kiley says that at this stage – 'it was the Stockholm syndrome, stay with your jailer long enough and you will identify with him' – he had suggested the creation of an organisation called London Underground Maintenance, with which all three infracos would have contracts: 'Then we would have controlled LUM jointly with the infracos and finally they could not agree to that.' He even tried dealing directly with the infracos over it and Metronet was keen, but its boss, Rod Hoare, eventually thought too much water had passed under the bridge, while Tube Lines always steadfastly refused to speak to Kiley.

At the end of March, the talks collapsed with Kiley saying the whole process had been 'boring' because the key issues had never been on the table. He dismisses the suggestion that he was merely going through the motions but accepts that the Hatfield disaster which occurred during his first week in London was a defining moment in holding firm over the issue of management: 'The line I could not cross was the track wheel separation' which had caused so much trouble on the national railway. Several on the other side, however, remain deeply sceptical about whether Kiley would ever have been prepared to move once he could not persuade David Gunn, the man he wanted to run London Underground, about what was on offer. Gunn, who previously ran the Toronto transit system and had worked for Kiley in New York, is described as 'one of the most brutally forthright people I have ever met whom you have to deal with by jabbing on the chin' and by a former colleague as having 'an absolute contempt for politicians who he thinks are ill-informed, which is unacceptable for a civil servant'. Gunn was completely immovable over the separation of infrastructure from operations, the heart of the PPP. Gunn would have had, says one of the veterans of the talks, 'a devastating effect, possibly good, possibly not' on London Underground but it was not to be. He had an argument with Kiley in the middle of the negotiations and went back to North America where he now has, ironically, the worst railway job in the world – running the heavily indebted and loss-making US passenger service, Amtrak, where every decision is likely to be reversed as a result of interference by politicians.

The recriminations over the breakdown of talks were mutual. Prescott accused Kiley of megaphone diplomacy. In response, the commissioner wrote a lengthy letter to the Deputy Prime Minister setting out the minimum conditions for accepting the PPP and threatening court action through a judicial review of the PPP process if they were not met, a threat which Kiley and Livingstone had begun to make publicly. Whatever the details, it is obvious, with the benefit of hindsight, that the fixed positions, of the Treasury on one side and Kiley on the other, made a deal unlikely. But was Kiley merely being obdurate and refusing to move, or had the other side made promises that they could not keep or later withdrew?

The evidence from independent sources favours Kiley. Early in March, Will Hutton, who had written the Industrial Society report mentioned in Chapter 9, said in his *Observer* column[9] that the government had offered 'Ken Livingstone the deal of his life. The scale of the concession is beyond anything mainstream opinion imagined when Livingstone was elected mayor.' Hutton was writing on the basis of a leaked letter from Prescott, dated 28 February 2001, which set out an offer that seemed to meet Kiley's key demand, control of the investment programme to be undertaken by the infracos. In particular, said Hutton, the government had given TfL 'votes, vetoes, assurances of money and *de facto* board control of the infracos, while retaining the PPP structure. The infracos would now be 'public interest stakeholder companies' with day-to-day management by London Underground which would have a stable funding regime for 7.5 years: 'Livingstone has the government on the run,' concluded Hutton, and he should show magnanimity. The Department so liked Hutton's piece that it was included in its next briefing to Labour MPs, but already by then the offer, if it ever existed, appears to have been withdrawn.

In fact, the government seemed to start retreating from the offer even before Kiley and Livingstone could properly respond. For example, while the Department claimed that LU would have 'closer oversight of asset management', according to TfL the government withdrew its original offer to provide LU with the right to approve bidders' 'annual business plans and budgets' and 'explicit approval rights over maintenance plans'. Instead LU was offered only the right to approve the first annual plan of each infraco as part of the bidding process. Indeed, most of the 'rights' on offer to TfL proved to be much weaker than suggested.

A group of London Labour MPs who had tried to mediate between the Department and Transport for London went to see Kiley to try to get to the bottom of the story. One MP said: 'We had two or three sessions with him over a fortnight and were doing quite complex comparisons, sitting down with government briefs on the one hand, and what Kiley was saying, and trying to work out the truth. We came to the conclusion that what the government was briefing was completely untrue and that what was in this notional deal never really existed.'[10]

The nub of the issue is the status of the 'offer' made by Prescott to Transport for London in the 28 February letter. Crucially, although the letter had been shown to a relatively senior official at the Treasury, it had not been approved by either Brown or Vadera. Moreover, the bidders, in particular Bechtel, part of Tube Lines, were not happy with the deal, feeling that they could not put their shareholders' money at risk in an arrangement which effectively gave TfL control over what they could do, and quickly started lobbying against it once Hutton's article had appeared.

In a letter to Kiley after the negotiations had broken down, Prescott suggests that the concessions did not constitute a firm offer. He wrote, on 27 March:

> These proposals formed the basis of my letter of 28 February. I made it clear that they were 'a basis on which it might be possible to find common ground within the framework of the PPP' and that the proposals were also 'at the limit of what I could contemplate by way of making modification to the PPP while remaining within its framework and may even go beyond that limit depending on the detailed way in which they might be implemented'. I went on to say that any changes to the PPP should not 'significantly reduce performance risk transfer nor preclude privately owned and privately financed infrastructure companies'. The ensuing discussions based on the framework of the major concessions in my letter did not end in agreement. We worked through in detail how the concessions we offered could be made to work within the structure of the PPP, which we understood you accepted.[11]

This suggests very strongly that the deal in the 28 February letter did not constitute a firm offer but was merely a set of negotiating points that would only be taken forward if they could be fitted into the framework of the PPP, or that Prescott was nobbled after sending the letter to Kiley. Stephen Glaister, who has viewed the whole PPP process both as an academic and as a member of the Transport for London board, is convinced it was the latter: 'Prescott made what he thought was a firm offer, but the Treasury forced him to backtrack'.[12] Hutton feels that Livingstone may have missed a trick: 'Livingstone should have gone public, proclaiming victory as quickly as possible. He needed to make it too politically difficult, as fast as possible, for the government to withdraw the proposal, therefore locking it into its offer. Instead he hesitated and the Treasury and the infracos ensured that the deal was killed off.'[13]

Although sceptical of the government's case, the London MPs were not wholly convinced by Kiley either, finding him at times 'disingenuous', and felt that the personal antagonism between him and Prescott had been unhelpful. Nevertheless, they were concerned enough about what they saw as government dissembling to take their concerns to the Prime Minister: 'We felt there was less to the deal than met the eye and so a group of us London MPs went to see Blair, a week before Easter. We took all the documentation that we had done and spent an hour with him. He said, "I promise to come back to you."' Like it or not, Blair was to be dragged into the PPP controversy.

CHAPTER ELEVEN

Nothing to do with any of us, guv

The intervention of the London Labour MPs prompted Tony Blair into taking a personal interest in resolving the issue. With a general election in the offing, he was becoming increasingly concerned that the controversy might be a heavy vote loser in London. Ministers had tried to wrest the initiative with a campaign to sell the PPP's benefits, something they had singularly failed to do over the previous four years; but as with every announcement over the PPP, it left more unanswered questions than before.

Prescott had launched an eight-page document setting out all the goodies in the PPP on 11 April 2001. But the government had already been pushed onto the defensive after the collapse of the talks by the resignation of Derek Smith, the managing director of London Underground. It was a victory for Transport for London and for Livingstone, who had already made clear privately that he could not work with Smith ('When I appointed Bob, I had not made up my mind whether to keep Derek Smith and asked Bob to find out, and within a month he told me we needed to let him go. It was not that I vindictively got rid of him.') and had consistently attacked the top management as 'dullards' and 'knuckleheads'. Smith, who had been infuriated by these attacks, was now free to vent his fury at Livingstone, saying they had had 'a disruptive and unsettling effect on morale in the company'. The departure of Smith, who stayed until the end of the year before going off to run an NHS trust, was not the only one. At least half a dozen other leading Underground managers had left in the previous few months, some to work for the companies who were to take over the maintenance of the system under the PPP.

To make matters worse for Prescott, on the very day of his announcement, Transport for London learnt that it had won permission in the High Court for a judicial review of the PPP. Nevertheless, Prescott gamely outlined the details of the timetable for improvements, promising the introduction of new or refurbished trains on most lines by 2019 and a programme of refurbishment for fifty-six stations by 2006. Litter would be cleared within one hour, escalators and lifts would be repaired within a day and signalling equipment within two. The scheme was now said to be worth £13bn over the first fifteen years, £20bn over thirty, a big increase from the £7bn when it had first been announced. But it was unclear precisely how much of that money was to be provided by the private sector. The government later conceded that it was 75 per cent public money: 45 per cent government grant and 30 per cent from London Underground revenues, with just 25 per cent coming from the infracos which, of course, was not free money since it would be repaid with interest and profits.

Livingstone's response was that too much money was being budgeted for stations and not enough for major line upgrades, a point he and Kiley would reiterate over the coming months. Indeed, the scheme seemed relatively thin gruel, with a huge amount of money producing relatively little improvement within the first period of the PPP. Moreover, the commitment to improve capacity on most lines by 15–20 per cent, cited in the Invitation to Tender document, had been dropped with only the Northern achieving that target in the first 7.5 years. As the *Financial Times* put it, 'Tube travellers face long wait for arrival of new trains.'[1]

The other lines were to be refurbished during the second and third periods, which highlights a major point on which the two sides were bitterly divided. The supporters of the PPP argue that the timing of the improvements makes little difference since the infracos have thirty-year contracts with which they must comply. The opponents say that the review points at every 7.5 years effectively mean a total renegotiation of the contract, and therefore anything beyond the first period is merely an aspiration, not a commitment. TfL's argument is that there is no fixed pricing arrangement beyond the first period and therefore any schemes scheduled for future periods may prove to be unaffordable. LU's PPP team responds that much of the relevant work will begin in the first period and therefore the infracos will already be committed when the review is carried out. Obviously, it is impossible to judge which argument is correct because there is so much uncertainty about the review process, but again it is difficult to support London Underground's uncritical optimism about the ability of the PPP to deliver these improvements over the full thirty years. As with so much about the PPP, we are in uncharted territory. (The issue of what the contracts will deliver and how the terms appear to have moved against London Underground and in favour of the infracos over time is examined fully in Chapter 2.)

Still the government tried to press blithely forward, ignoring the increasingly detailed arguments querying the whole concept of the PPP. In early May, ministers announced the preferred bidders, even though Kiley counselled caution arguing that, once there was no longer competition, London Underground's negotiating position would be greatly weakened.

In a letter to London Transport's chairman, Sir Malcolm Bates, just before the 2 May London Transport board meeting at which the selection of the preferred bidders for the two deep tube contracts was to be confirmed, Kiley warned that LU would lose 'invaluable and necessary leverage to protect the public interest' over a series of points in the contracts which remained outstanding.[2] To no avail. Tube Lines, which was formed by Jarvis, Amey and Bechtel, won the Jubilee Northern Piccadilly contract, while Metronet – a consortium of W.S. Atkins, Seeboard, Adtranz (which later became Bombardier), Thames Water and Balfour Beatty – was allocated the Bakerloo Central Victoria infraco[3] and, in September, was announced as the winner of the competition for the sub-surface lines. Metronet was run by Rod Hoare, a former BAA executive who had been responsible for the Heathrow Express project, while Tube Lines was headed by Iain Coucher, who had previously run TranSys (the company that was installing Prestige, a complete new ticketing system for the Tube, under a PFI contract) but would later, in the spring of 2002, join Network Rail as its managing director.

The consortia were predictably delighted and the share prices of their constituent firms soared. In contrast, Livingstone and Kiley were furious, especially as the former had once called Balfour Beatty 'capitalist scum' in the wake of the Hatfield crash. The company subsequently lost the £250m contract for maintenance on the East Coast Main Line, although it strongly denied responsibility for the accident. Balfour Beatty's record was, indeed, unenviable, as it had a string of previous convictions for breaches of health and safety regulations on the railways. Balfour Beatty had bought three of the thirteen infrastructure units sold off when British Rail was privatised in 1996 and their safety record was patchy. In a series of high-profile cases, two of its subsidiaries were fined nearly £200,000 for having caused the derailment of a freight train, parts of which subsequently toppled off a viaduct, in Bexley, south-east London, in February 1997; six months later a freight train was again derailed, this time at Chelmsford in Essex, as a result of incompetent track work, resulting in a conviction for another subsidiary and a £500,000 fine; and worst of all, the company was fined £1.2m for serious breaches of the Health and Safety Act after a tunnel collapsed during the construction of the Heathrow Express. The subsequent Health and Safety Executive inquiry found that 'the collapses could have been prevented but for a cultural mind-set which focused attention on the apparent economies and the need for production rather than the particular risk'.[4]

By coincidence, Jarvis, one of whose directors is Steve Norris, the former Tory transport minister and failed mayoral candidate, also had a blemished record, having incurred a huge fine for health and safety breaches on the railways. Jarvis Fastline was fined £500,000 in August 2000 following two separate incidents in 1999 that resulted in freight train derailments. Following maintenance work, the company had failed to check the track before trains were allowed to run, thus endangering the lives of employees and passengers. In a more minor incident, the company had been fined £7000 after a contractor lost an eye while working on renewing rail.

Perhaps more significantly, Jarvis was to be widely criticised for its attitude to the Potters Bar train crash in May 2002 in which five people were killed. The accident was caused by the failure of points from which two sets of bolts had been removed. Jarvis, which had taken over the contract from Balfour Beatty for the maintenance of that section of the East Coast Main Line, briefed journalists that the bolts were likely to have been undone by saboteurs because the process did not accord with any known type of maintenance work. There was, however, widespread scepticism over this claim within the rail industry, not least because Jarvis's statement was based on photographic evidence, as the company had not been allowed onto the track in the immediate aftermath of the accident; and at the time of writing, summer 2002, the cause of the disaster remains unknown. It was widely felt among railway executives that Jarvis had done itself and the industry far more harm than good by issuing statements about the accident on the basis of scant photographic evidence and that it was a PR exercise intended to boost the company's falling share price. As one industry insider told me at the time: 'It would have been much better if Jarvis had just kept quiet like the rest of us until the cause of the accident was known.'

Defenders of the PPP argue that it is to be expected that such large firms should have occasional lapses and note that London Underground itself was fined £225,000 under health and safety legislation in January 2002. The case involved a project manager, 'Dangerous' David Elkington, who made workers undertake track maintenance next to live rails and train services when the jobs should have been carried out at night when the line was closed. However, the seriousness of the cases involving Jarvis and Balfour Beatty seem to reveal a pattern of slapdash approach to safety that raises concern about these companies' future behaviour. Moreover, it will be a matter of huge political embarrassment should there be any similar cases once the PPP contracts have been signed, especially as Livingstone has made safety one of his primary concerns about the PPP.

Bombardier also has a controversial recent record, as its subsidiary, Alstom, had developed an unenviable record for late delivery of trains before it was taken over. The parent company also gained a reputation for being litigious after it counter-sued when Amtrak, the US government-owned passenger train service, had filed a suit over the late delivery of a set of high-speed trains. Bombardier replied, in what Amtrak called 'a stunning demonstration of irony',[5] by trying to sue Amtrak for failing to ensure that high-speed track was available in time. Moreover, when the trains were finally delivered, all eighteen sets had to be withdrawn twice in August 2002 because cracks were found in a vital bracket, causing chaos to Amtrak services.

These failings by the bidding companies were regularly highlighted by Livingstone and Kiley in the growing controversy over the PPP. While the public slanging match escalated over the demise of Derek Smith and the announcement of preferred bidders, Blair was trying to patch things up behind the scenes. He asked Anji Hunter, who as director of political and government relations at No. 10 was a key backroom figure in the government, to phone Kiley and ask him to drop in at Chequers, the Prime Minister's official weekend retreat, on Easter Monday. Kiley was a bit taken aback, especially as he was told not to inform Livingstone. He agreed to keep it quiet until the first meeting but then told Blair he would have to keep his boss in the picture. There were just the two of them at that initial meeting: 'He had the contracts strewn all over his worktable, which covers two walls of his study, which is a big study. The Northern Line PFI contract was there as well as the PPP and he remarked: "The language in this Northern Line contract is a lot better than the language in this PPP contract." I agreed.'[6] Blair is, of course, a lawyer and well able to understand such nuances.

The PM said that he would like to name Kiley as chairman of London Transport for the purpose of finishing the negotiations with the bidders but on the understanding that the basic elements of the PPP had to be preserved and that the government would have to make that judgement in terms of any deal. Kiley demurred: 'I said I didn't think I was going to be on secure ground if those were the constraints because there was still no clear definition of what the PPP was. He said I could have my own consultants, but I countered by asking for the Tube to be transferred to TfL straight away. I told him: "You keep the discretion on whether the outcome is or is not PPP and you are going to fund it. So you keep the key cards, money and decision over PPP." I felt the contractors would think that was a serious move, but not my simply going over to 55 Broadway [LT's HQ] every day to talk to them.' For a fortnight, over a series of three or four meetings and a similar number of phone calls, Blair and Kiley argued over that issue. In the end Kiley had to give in and took on the role of chairman reluctantly: 'When the Prime Minister asks you to do something, sure you can argue and say what about getting Gordon Brown involved but at the end I felt that just to say, "Sorry, Prime Minister, bad idea," would be the end of any kind of conversation so I thought I had to go through with it.' No whiff of these meetings reached the press and Blair kept firmly out of the public controversy over the PPP, knowing it was an issue that few could understand and even fewer supported. By appointing Kiley, he had achieved the key aim of keeping the issue out of the political agenda for the duration of the campaign for the election, which was due to be held in May but was postponed until June because of the foot and mouth outbreak.

In a move widely interpreted as showing that Kiley's tenure in his new job was going to be short, he did not withdraw from the court case – which effectively meant he was preparing to sue himself since he represented both TfL and London Underground. While the government's decision to appoint him could seem equally cynical given the short-term political needs, Kiley reckons there was more to it: 'I think there was a mixture of motives. There was the politics, but there was also the feeling that there was no point having a hostile Transport for London. Blair had an appreciation of the various aspects, it was not just a political point, but I still don't know how much to weigh these factors.' Livingstone, though, had lost what could have been a key bargaining point during the election campaign but he was probably not too concerned about this as he wanted to keep open his prospects of rejoining the Labour Party in time for the next mayoral election. Had he campaigned strenuously against Labour's plan for the Tube during the general election hustings, any return would probably have been ruled out for ever.

In the event, out of the three, only the government achieved its aim. The Tube did not feature in the election campaign but Kiley was gone from London Transport a month after the election and Livingstone failed in July 2002 in his attempt to overturn his five-year banishment from the Labour Party, largely because he had embarked on a second court case against the government.

Whatever the motives, Kiley effectively sacked himself from the chairmanship of London Transport – though, of course, he remained as Transport Commissioner at TfL – within a month of the general election when he wrote to Tony Blair that he had been unable to reach an agreement with the bidders which met his objectives for modernising the Tube but fitted within the framework of the PPP. Stephen Byers, the new transport secretary appointed after the 7 June election, publicly dismissed Kiley's objections by announcing to Parliament on 5 July that the government was proceeding with negotiations whatever Kiley's view and was going to impose the PPP come what may. He told MPs: 'Having carefully considered everything Mr. Kiley had to say, the Government have concluded that the best course is to proceed with plans for the modernisation of the underground, to create a 21st-century tube which will be publicly run and privately built.'[7]

Kiley clearly had to go and was sacked on 17 July, just six days before the Judicial Review into the legality of the way the PPP was being introduced was due to start in the High Court – at which point his post as chair of London Transport would have been untenable anyway since he would have been party to both sides in action. The case, which attracted considerable publicity and a fair-sized demonstration outside the High Court, was really fatally flawed from the outset, with even Livingstone giving himself only a 30 to 50 per cent chance of victory. The judge, Mr Justice Sullivan, who was something of a railway buff, made clear that his hands were tied by the legislation which expressly said the government would complete the PPP deal before handing it over to TfL. In the key passage, he said: 'Whatever Londoners' expectations may have been, the statutory code transfers full democratic control to their mayor but only after the government has been able to introduce its version of PPP.' However, the judge criticised ministerial dissembling in Parliament over this fact, singling out the then junior transport minister, Glenda Jackson, for failing three times in a 1999 Commons debate over the legislation to make it clear that the mayor would only assume control of the Tube once the PPP was in place. In effect, Labour's decentralisation was a sham, as Kiley had spotted when he addressed the Policy Unit in No. 10 (see Chapter 10). The result, as Tony Travers, the head of the Greater London Group at the London School of Economics, put it, is that London 'is treated as if it were a small *commune* in rural France'.[8]

The judge's sympathetic remarks drew TfL into a trap by encouraging a foolhardy attempt by Kiley to challenge the PPP yet again in a reprise of the action almost exactly a year later in July 2002 which was to end abruptly when the same judge made clear that his case was legally without merit.

Despite their party's overwhelming election victory and relatively good performance in the capital, the London Labour MPs remained extremely concerned about the PPP and pressed Byers not to foist it on their constituents. At a meeting of the 55-strong group, Byers was warned that he should try to find a workable compromise rather than simply imposing the PPP, but while he told the meeting that he would 'reflect' on what he had heard, he was in no position to do anything about the PPP. When he had accepted the transport brief from Blair after the election, it had been made clear to him that the one policy that was not open to change was the PPP.

Byers had some personal doubts about the scheme, which he had examined in some detail back in 1998 as Chief Secretary at the Treasury. As another of New Labour's lawyers, he was able to grasp the detail of the contracts and their shortcomings. According to a former aide, Byers's view was that the PPP – and indeed the controversial part-privatisation of the National Air Traffic Services which was going through at the same time – was not the optimum way forward, but he had no choice: 'He felt strongly that the PPP for the Tube was not the best approach but the biggest supporter was the Treasury, not the Department of Transport. Prescott had dithered and found it difficult to make a decision and by the time Byers got in, it was too late.' Byers, the aide added, 'was told that the PPP was off-limits and there was nothing he could do about it'. The reality was that Londoners had been promised investment for four years and nothing had happened, which meant Labour ministers felt it was too late to scrap the plan. Indeed, Byers effectively confirmed this when he met Livingstone, who says: 'At my first one-to-one meeting with Byers, I said I have fourteen issues I wish to raise, and he said let's leave the Tube to last. We agreed on the first thirteen, and then he said, "We've got two minutes, I have to tell you I am not authorised in any way to vary the PPP, so we should put it to one side and get on with working together." And that's what we did. We made good progress on everything else, on capital projects, the congestion charge. The PPP was further up the food chain. I liked his honesty. But he had been told when he took that job, the PPP was fixed as an issue.'[9] Interestingly, Byers felt so constrained in what he could do on the PPP that he never even bothered to meet Kiley privately during his whole year at the Department of Transport.

While Blair was agnostic about the PPP, he wanted to see the issue resolved as quickly as possible. Brown, on the other hand, was a PPP evangelist, but he, too, was concerned about being directly involved. He has, famously, refused to see Kiley throughout the whole controversy, and has operated indirectly through such interlocutors as Geoffrey Robinson and Shriti Vadera. He infuriated London Labour MPs just before the 2001 election by refusing to reply to questions about the PPP when he spoke at their meeting, saying it was nothing to do with the Treasury. As one MP at the meeting put it, 'He got up and said, "Nothing to do with us, the Treasury is not involved." These are the sort of reasons you lose faith in your own side, even if you don't have faith in Kiley always telling the truth, because I know that they lied and I don't know he has.' The MP paused for breath, face reddening with anger: 'How can they say that? But you can't say to the Chancellor, "Sorry, but you are lying."'[10]

Indeed, Brown's advisers seem to have gone on a charm initiative in the run-up to the court hearing in an attempt to distance their boss from the PPP. Polly Toynbee reported wittily: 'As I write, calls rain in from Brown's people claiming incredibly that the PPP has nothing to do with the Chancellor, nothing at all. It was all John Prescott's baby – as if. Last week, they told me it was all Stephen Byers's responsibility forsooth.' She was not fooled: 'The Chancellor's fistprint on this one is indelible: his people have done the negotiating . . . . Macavity the mystery chancellor has a habit of vanishing from scenes of crime, but this time he is right here.'[11] She recalls: 'It was a surreal experience. Here was this person ringing me up from the Treasury with whom I had discussed the PPP several times telling me it was nothing to do with them, it was the Department of Transport. I said: "But we have talked about this many times," and they simply replied: "We've talked about lots of things in the past."'[12]

Certainly the Treasury's hand seemed to be all over the deal according to one of the failed bidders. Michael Cassidy, who headed the Linc consortium, gave particularly revealing evidence to the Commons Transport Committee in November 2001. Although Cassidy remained broadly supportive of the PPP concept, he was unequivocal about its origins: 'This was a scheme that was, in my view, conceived, designed and manufactured by the Treasury. This was a Treasury project. It was almost like designing a new racing car. They were the designer, they manufactured it, the chassis may have come from a previous model, subsequently found to be disappointing, the steering was completely different but this was a Treasury-conceived motor car and it was assigned to the Department of Transport to actually manage the project and London Underground were the drivers.'[13] Eloquently put. During the initial negotiations, Cassidy at first thought that the Treasury would remain in the background, but at various stages in the bid process it took an active role. So while on a day-to-day basis he was meeting with London Underground officials, at various times the Treasury 'decided it was appropriate to make an intervention'.[14] But these were not direct interventions as they came through London Underground or Department officials.

The key Treasury intervention came at Christmas 2000 when, as mentioned in the previous chapter, the bids proved to be too expensive. The Treasury, according to Cassidy, told all the bidders 'that the totality of this project was now too expensive for the nation to afford, please go away and readjust your bids by taking out sectors of the work or delaying expensive parts of the work to later years, so that the overall figure was less'.[15] In particular, Cassidy said, delivery of trains was delayed into years 8 to 12, rather than being scheduled for the first period. In fact, London Underground had rejected the 'best and final offer' (BAFO) bids for the two deep tube lines in November 2000 at the behest of the Treasury, and the bidders had been required to submit cheaper alternatives by early January 2001, which they had done, resulting in some of the investment plans being postponed or scrapped.

But despite the continued involvement of the Treasury, Brown managed to keep out of the fray, even after the 2001 election. It was Byers, the reluctant foot soldier – ironically a Blairite rather than a Brownite – who was forced to carry on pushing through the plan. Following the government's victory in the Judicial Review, Byers said that there were three conditions that had to be satisfied before the PPP could finally be implemented. There had to be value for money, the scheme had to be approved by the Health and Safety Executive and the Tube must not be privatised. Of the three tests, two were meaningless and out of his hands. The Health and Safety Executive was assessing the safety case for the PPP but there was little doubt that eventually it would grant a seal of approval, which it duly did in July 2002. As for the Tube not being privatised, that was a manifesto commitment, but clearly New Labour had managed to convince itself, if no one else, that the PPP did not mean privatisation. That was just a bit of semantic sophistry which troubled no one.

Value for money, however, was potentially a real test, a reprise of the assessment of the public sector comparator against the bids from the private consortia which was considered in detail in Chapter 8. The test was to be carried out, at the behest of the government, by yet another consultant, Ernst & Young, and was eventually published in February 2002 after much misplaced speculation that it would lead to the scrapping of the PPP.

In the meantime, the battle between the two parties intensified but was largely fought, like the Cold War, through proxies with the role of the

Vietcong in Vietnam and Unita in Angola being taken, almost as expensively, by Deloitte & Touche, PricewaterhouseCoopers, Parsons Brinckerhoff, Ernst & Young and several other overpaid guns for hire. No sooner had Kiley lost the judicial review than he was back in court seeking permission to publish a report by Deloitte & Touche which was supposed to be presented to the London Transport board. However, he was sacked on 17 July, the day before the board meeting, and the report had subsequently disappeared. As a result Kiley was the subject of an injunction obtained by London Underground forbidding him to talk about the Deloitte report and another one, on engineering and safety standards, by Parsons Brinckerhoff.

This time Kiley won. London Underground argued that the report was commercially confidential but on 23 August was slapped down by the Appeal Court which allowed the publication of a version with a few 'commercially confidential' figures withheld. The report, as we saw in Chapter 9, was critical of the way the public sector comparator had been increased through assumptions that were used to negate the effect of the public sector's access to cheaper borrowing: for instance, the public sector's poor reputation was supposed to cost £700m, according to a concept of 'reputational externality' introduced into the equation, and if the investment were retained in the public sector, it would cost £1.17bn in lost performance; it was further assumed that while the private sector would learn from its mistakes, London Underground could not, and this would cost a further £1.6bn; and there would never be any upward renegotiation of contract prices because private contractors always deliver what they promise to budget. The Ernst & Young report would rehearse these issues yet again six months later.

Then, not for the first or last time, it all got silly as the two sides waved their consultants at each other. Derek Smith, the outgoing managing director of the Underground, criticised the Deloitte report, pointing out that it contained a caveat which said: 'Our work has been limited by the time available, scope, information available and limited access to information sources.' It was, Smith concluded, 'rushed, wrong and riddled with errors'. He also laid into the Parsons report, suggesting that Kiley had doctored the executive summary which, at times, seemed to contradict the main body of the report – a criticism, incidentally, soon to be levelled over the Ernst &

Young value for money report by the other side. All this shed little light for the London taxpayers and the users of the services that were the subject of this increasingly arcane row. It was a dishonest argument that merely emphasised the point that consultants tend to come up with the answers which their paymasters are seeking, not least because it is those who commission the reports who have control over the information available as well as the eventual use to which the report is put.

Kiley's pleas and arguments did not fall entirely on deaf ears. The government, constantly on the defensive over the PPP, let slip that it had changed the contracts to give the operator, the London Underground, the power to insist that improved safety standards should be introduced more quickly and the right to 'step in' if work were not carried out by the bidders. As part of the overall scheme, these were minor concessions which the bidders appeared happy to accept.

Over the autumn of 2001, the opponents of the PPP had occasional bouts of optimism that the scheme might yet fall apart or be shelved because it would fail to overcome the value for money hurdle. Indeed, Byers stoked up the fire on this issue by intimating to the Commons Transport Committee which was, yet again, examining the PPP that he might be prepared to drop it. Giving evidence on 5 December, he told the MPs that if the bids failed the value for money test, the government was ready with alternatives that would not involve 'a year or two years further delay'.[16] Although this was really nothing new, the press got very excited and even more so when, at his next appearance, a month later, he went one step further by indicating that the government had even considered that it might back a bond issue to finance London Underground should the PPP fail the value for money test.

But all this has to be taken with a pinch of salt as this was the time when Metronet and Tube Lines were negotiating hard on their final bids, and a bit of political noise suggesting that they might not get the lucrative contracts, which they had begun to build into their business plans, could only strengthen London Underground's hand during these final negotiations. A senior London MP was not convinced there was any real movement: 'Sure, there was the value for money process but that answers in whatever way you want, and I presume the drip drip of letting it be known that the contracts might be at risk was designed to put pressure on the companies to lower their prices, on the one hand, and to make the government seem terribly reasonable on the other.'[17]

In reality, with hindsight, there was little chance of the PPP being ditched because the government had invested so much in it, both financially and politically. 'It would,' as one senior insider put it, 'have needed something very big coming out of left field to stop it.'[18] Byers was, as we have seen, a prisoner of the Treasury who was being disingenuous when he told the select committee that the decision 'will rest with myself'.[19] There was a brief flurry of activity during Brown's absence for a few weeks in January 2002 while he was in mourning for the death of his baby daughter, with John Spellar, the junior transport minister, suggesting to Livingstone that changes might be made to the PPP should he ditch congestion charging, but the mayor would not accept the plan and, in any case, the idea petered out on Brown's return.

Byers was already in deep water with the Treasury which had been infuriated by his behaviour after the decision to stop funding Railtrack and force it into administration. While that move, in October 2001, had been sanctioned by both No. 10 and No. 11 Downing Street, Byers had tried to make himself popular in the parliamentary Labour Party by stressing that Railtrack shareholders would never receive any public money to compensate for the losses arising from the suspension of the shares. Moreover, Byers had suddenly become public enemy number one in the media, largely through his failure to sack his special adviser, Jo Moore, when it was revealed that she wrote an email to the Department's press office suggesting that the aftermath of the 11 September attack in New York would be a good time to 'bury bad news'. Moore remained, for the time being, in post, but the episode, which ultimately cost both of them their jobs, together with the growing anger of the Railtrack shareholders, meant that Byers was on the defensive for the months leading up to his eventual departure in late May 2002.

The Treasury was incandescent over Byers's playing to the gallery in the Railtrack affair. His grandstanding ultimately cost the government £500m, which it had been forced to hand over to Railtrack shareholders, supposedly for getting the company out of administration early. It was not, therefore, in a mood to tolerate any compromise over the PPP. Indeed, the government's real intentions were demonstrated by the fact that the

Treasury sanctioned a remarkable addition to the contracts to make them Kiley-proof. A new clause, which came to light in January 2002, would guarantee an infraco thirty years' estimated profits – worth £500m according to TfL – if the operator, London Underground, was found to be acting unreasonably in its management of the contract. If London Underground failed twice in two years in complaints about safety or more effective running of the Tube, it would be faced with the possibility of having to pay up. Kiley was infuriated: 'The clause invites, indeed demands, the most passive contract enforcement imaginable.'[20]

Byers then took a further step the following month, again clearly with Treasury support, in what appeared to be a desperate effort to keep the bidders on board by issuing a 'comfort letter' pledging that the government would underwrite 95 per cent of the bank loans taken out by the infracos. In one of the smoke and mirrors games beloved of the Treasury, the Department of Transport insisted that the comfort letters were 'not an absolute guarantee' of government liability but a statement of the Secretary of State's 'current intent'[21]. The move was necessary to reassure the bidders and their banks that there would be enough funding for the Tube, which was no longer making an operating profit to cover interest payments on the £4bn of borrowing to which the private sector was committed to help fund the investment in the system. The move, which received little attention at the time, suggests that the amount of risk being borne by the infracos was fairly minimal and may indeed be insufficient to get the PPP scheme off the government's balance sheet (see Chapter 12).

In early February, the delayed Ernst & Young report was eventually published. Rather than the Beecher's Brook for the PPP which ministers had suggested, it turned out to be a low hurdle that would never have toppled the project. The conclusions, published in February 2002, though by no means unequivocally in favour of the government's argument, were sufficiently positive for ministers to say that the PPP had successfully cleared the final obstacle. But that was inevitable from the way the report had been conceived, as the commissioning process for the report was inherently flawed. Ernst & Young worked 'on the instructions of the Department for Transport, Local Government and the Regions and for the DTLR's purposes'.[22] Therefore when Transport for London sent evidence on a lot of issues which it wanted examined, Ernst & Young simply wrote back saying that it could not consider material from third parties. The very subtitle of the document, 'Independent review for the Secretary of State for Transport, Local Government and the Regions' was, therefore, an oxymoron. As Patience Wheatcroft put it ironically in *The Times*: 'Well fancy that. A firm of accountants hired by the Government has looked at the various proposals for funding the London Underground and decided that the one favoured by its client is the most attractive.'[23]

The report again took it for granted that the private sector would improve performance and the public sector would fail to, an assumption that adds some £2.1bn to the public sector comparator over thirty years, around 15 per cent of the total which had itself risen yet again, to over £16bn for the first fifteen years, rather than the £13bn that had been used by the government for the previous year. Broadly, the figures, which remained opaque, indicated that £4.5bn would be raised from the private sector, £5bn from Tube fares and £7bn from the taxpayer.

As a result, broadly – the report analyses a series of different scenarios and, possibly deliberately, avoids setting out a clear conclusion – the PPP comes out cheaper over thirty years, although the calculation gives a very marginal result for the first 7.5 year period – £9.4bn versus £9.6bn, the bottom of the public sector comparator range. Using a simple calculation, omitting the cost of finance over the full thirty years gives an even closer comparison, a figure of £8.44bn for the private sector and £8.39bn at the bottom of the public sector range. In other words, the test was only just passed, even with all the weighting of the public sector comparator explained above. Ernst & Young's conclusion is lukewarm to put it mildly: 'Overall the methodology adopted for assessing the value for money by London Underground has been robust and appropriate and London Underground's recommendation that the PPP proposals deliver value for money is a subjective one supported by its analysis.'[24]

Not surprisingly, the commentators remained unconvinced. In an unequivocal leader, the *Financial Times* said there were four serious problems with the value for money tests: 'First, the odds were stacked against the notional public sector alternatives; its costs were assumed to overrun by 11 per cent and it was also forecast to perform so badly that another 15 per cent of public inconvenience costs should be added. Second, the PPP bids are subject to review after 7.5 years, giving the private infrastructure companies a strong incentive to bid unrealistically low for the remaining period. Third, the contracts have not yet been signed . . . . Fourth, the government bears the risk of infrastructure company bankruptcy but this contingent cost is ignored.'[25]

The Ernst & Young findings, never the most convincing of exercises, were published almost simultaneously with yet another damning report from the Labour-dominated Commons Transport Committee[26] which was highly sceptical of the value for money test and even at this late stage recommended the government should 'develop alternatives to the PPP in conjunction with Transport for London and the Mayor'. In particular, the MPs expressed doubts about where the £5bn contribution from fares was going to come from given that London Underground was now making a loss. As the irrepressible veteran Labour MP Gwyneth Dunwoody put it at the press conference launching the report, 'it was difficult for us to find anything good in this deal. There were so many areas where we were not able to say to the public exactly what it will eventually cost.'[27]

The government was never going to win the propaganda war, but that did not stop it proceeding with the deal. The signing of the contracts[28] for the three infracos subject to final details and financial backing went ahead as planned on 8 May but even then there was more controversy when it emerged that the infracos would receive millions of pounds of public money to cover success fees and costs of bidding. Tube Lines sought to get £109m shortly after signing and a further £60m later: this included £36m to be passed to the three consortium members; £11m in success fees for financial and legal advisers; and £55m for 'development costs' with the rest being made up of financing costs.[29] Since Metronet was understood to be seeking a similar sum for both its two contracts, the total bill could be in the order of £500m, but in Parliament the transport minister, David Jamieson, refused to confirm the amounts, merely saying that it was 'perfectly normal commercial practice'.[30]

Even at this late stage, with Kiley threatening a second judicial review on the basis that the contract terms had changed so much in the bidders' favour since the selection of preferred bidders that the normal rules of administrative law had been breached, there were still a series of meetings between the government, TfL and the mayor, and again Blair was involved. Livingstone had gone to see the Prime Minister in March for a routine meeting over a series of issues and raised the fact that the contracts now seemed to offer little benefit in return for the vast expense. Livingstone reiterated his concerns about safety and stressed that the PPP programme of investment had been greatly reduced in order to fit in with the Treasury's budget ('descoped' in the jargon) during the past six months of negotiations. According to Kiley, 'Blair was taken aback as Ken had taken some examples to give him, which flustered him.' Livingstone 'wanted him to look at it personally and he undertook to do it'.

Sally Morgan in Blair's office and Matthew Elson, the sharp young ex-McKinsey man who is the No. 10 transport adviser, organised the meeting, which had the three or four top people from both London Underground and Transport for London together, with David Rowlands from the Department of Transport who did not like being there as it was really a political arrangement. But the meeting quickly fell into chaos when a slanging match broke out between Steve Polan, the sharp bruiser New York lawyer with a nasal Brooklyn whine who has examined the PPP in great detail, and Martin Callaghan, LU's PPP director. As one of those present recalled, 'Martin and Steve went for each other because he felt Martin was not being as accurate as he could be and that Martin was just philosophising about it.' Although a second meeting was held, attended by PricewaterhouseCoopers, there were too many people there and the hope of reaching a deal fizzled out.

Blair eventually sent Livingstone a letter which the mayor regarded as quite positive: 'I don't have the slightest doubt that he shares some of my doubts, because he was prepared to go back and look at it, and the letter he wrote back was very friendly. It did not say that this will work, but said, on balance, "I have looked at this and I think your fears are overstated."'[31]

As the day of the hearing for the second judicial review, which was scheduled to start on 23 July, approached, there was a last-ditch attempt to avoid the proceedings. Transport for London's principal complaint was that when the PPP was handed over there would be a funding gap in the first 7.5 years amounting to over £1.4bn. TfL had been given an 'Illustrative Funding Statement' by the Treasury setting out the Department of Transport's intended level of grant until 2009–10. However, according to TfL, there is a shortfall in the amounts promised compared with the likely costs of the PPP. Moreover, there is no guarantee that all the costs of the

PPP, such as extra spending by the infracos which is deemed, in the jargon, 'economic and efficient' and therefore the responsibility of TfL, will be met.

The negotiations, held in June between senior officials of both sides, centred around whether the mayor, like the infracos, could be given a letter of comfort guaranteeing payments over this period. Livingstone recalls: 'I wanted a clear letter of comfort that the government would actually fund the full cost of this scheme for the first 7.5 years and I thought I was being very reasonable in not asking for the full thirty years.'[32] Instead, they offered just two years' guaranteed money, enough to get Livingstone up to the next mayoral election in 2004: 'I imagine someone in the New Labour machine thought that one up, that I did not need to think beyond the election. Why should I impose on my successors this nightmare funding gap which means you either have to increase fares by 20 to 25 per cent or put £1.50 on the council tax weekly bill?'

In addition to the funding gap, TfL raised two other issues at the Judicial Review. Kiley challenged the way that the contract terms had allegedly moved so favourably towards the infracos in the period since the selection of preferred bidders. For example, TfL found that the infracos' costs for the three contracts were now £925m higher over the thirty-year period when compared with the bids tabled at the 'best and final offer' stage which was the basis of the selection of preferred bidders. Yet, according to TfL, the scope of the contract had been greatly reduced, with much work such as station modernisations and line upgrades being deferred from the first period into future ones. According to Kiley's witness statement, in the three contracts 'over 125 station modernisations have been dropped since BAFO. One of the line upgrades on each of the Jubilee and Piccadilly lines have been eliminated [and] where work has not been eliminated altogether, it has been deferred to later review periods.'

TfL also picked up on the fact that Metronet's rate of return on the equity part of its investment had risen significantly since BAFO for both of its contracts, from 15 per cent on BCV and 16.2 per cent on SSL to 17 per cent and 19.5 per cent respectively, figures which, in any case, Kiley argues are high for PFI deals. TfL also pointed out that the caps on bonus payments had been removed, leading to possible increased liability, and that an allowance of service points (see explanation in Chapter 8) of 30,000 to

40,000 for each four-week period had now been granted to the infracos. At £50 per service point, this could be worth as much as £1.5m to £2m for each period and, according to Deloitte & Touche, this concession could be worth up to £486m for the infracos. As Kiley's witness statement put it, 'It would be surprising to see an increase in scope costs where the scope of work had been simultaneously reduced. Yet this is exactly what has happened since the selection of preferred bidders in the London Underground PPP.'

All this detailed scrutiny of the contracts proved a waste of time. In the event, the second judicial review was a formality, as TfL was floored in a legal first-round knockout. Technically, it was a review of the decision to sign the deal on 8 May 2002. Kiley, who as an American was used to employing litigation as a tool of negotiation, had been more enthusiastic about it than Livingstone, but there was no real falling-out. The judge, though, gave Transport for London short shrift at the hearing which opened in late July. Within three days TfL's counsel, Lord Lester, had to make an embarrassing announcement accepting that TfL's case was likely to be thrown out and that 'the claimants have therefore been advised that they have no reasonable prospect of obtaining an effective remedy for the breaches of the procurement rules they have raised in these proceedings and . . . have decided not to continue further with these proceedings'.[33] It was an abject and embarrassing climbdown that would cost London taxpayers several million pounds.

The judge threw out the case for a judicial review because of a fundamental blunder on the TfL side rather than because of the case's merits or lack of them, although the government side had been confident of winning on the substantive issues, too. According to one well-placed source in the Department for Transport, 'barristers who usually counsel caution had been telling us the odds were 95–5 on winning this one'. The case for a judicial review has to be based on the fact that a decision has been taken which the complainant has not had the opportunity to challenge. However, TfL had long been aware of what it saw as the deficiencies in the procurement process and, indeed, was using these as the basis of the case in Brussels, but did not complain at the time to London Underground. Therefore seeking relief through a judicial review was not the right remedy, according to the judge who promptly ruled that TfL should bear all the costs of the case, a relatively rare decision which demonstrated the weakness of TfL's argument. Kiley was blamed by many London political insiders for the fiasco, as it was widely felt he should not have gone to court.

London Underground crowed over the victory, saying that the decision showed that the contract changes since the selection of preferred bidders had not damaged the Tube's future interests in the way that Kiley had argued. There was, however, one fascinating fact revealed during the course of the case when London Underground's barrister, John Howell, QC, let slip: 'Whatever view one may take about the merits of these contracts . . . they are contracts that have taken a considerable time to evolve, and in which very considerable amounts of money have been engaged in negotiations. Some £400m since the beginning of the process, £100m since the selection of the preferred bidders' – precisely the value of the Northern Line PFI contract for over 100 new trains and their maintenance over twenty years.

In October 2002 as this book was going to press, the last hurdle was crossed successfully. The European Union, which has to look at the issues of the procurement process and state aid, gave its approval. London will get the PPP when the contracts are signed, some time in the winter of 2002–3.

CHAPTER TWELVE

PPP: bog standard but incomprehensible

I set out on the research for this book in a genuine spirit of inquiry. Sure, my misgivings about rail privatisation meant that I would scrutinise the PPP case intensely but I was truly open to persuasion. Listening to London Underground's argument in favour of the idea, there were moments when I thought that it might have merit. Or at least I did for an instant. But as the explanations led on to further complexities and explanations, I just wanted to say, in the words of John McEnroe, 'You cannot be serious.'

I have had several such moments, but the best one came towards the end of my research after I had looked at the contracts and how they deal with the capability measure, explained in Chapter 8. In a telephone briefing to deal with a series of detailed questions about various aspects of the PPP, I asked for an explanation of the three components used in the formula to measure capability. The main one is journey time, which, though it leads to a host of complexities, is at least understandable. The other two are consistency and control. The latter refers to the flexibility of the system and the ability, for example, to turn around trains at intermediate points in the network and the number of junctions. Consistency is concerned with the regularity of the service provision and is made up of 'eight or nine' factors, one of which is the distance between the cab at a station where the drivers clock on and off and the toilets.

This is really, to put it crudely, taking the piss about taking a piss. But within the world of the PPP, it makes sense. If the distance between the cab and the toilet is a factor in determining how consistent the train service is, then it will have an effect on how much London Underground has to pay for the contract. Consequently, it has had to be factored into the formula that covers these issues. So, imagine the scene: the teams of suited consultants and lawyers, all on City rates, working out what should be the standard distance between the cab and the toilet; the speed at which drivers would walk; whether the number of stairs (are they up or down?) should be taken into account; the number of doors which have to be opened to gain access to the facilities; how to accommodate female drivers and arrive at a formula which takes into account possible changes in the percentage of women drivers; the possibility of moving the point where the trains stop; and much more. All this to ensure that an infraco is sufficiently – but not overly – rewarded should it decide to replace a set of toilets with facilities nearer the end of the platform.

One could call this the 'bog standard'. From the point of view of those paid to construct the PPP, you can understand why the bog standard is essential. The infracos will need at times to renew the facilities for the drivers (who, incidentally, in an extra bit of complexity will not actually be working for them but for London Underground) and will need to be remunerated for doing so. In a sane world, there would be a contract for a specific job and that would be paid for. In PPP land, you can't do something so simple. Instead, you have to pay by outcomes and therefore the bog standard has to be part of the capability score. But think what will happen if the reward has not been properly calibrated? If the infracos are not paid enough in terms of the complicated capability formula outlined in Chapter 8 to offer them a sufficiently large incentive to compensate for the cost of the works, then there will be no new toilets for drivers for the next thirty years. (Indeed, what if they rebuild the toilets in the same place?) On the other hand, if the formula is too generous, then we may expect to see toilet facilities sprouting up at every platform on the system where drivers clock on or off. They might even become a tourist attraction: 'Look, my son,' the tourist daddies taking their children out to Cockfosters or Edgware will say, 'here is a monument to a 21st-century folly, the PPP. One day you will understand.'

This is not an academic book and therefore I will not trudge through each issue, weighing the pros and cons of the PPP and coming to refined conclusions. Indeed, that would be a dishonest exercise. The whole point is that the PPP is a massive gamble and only in practice will it be possible to assess whether it is a viable concept. Instead, this chapter looks at some of the more obvious flaws of the scheme, and attempts to examine what its ultimate impact on the Tube will be. In reality, there is little need for massive amounts of detailed analysis. It has all been done already. In the five years' worth of press cuttings on the PPP, there is barely an article which supports the concept unequivocally. And even those that give qualified approval can be counted on the fingers of both hands. The PPP is a credo in which only a minority, even among its evangelists, believes. Martin Callaghan at London Underground really has the faith, so does Tony Poulter of PricewaterhouseCoopers who has worked on it throughout, and there are a few others. But most of the people involved with whom I have talked, informally and formally, have doubts or misgivings. I have lost count of the number of MPs, ministers, civil servants and advisers who, when pressed, say, 'it's not ideal but . . .'. How could they not when commentators and practitioners as varied as Anatole Kaletsky, Will Hutton, Patience Wheatcroft, Jeremy Warner, Simon Jenkins and Polly Toynbee have all, in their separate ways and from their differing political perspectives, damned the thing?

The PPP is based on a fundamental misconception of the nature of a transport system. As Brendan Martin, an expert on privatisation,[1] put it, 'They see the object being privatised as a machine when, in fact, it is an ecosystem.' That is exactly what those who privatised the national railway failed to recognise. Ecosystems are fragile affairs, with various elements in balance with each other. Privatisation, quite deliberately, rips out all the connections and attempts to impose a whole new set, based on legal contracts and performance requirements.

That the PPP is a mistake is such conventional wisdom that it has become almost a truism. But what is wrong with it? The 'bog standard' tale may be a minor detail and largely retold here for a bit of necessary light relief, but it points the way to the fundamental problem with the PPP. Remember, the idea started out to solve a conundrum. The Tube could not be privatised, because that was a Labour manifesto commitment; yet everyone knew it needed massive amounts of investment. The basic concept of splitting up the infrastructure into three and keeping the operation in the public sector was the device used to overcome that political dilemma. The scheme fitted in with another political requirement, to harness the private sector in the upgrading of the system.

Splitting it into four parts is not an obvious solution. It is a political fudge, but perhaps, in itself, it may not be a completely ridiculous concept. Martin Callaghan, London Underground's PPP director, went on at great length about how it was a way of ensuring that engineers would still be attracted to work on LU. That seemed a pretty obscure reason for such a radical move, but let us, for the moment, give the architects of the PPP the benefit of the doubt.

OK, so we have this odd split which, incidentally, leads to the complexity of the performance regime because it requires a system of fault attribution between the operator and the infraco that makes simple indicators, such as the percentage of trains run on time, useless. The next step in the argument is the crucial one. The infracos have to be contracted out because we all know that London Underground is no good at running massive investment schemes. Again, let's leave aside the fact that London Underground will still be managing the contracts and that, in any case, the past management of the Tube has not always been such a disaster as the PPP supporters would like to think. The key problem here is that LU could not simply contract out the infracos to the private sector in an ordinary management contract. Why not? Because this would have kept the whole shebang in the public sector and would leave it on the government's balance sheet *since there would be no risk transfer*. The argument about the failings of LU management is no more than a device to disguise the fact that one of the key aims of the whole process was to ensure the Tube investment did not count against government borrowing. So the infracos had to be contracted out through a PFI or PPP type process and this is where the real difficulties with the concept arise. In order to do this, there has to be a transfer of risk. Now the Tube PPP is not like a conventional PFI where most of the spending is on a large construction project and then the scheme is managed and maintained by the PFI consortium over the ensuing twenty-five or thirty years. The Underground is a massive existing set of ageing assets which have to be managed from the day that the contract is signed. Therefore, unlike conventional PFI schemes, where a large chunk of the risk is in the construction phase, on the Underground it is the risk of falling short in routine day-to-day operations which has to be transferred together with the risk of not achieving the incremental improvements that will lead to reduced journey times – broadly the capability measure.

This is where the PPP architects began to plunge into extremely muddy waters. To work out a way of rewarding or penalising the contractors for their performance, they had to resort to the concept of lost customer hours, a theoretical idea measuring the minutes of passengers' time lost by any given delay and attributing a cost to that by assuming a rate of £6 per passenger hour. This, in the jargon, is a form of cost benefit analysis used widely by transport planners to assess whether it is worthwhile to build a scheme such as a bridge or a new railway line. The trouble with cost benefit analyses is that the cost side consists of hard dollars, real money that will have to be spent to build the scheme (leave aside the fact that the cost is nearly always an underestimate) while the other side, the benefit, consists mostly of wooden dollars. Part of the benefit of a rail line or a toll bridge, but not a motorway, is reflected in the income that the scheme will generate through fares or tolls, but mostly the benefit, as in the case of the PPP, is notional – it is time saved multiplied by a set sum per hour. The money never exists. Yet the creators of the PPP have put this type of cost benefit analysis at the very heart of the whole scheme.

Now let's be generous again. It is not an entirely stupid idea to try to 'incentivise' the infracos to improve their day-to-day operations. There are, however, as there have been throughout this whole story, complexities and details which turn a relatively simple idea into an administrative nightmare. Martin Callaghan tried to dismiss this, but any dispassionate assessment of the PPP contracts would conclude that they are highly complex and replete with areas of potential conflict, despite the lengthy period of shadow running. Moreover, the terms of the contracts seem to have moved in favour of the infracos since the scheme was first dreamt up. But again, leaving all these doubts aside, it is the other principal measure of performance, capability, where the total madness begins and the notion of the PPP really falls apart.

Again, we are back to why the system was designed in this particular way. Conventional contracts require a set output – build me a new line between Green Park and Stratford – and are paid for accordingly. The problem, as we saw in Chapter 6, has been that the public sector has not always been very good at specifying what it wants and sticking to that. Moreover, the risk of cost overruns largely remains with the public sector which, again, has not been very good at making contractors responsible for their own mistakes. So, rather than try to correct these deficiencies, a relatively much simpler task, the PPP is an attempt to ensure that the contractors pay for their own failings. But it is also much more than that. Instead of rewarding them for work carried out, it is a way of paying them in a completely novel way, as we saw in Chapter 8. Instead of being simply paid, say, £10m for £9m worth of work (to give them a profit) the contractors are being paid through a complicated formula which rewards the various ways in which they manage to reduce journey time or improve what marketing people call 'the travel experience' for passengers. Here the problems are legion. From the detailed analysis of this issue in Chapter 8, we have seen how complexities quickly multiply. The bog standard is just one extreme example. At root, there is a basic incompatibility between the two sides of the equation which no end of discussion by people far cleverer than you or I, but much more stupid, too, will ever resolve. The cost of making these improvements is largely determined by engineering factors and the particular problems to be faced in, say, fitting extra signals or improving track layout. The benefit side is calculated through a complex formula which multiplies each second of the journey time reduced as a result of the investment by a large sum, itself calculated by assuming that every passenger's time is worth £6 per hour, and then working out how many journeys will be shortened each year and making an extra annual payment to the infraco on that basis.

Now if there is one central intellectual problem with the PPP, it is that these two figures come from different planets. There is nothing to link them and therefore the model may lead to all kinds of silly decisions being made because there is no particular reason why the cost of the engineering project should be anywhere like the notional benefit calculated by the formulae, which involve equations that include sums of money in the order of hundreds of thousands of pounds. An error one way or the other in the devising of these formula could mean windfall payments for the contractors or, alternatively, give them no proper incentive to carry out the improvements. The very complexity, adding in bog standards for example, is a way of trying to mitigate the most obvious errors, but the whole PPP is such a novel concept that only in practice, when profit-maximising consortia are on the other side of the table from public-sector London Underground, will the real pitfalls be revealed.

The infraco will be able to calculate, broadly, what an improvement will cost and probably be able to muster a good estimate of how much benefit that will bring through these baroque equations. Of course, there is a certain amount of risk if it gets these calculations wrong, but as we have seen, for an 'economic and efficient' infraco, that risk has been capped at a relatively low level. For Transport for London, the risk is that the infracos will find ways of making such improvements cheaply and therefore gather in massive sums for relatively little outlay.

Moreover, this process incentivises the infracos to carry out investment as early in the contract as possible. The concrete example given in the Invitation to Tender is that a two-minute saving on the Victoria Line would be worth £12m per year. So if that work could be carried out early, it will be worth more to the contractor. The Treasury suddenly cottoned on to this in late 2000 and ordered London Transport to make clear in the contracts that various upgrades and refurbishments should not be carried out before set dates. Nevertheless, according to an analysis by Deloitte & Touche for Transport for London,[2] of the three aspects of the performance regime, ambience has an almost trivial impact, and availability, while quite important, is completely overshadowed by capability. The analysis suggests that should the infracos achieve half the capability maximum in the first 7.5 years, they would be entitled to an additional £100m per year. In other words, if they make the improvements early, London Underground will be in financial trouble. That is why the Treasury sussed that, as some mandarin pompously told the bidders, 'the country could not afford the scheme'. Of course, such rapid improvements would theoretically be great for passengers, although it must be noted that increased payments may result from infracos' ability to manipulate the performance measures – by, for example, building lots of toilets for drivers or simply making sure that the best trains carry out the journey time tests – rather than from really making the lot of the passenger better.

Moreover, this type of calculation does not take into account wider factors as to what might lead London Underground to want some bit of infrastructure improved – or not. There may be countless good reasons for making an improvement that would not necessarily be reflected in this type of calculation. On the other hand, there may be investments which score well in this model but which are not really that worthwhile.

There is a final irony to all this. There is a debate over the amount of risk transferred (outlined below) and it does, indeed, seem that the infracos are taking on little real risk. But even if they are, every part of that risk is paid for. It has a price. The infracos cost the risk into their bid. Therefore, the actual risk is greatly mitigated. The prospect of an infraco seeking to be bailed out is an extremely unlikely one, especially as enormous contingencies (see below) have been built into the system.

The myth of risk transfer is explained by a fundamental conundrum with the PFI. Schemes financed through the PFI generally involve the building of a long-term asset – say a hospital or a tram line – and its maintenance over, say, thirty years. If the PFI contractor starts performing badly or if there is a major fault with the facility, then the health authority or transport operator has the right to terminate the contract. However, it would then get the hospital or tram line for free for the remainder of the contract length and therefore has to pay a termination sum as otherwise it would be getting a windfall. However, it also has to pay for the problem to be rectified. Therefore the payment is equal to the remaining worth of the asset, minus the cost of solving the problem. This creates a major risk for the contractor and, in particular, the lenders who have financed the construction of the asset because they may not get their money back if the cost of rectification is too high. Therefore the government has been forced always to cap the cost of rectification in order to allay fears of the lenders (who generally put up nearly all the finance, with very little – 10 or 15 per cent – coming from equity investors) that they have a high chance of losing their money. This effectively means that the risk remains firmly in the public sector.

The conceptual problem with the PPP is that it is an attempt to know the unknowable, to explain the inexplicable. It is difficult to quibble with Bob Kiley's rant in a letter to the chairman of London Transport, Sir Malcolm Bates, sent in November 2001,[3] which is worth setting out in some detail (slightly edited) because it asks a lot of the right questions and is one of the best available summaries of the problems with the PPP. Kiley starts off by pointing out that metro systems in the past have been improved through the conventional model of paying contractors to carry out work:

> The PPP turns tried methods on their head, resulting in systems analysis run amok. LUL is to pay the infracos based on how the system is doing and whether the improvement or deterioration of the system is contractually attributable to the infracos. But how do you figure out how the system is doing and who gets the credit? Well, if you are going to have a chance of succeeding, you have to be able to measure the performance of the Underground in excruciating detail. You need to measure things like how quickly the customers can get from place to place on each line, how quickly they *are* getting from place to place, what the system looks like to customers and how comfortable the ride is on each line. You need to measure all the minutiae that make up the Underground network as a whole, and put them in a formula that assigns proper weight to each element, and allocates pounds to each category of performance. Then you need to gather the data. And you need to figure out who gets credit or blame for each incident that arises. Finally, you must reach common agreement or pursue dispute resolution for each attribution of responsibility. 'Very complex' is an understatement. The mathematical model LUL intends to employ is scattered throughout the 200-plus page Performance Measurement Code, the massive Service Outputs Schedules, Line Specific Performance Measurement Schedules and Nominally Accumulated Customer Hours Tables, the Capability Model and finally the Performance Payment Mechanism Schedules. Key elements require cross-reference to other lengthy and complex documents.

He then goes on to cite a particularly complex equation.

When Transport for London released some of the mathematical formulae, which centred around measurement of litter, London Underground replied that they are easily comprehensible by someone with GCSE maths. This is only partly true. While they are indeed relatively simple, but for an A Level student rather than a GCSE one, the explanations of how the variables – like the bog standard – which go into them are calculated and how they interact are exceedingly complex and require an understanding of how the Underground system works. As Jon Shaw of Aberdeen University who read the draft of this book put it:

> The over-riding thing I can't get out of my head is that this is complexity for the sake of it, rather like rail privatisation. I am specifically avoiding the Luddite argument here of not wanting to approve of anything complex: the obvious drawback of that is that we wouldn't have invented things like aeroplanes. What I mean is that if you can get the same outcomes in a straightforward manner (i.e. leaving it as it was and correcting the obvious faults) why complicate matters?

PERFORMANCE PAYMENT MECHANISM FOR JNP CONTRACT (PART OF THE EXTRACT FOR THE JUBILEE LINE)

For any line grouping, the Actual Aggregate Capability Score, T* is the sum of K* (actual journey time capability), Y* (actual service consistency) and L* (actual service control) as calculated in accordance with paragraphs 1.1.1., 2.1.1. and 3.1.1. of section two and schedule one of the Performance Measurement Code.

[*Note: This simply gives the starting point for the contract, and the bases on which annual adjustments are made are given by the formulae outlined below. At the start of the contract a value of around 18 (it has varied in the negotiation) has been given for K*, around 1 for Y* and 2.3 for L*. They are each calculated on the basis of a series of complex performance indicators, which take in a wide variety of factors, with the most important being the journey time capability – a measure of how fast a train can get from one end of the line to the other and how many people it can carry per hour. The consistency and control measure factors that affect the regularity and frequency of the trains.*]

The amount of aggregate capability adjustment for each payment period shall be the sum of aggregate capability adjustment for the Jubilee line grouping, Northern line grouping and Piccadilly line grouping as calculated in accordance with the formulae in the paragraphs 2.3 to 2.5 below. [*Note: This just means that the amount payable to the infraco for capability is the sum of the amounts due for each of the three lines.*]

[*The formula then goes on to say that for the Jubilee Line*]

$$JT^* = JK^* + JY^* + JL^*$$

[*where J refers to the Jubilee Line and the other letters refer to the definitions above*].

2.3 Calculation of the Aggregate Capability Adjustment for the Jubilee Line Grouping.

The Actual Aggregate Capability Score for the Jubilee Line Grouping for each payment period (JT*) shall be calculated in accordance with the following formula.

a) If the Actual Aggregate Capability Score for the Jubilee Line Grouping (JT*) is greater or equal to the Unacceptable Aggregate Capability (J*tunac*) then the Aggregate Capability Adjustment for the Jubilee Line Grouping for each payment period shall be:

$-jt3.(JT^* - Jt\mathit{unac}) - jt2.(Jt\mathit{unac} - JT\mathit{bmk})$

[*Note: JTbmk is the benchmark and jt3., jt2. and jt1. represent sums of money which are around £440,000, £885,000 and £1.36m respectively at the start of the contract and in some cases increase after 2010.*]

[*There are three other similar formula*] If the Actual Aggregate Capability Score is less than the Unacceptable Aggregate Capability Score but more or equal to the benchmark Aggregate Capability score (JT*bmk*), then the Aggregate Capability Adjustment for the Jubilee Line Grouping for each payment period shall be

$-jt2.(JT^* - JT\mathit{bmk})$

[*Similarly, when the score falls between benchmark and the cap (Jtcap), the formula is*]

$+jt1.(JT\mathit{bmk} - JT^*)$

[*and if it the score is less than the cap then the formula is*]

$+jt1.JT\mathit{bmk} - JT\mathit{cap}$

[and similar calculations are made for the Piccadilly and Northern lines.]

The answer, of course, is the Treasury and its two obsessions – the inability of the public sector to run anything properly and getting capital projects off its balance sheet.

Livingstone is unequivocal about this, stressing that it is not the personal animosity between him and Gordon Brown which has resulted in deadlock over the PPP: 'I don't think my relationship with Brown is a factor at all. The same officials that advised on rail privatisation pushed this through. That is not something that happened with Brown, it is the classic Treasury approach to projects. When we still had a cold war, one of my lines was that we would discover the Treasury was being run by the KGB all along, undermining a powerful western economy. That predates Gordon by decades.' He is, alas, only partly right. It is a fact that Brown's 'fist-print', as Polly Toynbee put it, is all over the PPP.

In the course of my research, as I began to understand the sheer scale and complexity of the concept, it became clear that, as with the poll tax and rail privatisation, the PPP was an idea that should have been left on the shelves of the think tanks and consultants who dream up such outlandish schemes. So how come it wasn't?

The explanation is largely cock-up and part conspiracy. The idea was dreamt up and developed by a mix of Treasury intellectuals who sought to get transport off their agenda, ministers eager to bring about rapid improvements on the Underground, London Transport executives who never wanted to experience the vagaries of unstable funding again and consultants who easily get in to the habit of exercising power without responsibility. They were motivated by the desire to revolutionise the whole structure in order to ensure that the past mistakes of bad management, unstable funding and the inability to run large projects were not repeated. To complicate matters, the PPP had to fit in with a political fudge over privatisation that was unsatisfactory to all sides. The scheme then got into the hands of people at London Underground, such as Martin Callaghan and Denis Tunnicliffe, who saw it as an intellectual exercise to solve the long-standing problems of inconsistent and insufficient funding of the Underground. Callaghan is a genuine blue skies thinker while Tunnicliffe always wants to get to the bottom of things, to find out the reasons – unlike Callaghan, he is not an intellectual but would like to be and this, one suspects, was why he became enamoured of the PPP. PricewaterhouseCoopers also had a strong input during this stage. It seems to be during this working-up of the basic concept that it slipped from something workable and feasible to an ever more Byzantine structure that seemed to be designed as part of a Mensa puzzle. The detail, note, was devised by London Underground and its consultants, rather than the various government departments involved. This too was problematic in that ministers, particularly the ineffective and indecisive Prescott, crucially lost sight of the detail of the project, which slipped from being self-funding and delivering large and rapid benefits to an expensive mess that appears to deliver little that could not have been provided much more simply and cheaply. Blair, as with rail privatisation and transport generally, subjects which he largely ignored in his first term, paid little attention to what was happening. Even the media were slow to react and therefore much of the scheme had been devised and pushed through Parliament before any concerted opposition emerged. Labour MPs were bemused by the detail, as were most people who tried to understand it. So, in effect, much of it went through by default without proper public scrutiny.

There was, though, and this is where we get to the conspiracy bit, a constant impetus from the Treasury, which was not prepared to countenance any alternative. The extent to which the hatred of Ken Livingstone in some parts of New Labour, notably Gordon Brown's office, fuelled the headlong rush into PPP should not be underestimated. Nor should the Treasury's obsession with the failings of public sector management. Ed Balls, Brown's economic adviser, is known to look at the decaying housing estates of Pontefract in the constituency of his wife and junior law minister, Yvette Cooper, and go back to Whitehall vowing to do everything possible to ensure that the public sector never manages anything ever again.

The other part of the conspiracy is well expressed by Kiley. He is not overly impressed with consultants and with good reason. Look, he says, at the role of PricewaterhouseCoopers, which

> wears enough hats to support a lifetime of visits to the Ascot royal enclosure. Most notably, it is financial adviser to the London Transport board, and therefore to London Underground. But it was also commissioned by the Department of Transport to look at the financing of London Underground. Meanwhile, PwC also promotes itself as the leading adviser to the PPP community [employing 500 people across the world in that role], a role it could hardly maintain were it to conclude that the largest such transaction did not provide value for money.

You do not need to be a Leftist conspiracy theorist to see that consultants tend to come up with schemes that require more consultants and which err on the side of complexity. The PPP was first put forward by PricewaterhouseCoopers and it has worked on the concept ever since. Dozens of other consultants have been brought in. The bill has been enormous. And yet their advice is very unlikely to suggest: 'Look, actually, just hire a contractor on a straightforward basis making sure you get the specification right at the beginning.' As Kiley put it, 'intellectualism can be your enemy . . . you can't mortgage the Tube for thirty years on the basis of an untested PwC theory'.[4] It is, indeed, hard to have faith in an organisation which decided to rename itself 'Monday', though, in that case, it did have the sense to think again.

Philip Stephens in the *Financial Times* neatly questioned the role of the consultant: 'An adviser intimately involved in the plan started to explain to me how many thousands of interlocking contractual obligations, incentives and penalty clauses could force four different managements to collaborate – just. After a few minutes, he stopped in mid-sentence and frowned. He could not complain – the fees paid by the Treasury were top dollar – but it would have been better to keep a single system.'[5]

A very senior US consulting engineer who has worked on many deals in the UK was frank about what went wrong with rail privatisation and how much of it is echoed in the Tube scheme: 'First, there was an obsession with consultants who have no responsibility but a lot of power. Secondly, the Treasury is obsessed about the benefits of competition[6] which often means that it kills innovation; and third, the leadership on the political side has been lacking.'

Susan Kramer, the LibDem candidate for mayor and herself a merchant banker with experience of both sides of the Atlantic points out that the PPP scheme would never have happened in the US: 'It seems to be the norm here that with an area like the railways the Treasury drives the process, essentially shaping it with people who are economists, academics, accountants and lawyers. They come up with a conceptual, legal and financial structure and the operating people are meant to shoehorn what they do into that structure. In the States, it would be the other way around. They care about what actually happens at the operating level and the financial and legal work is designed to back up what you want done at the operational level'.[7] Here, as she puts it, it would never occur to the Treasury to try to understand operations and then back it up with the right structure. Indeed, on rail privatisation, the railway people were specifically excluded from the process: 'In the States, when the chief operating officer walks into the room, the finance director shuts up. Here it is the opposite.' She reckons there is something peculiarly British about this, part of the general disdain for trade and people who get their hands dirty: 'I get the sense that these accountants and lawyers somehow think that the operations people are not as smart, they don't have the vision and intelligence to solve problems.'

Kramer's criticisms of the PPP are thorough and well-informed. She also points out that in the PPP it is the accounting firms, who put nothing in and are guaranteed a fee, who drive the process: 'That is one of the big question marks behind a lot of the problematic structures you see in both the public and private sectors; they are being done by people whose instinct and rewards are a transaction being done, rather than with people who stay with the deal long enough that they are going to lose if it goes wrong.'

She is shocked about several specific aspects of the performance targets in the contracts:

> I knew they would never be very demanding. The financial institution will say, make sure the companies get paid unless the bottom drops out of the world. A financial institution would insist benchmarks are set where a mediocre company can achieve them on a mediocre day. No one was going to finance a contract that had operational standards which were above mediocre. It is a given before you begin.

Moreover, she is bemused that they will have a guaranteed rate of return: 'The guaranteed rate of return will come off the top. My understanding is that if there were a lot of inflation and wages go up, that will not be a problem for the infraco. They will still get a guaranteed rate of return. What these contracts were supposed to do was transfer all kinds of risk which justifies the high rate of return. But none of that risk, as far as I can tell, has been transferred.'

Indeed, the only way that the contractors can lose out is if their behaviour is shown not to be 'economic and efficient'. But that is a terribly difficult condition to assess. Cost overruns result from all kinds of factors and it will be very difficult for the London Underground management to unpick exactly what has happened. At the end of each 7.5-year period, there will be an arbitration process to examine whether the price of the contracts should be raised or lowered. It will be up to the arbitrator to judge whether they have been 'economic and efficient', which will be an almost impossible task. The arbitrator faces two fundamental problems. One is that, as Railtrack has discovered, there are very few suppliers to the rail industry and many products are so specific that there is no real market for them. Secondly, many of the suppliers will be part of the consortia which make up the infracos. Finding out the true value of what they are supplying will be a tough paper chase. For example, Bombardier will be supplying all the coaches in the early part of the Metronet contract and since Tube rolling stock is so specific, there is no market that determines a fair price. Not surprisingly, Kiley predicts a wealth of arguments over the precise meaning of 'economic and efficient'. The cost, incidentally, of each arbitration process has been calculated at £36m,[8] enough to buy at least a couple of dozen Tube coaches.

The contracts are so lucrative that the share price of Amey, part of the Tube Lines consortium, plummeted in July 2002 after concern that the PPP would not start because of the intervention of the European Commission. The company had forecast a massive 'cash inflow' as a result of the deal but when on 8 July news that the deal might be delayed was released by the company, shares went down by 11 per cent (but then went up when the second Judicial Review collapsed). In a revealing analysis in the *Daily Telegraph*,[9] Alistair Osborne, under the headline 'Tube gravy train for the bidders', points out that Amey's cost of capital is around 8–9 per cent while it is earning nearly 20 per cent.

This is another bemusing aspect of the PPP, making the infracos provide the finance which they can only do by raising money more expensively than the Treasury. This has been a core complaint by opponents of the PPP, to which there is little sensible response. The government can borrow more cheaply than anyone else and therefore even if the work is to be carried out by the infracos, why insist that they are responsible for arranging the finance? It would be much cheaper simply to allow TfL to raise the money itself. The explanation, of course, lies in the fact that the risk is thereby notionally transferred, which allows the government to count the borrowing as off-balance sheet. This process is a sham that is not only expensive to the taxpayers, but also creates a structure that reduces accountability and transparency.

There, incidentally, is a risk that the PPP may not be off-balance sheet. The changes to the contract made by Stephen Byers, such as allowing step-in rights for London Underground and backing 95 per cent of the loans, may mean that the Office of National Statistics will insist on treating the whole scheme as government spending. That would be a rich irony but at the time of writing is, as yet, undecided because the ONS says it can only make a decision once the contracts are signed. The fact that the ONS allowed Network Rail, Railtrack's replacement, to be off-balance sheet despite the fact that it is essentially government-controlled, augurs well for the PPP, but nevertheless one well-placed source in the Department of Transport said in July 2002: 'I think that Byers may have done too much and messed it up.'[10]

Osborne also spotted another bit of generosity to the infracos: 'Amey would receive £6bn a year for seconding staff, implying £400,000 per person, well above typical market rates.'

There are more serious ones: there is a contingency of over £300m for each contract for each 7.5-year term. Uniquely in such contracts, according to Steve Polan, the TfL lawyer, the contingency will go to the infraco should it not be spent: 'If none of the contingency is spent, this will push the rate of return up around the 50 per cent mark. It does get you to ask, what real risk are these people taking?'

There are a host of other details in the contracts which could be examined, but space – and sheer boredom for the reader – precludes it. Suffice to mention one more. What happens at the 7.5-year review points? TfL argue that effectively a whole new contract starts because the pricing may be completely changed. LU argues that the commitments will remain and that the process is a review, rather than a total reconstitution of the contract. Polan says the real problem will come if the infracos are unable to raise further finance. The contract says that they can then walk away, passing on their debt to London Underground, which by then will be part of Transport for London: 'In practice, LU cannot take that debt. So it will give the infracos enormous leverage to get LU to accept whatever price they say is fair. The PPP arbiter is supposed to determine the price, which is problematic as there is not a lot of transparency in the industry, but that aside, the leverage the infracos will have at the review point is extraordinary.'

There is no doubt that the contracts have moved in the infracos' favour since preferred bidders were announced. In his witness statement for the 2002 Judicial Review, Kiley cited several ways in which the contracts had changed since the selection of the preferred bidders. These included, as we saw in Chapter 11, a rise in the contract prices; an increase in the rate of return on share capital for the infracos; the removal of caps on bonuses; a reduction in the scope of the work; less risk to the private sector; and the introduction of allowances in the performance regime which reduced its effect. Even London Underground admitted there had been some changes. However, LU argued that this was all part of the negotiation process and refused to discuss details, saying these were 'commercially confidential'.

This process of renegotiation, however, seemed to be in one direction, as Kiley had complained it would be when the preferred bidders were selected – according to Kiley, far too early in the process. When I asked LU whether any of the terms of the contract had moved against the infracos, one of the PPP team highlighted a more onerous performance regime for the failure of infracos to hand back work sites after a possession, resulting in delays to train services. 'But,' I asked, 'are the infracos being compensated for taking on that extra risk?' 'Of course,' came the reply. Therefore it is not that the terms have moved against the infracos but that, to put it simply, LU have gone into the infraco shop and made an extra purchase.

This raises the biggest mystery of all. Why is the government, especially the Treasury, which has so little faith in public sector managers, allowing them to undertake what is probably the biggest public procurement in British history outside of the defence industry? Anatole Kaletsky summed it up neatly: 'If there is one clear lesson from such bungles [various computerisation projects in the public sector] it is that civil servants are even worse at drawing up performance contracts than they are at managing projects themselves.'[11] No one was able to provide even a whiff of an answer to this conundrum.

Of all the arguments against the PPP, the least convincing have been those over safety. Partly this is because of the hyperbole that has been associated with them, with repeated statements about 'bodies on the tracks' and 'the Tube becoming a tomb'. Moreover, arguments about safety have been damaged by the cynicism of the trade unions who have used safety as a pretext for holding a series of one-day strikes which have served little purpose other than to inconvenience the public. However, just because the claims have been exaggerated does not mean that there is not cause for concern. During the run-up to rail privatisation, there were also many claims about potential risks being introduced by the new structure of the railways. And, while I was sceptical of them at the time, they have proved right. Although, overall, the railways have continued to become safer if measured by, say, the number of minor incidents occurring on the system, there have been a series of major and extremely high-profile accidents that have been directly attributable to the way the industry was restructured and sold off.[12] That is because of a concept called 'interface risk'. When you split up organisations into smaller parts, it requires efficient communication between the various parties and failure results in interface risk.

Fortunately, the Tube is only being split into four but there is still a potential risk that information will not be properly shared or communicated. The Tube is a far simpler system than the national railway and has an excellent safety record but, nevertheless, there is the potential for a major disaster, particularly as it is getting more and more crowded. The other risk introduced by the PPP, and one which contributed to the Hatfield disaster, is the emphasis on performance rather than safety. If the infraco managers become obsessed with meeting targets and neglect their primary duty, which is safe operation of the system, then extra risk will have been introduced by the PPP. It is, at this stage, impossible to judge whether the lessons of the national railway will have been learnt.

There are bound to be a host of practical difficulties in the operation of PPP as a result of having broken up the unified structure. One current manager in the Tube warns:[13] 'There are a lot of facilities which are in short supply. In the past, London Underground allocated these on the basis of what needed to be done quickest. Now, the infracos will be bidding against each other, and decisions will be made on the basis of seeking profit, rather than what is best for the passenger. There may even be long closures, if that suits the infracos. They are likely to build up a bank of lost customer hours, and then spend them.' One of those scarce facilities is the emergency response team, a heroic gang who clear up after people have fallen in front of trains and other incidents: 'How far will their work be subject to commercial pressures?' Inevitably, he says, the infracos will play to the contracts rather than to the public interest: 'They will try to demonstrate to LUL that they are doing a good job, rather than actually do one. That's very different.' He also predicts difficulties between the infracos and the existing PFI contractors: 'Formally, there is no relationship between the two. They will have to go through London Underground management to talk to each other.'

The biggest advantage claimed for the PPP is that it will provide long-term funding for the system in a way that has never happened before. This claim, incidentally, was also made at the time of rail privatisation, and there has, indeed, been a massive increase in investment on the railways, but much of it has come in the form of higher state subsidies, which, just as with the PPP, was not as originally envisaged. Moreover, much of that money has been wasted because every piece of engineering work on the railway, whether major or minor, costs considerably more as a result of the complexities introduced by privatisation. Ultimately, despite the promises made at privatisation, the long-term situation on the railways is no more stable than it was in the days of BR.

For the Underground, too, the claim that the PPP will provide a stable funding regime cannot be substantiated. Sure, as with the railways, a lot more money is going to be spent in the early years of the PPP. But as with the railways, the Tube has to run and any government will always have to bail it out in the last resort, a point which ensures that there never can be a real transfer of risk. Since rail privatisation, ten of the twenty-five train operators have returned to the government to ask for more subsidy and all have received it. As we have repeatedly seen, not just in the care of Railtrack, but also with the National Air Traffic Services and British Energy, the belief that the government can somehow shed its responsibility for essential services by privatising them is no more than wishful thinking.

Moreover, the idea that the tube is on the brink of some nirvana where there will be bucketfuls of money for capital investment is a myth. The following example provided by TfL demonstrates this. What happens if an 'economic and efficient' contractor finds that a set piece of work is much more expensive than anticipated, say because the world price of steel suddenly leaps upward? More money will have to be paid by London Underground through no fault of its own. Will the Treasury therefore necessarily cough up the extra money? No way. Instead, LU will have to make cuts in other parts of the investment programme, deferring or cancelling projects. Sounds familiar? It might not quite happen on a year-to-year basis as it used to, but the cuts will inevitably come.

The question which I have put to all the players in this game is why two highly intelligent and well-meaning groups of people, both with the interests of the London Underground and its passengers foremost in their minds, have come to such diametrically opposite conclusions. Martin Callaghan suggests it is a culture clash and that both sides are influenced by their past. The British lived through the Thatcher years of cuts in the public sector and the constant refrain that those who work in it are inadequate, which led to the creation of the PFI, while the Americans come from an environment where local government is able to raise huge sums of money through bonds. But Callaghan also has a little dig at Kiley: 'The first time we met, Bob told me we were all prisoners of our own experience. We start with two different experiences of history and Kiley is brought in by Ken, hailed as the world's greatest transport expert and does not want to fail. You have worked in a particular environment and succeeded, would you not try to persuade people to do it your way? All the people around him have worked with him before. I'm convinced he has given too little weight to the difference in political structure.'

Callaghan adds that there is the fundamental point that 'we have accepted the constraint that they have not which is that £4.5bn is coming into this railway from private finance. They want to raise a bond issue and we have accepted that in the public financing structure we have got, that is not a solution.' Kiley merely thinks that the other side have sold out to the government because they are so desperate to be freed at last from the yoke of annuality, those tortuous times waiting for the government to guarantee them next year's funding, that they will do anything to get out of that situation.

Even on the perception of the PPP, there is fundamental disagreement. Callaghan argues that there has not been a proper debate over the PPP and that if there had been, its virtues would have won everyone over. Kiley points out that there have been millions of words written about it and that they all broadly reach the same conclusion. The problem for Callaghan is that, ultimately, the vast majority of independent analysis suggests that the PPP is an expensive nonsense.

Let us, therefore, try to sum up, as succinctly as possible, the case against the PPP:

- It has cost at least £400m simply to devise the scheme
- Contrary to the promises made, it will deliver little extra private money, while leaving the taxpayer to foot an annual bill of £1bn – and there is still the prospect of a substantial funding gap
- It offers little more guaranteed long-term funding than the previous system and will not deliver the stable and reliable funding that was its original attraction
- It has passed the value for money test only by the narrowest of margins and with the help of financial sophistries that have been widely criticised
- The operation of the scheme is dependent on contracts so complex that they require some 300 mathematical formulae and countless volumes of legalese to define the relationships between the parties
- It is a system that has not been tried anywhere else in the world and has been opposed by virtually every independent expert who has examined it in detail
- It has been forced through by institutions who will not be responsible for operating it, despite the fact that there are many well-established and workable alternatives
- It splits up a unified system, which LT itself originally favoured, with consequent increases in management costs and potential risks to safety
- Minimal risks are assumed by the private sector infracos, which have been permitted to cost the risk factor into their bids; and, as Railtrack and other examples have shown, it is, in any case, totally impractical for government to shed their ultimate responsibility for maintaining essential public services.

And those are just the main points . . .

So will it work? The omens are not good. The battle over the PPP has already involved a major casualty: the travelling public. As we saw in

Chapter 1, the Underground's performance has been deteriorating quite markedly. To recap, the annual report published in August 2002 showed that during 2001–2, the percentage of scheduled services which operated was 92.9 per cent. This was a slight improvement from the 91.6 per cent of the previous year but still well below 95.5 per cent when the process started. In 2000–2001 on the six other criteria used to measure success, such as cleanliness, helpfulness of staff and waiting time to buy tickets, the performance was below the benchmark. The reduction in the percentage of services operated was largely caused by a rise in breakdowns on the Tube involving signals, points or track failures, the areas under the responsibility of the infracos, which went up by 35 per cent to 4738 in that year, three-quarters of which caused a delay to the train service. However, this was partly compensated for by a reduction of 10 per cent to 14,448 in the number of train breakdowns.

Interestingly, Martin Callaghan and other senior managers at London Underground say that the shadow running has resulted in an improved performance, even though the publicly issued statistics do not support that case.

Predictably, both sides used poor performance to back their case. Jon Smith, who heads LU's contract management team, blamed the continued attacks on the management by Livingstone who reiterated his 'dullards' jibe whenever he could, while Kiley and the mayor argued that the separation of the infrastructure from operations as part of shadow running had damaged performance. Londoners sighed.

Livingstone and Kiley could not be blamed for the remarkable collapse in the Underground's finances over the five years since the PPP controversy first arose. While income went up from £960m to £1244m between 1997–8 and 2001–2, the operating costs almost doubled from £695m to £1377m. Consequently, far from making a profit to help pay for the investment, the Underground had an operating loss of £133m in 2001–2 compared with a profit of £288m four years earlier. Part of the explanation for the deterioration in the figures was a change in the way that capital spending is represented in the books which is responsible for taking £135m per year off the bottom line, but that still does not account for the soaring costs which appear to be out of control. London Underground has no real explanation other than that wage costs have been rising above the rate of inflation as the unions have become more militant, but middle managers who have talked off the record say there is no doubt that a substantial chunk of the increase is a result of the extra layers of management that have had to be taken on to run the complicated new structure. The dire financial performance is an embarrassment and raises the issue of where the money for the 30 per cent of the PPP expected to be financed out of the fare box is going to come from. (Moreover, as an aside, since the high management costs of the restructured railway have been included as part of the public sector comparator when, in fact, an entirely public railway would have a simpler management structure, the comparison has been distorted.)

As usual the government grant has been anything but stable over the five years, ranging from £816m in 1999–2000 when the cost overruns of the Jubilee Line Extension had to be paid for, to £375m the following year and £520m in 2001–2. The system suffered, too, from the usual peaks and troughs of investment, with £415m available for the existing system in 1998–9, compared with just £162m two years later.

The patchiness of the money available for investment, of course, reinforced the argument of those managers who saw the PPP as the way out of these stop-go policies. Leaked correspondence published in the *Guardian*[14] suggests that the government originally promised £775m of grant for 2001–2 but cut it, possibly in response to the fact that the PPP had not yet been implemented, and then Byers cheekily presented it as 'doubling' of grant for that year when he announced the settlement after Labour's general election victory. As David Walker put it in the *Guardian* article: 'One of the many paradoxes of the PPP is that setting it up has consumed many hundreds of millions of pounds that might otherwise have been spent on infrastructure'. Indeed, £400m is not a sum to be trifled with.

Despite these financial problems which will have to result in a bail-out of some sort, there is a sense in which the PPP cannot fail. The expectations are so low that even a small amount of investment will be welcomed by long suffering Londoners. The PPP has been so damned before it started that even a modest success will be hailed as 'defying expectations'. The best that can be said for it, in the words of Jon Smith, is that 'it incentivises people to behave in the right way and we have put in as many things as we can to drive people on both sides to correct behaviours and to make it really painful for either party to go down wrong behaviours.' Livingstone and Kiley have promised that they will try their damnedest to make it work.

But there are structural problems ahead. Susan Kramer points out that joint ventures are unstable beasts, as they link people who do not necessarily have the same interests and tend to split up: 'If you want to find a more unstable structure for an entity than a joint venture, I just don't think there is one. Most JVs fall apart because they discover that they came together over a long negotiating period but their agendas are different.' On the other hand, these ones are so lucrative that there may well be a vested interest to stay together.

Interestingly, a senior member of one of the successful bidders reckons that the structure of the PPP will not survive long: 'When we start the contract, we will move towards an integrated system. Metronet and Tube Lines will not be able to do it on their own. People have not thought through how this is going to work.' In other words, all the trouble caused by the Treasury's insistence on having three infracos, which have already been effectively reduced to two by the bidding process, will come to naught.

Livingstone points to another problem, which is money. Indeed, the funding gap is a real one, as acknowledged by the offer he received for two years' guaranteed money. Livingstone envisages a reprise of Fares Fair: 'I don't think there is any way that there will be a majority in the assembly for a £1.50 per week increase in council tax. The Libs and the Conservatives won't vote for it. I wouldn't propose it, I am quite prepared to propose a real fares increase for a real improvement in service, but not to protect the profit margins of the infracos.' And, according to Livingstone, he has a real bargaining chip: 'The law is absolutely clear, only I can increase the fares on the Underground. No one else can and I can't be overridden. The only way if I refuse to increase the fares, is primary legislation. It is not like a local authority where the finance officers can step in. And to make it absolutely clear, I will not increase Underground fares to pay for the obscene profit margins of the infracos. The government either gives us the money to run or faces the consequences of that.'

Politically, therefore, the PPP has achieved nothing except a permanent state of war between Transport for London and the government. Moreover, the nastier the government is to Livingstone, the more votes he will attract at the 2004 mayoral election. Inevitably, the PPP will be a loser for New Labour. London Transport's inability to sell it to the public was demonstrated by the poll on its own website taken just before the second Judicial Review. Despite asking a question that was as loaded as the electoral system in Communist countries, 81 per cent of respondents (14,440 people) voted against the PPP and for the option of 'Transport Commissioner Bob Kiley says that he wants to go back to court to block PPP investment in the Tube', a quite staggering result.

Finally, the PPP may well get bogged down in arbitration and litigation procedures. When the infracos and the LU management are battling it out for real, rather than wooden, dollars, there are bound to be more disputes. But that will not bring the system to a halt. The Tube will keep on working – most Londoners will notice little difference apart from the odd bit of building. So the PPP may work in terms of a few modest improvements but it will be unexciting stuff. The promised transformation of the Tube will not happen until lots of today's commuters are pushing up daisies, and even then the cost is likely to have been prohibitive. The PPP will not solve any of the fundamental problems which led to its creation.

PPP supporters argue that TfL and other opponents have put forward no viable alternatives which do not transgress Treasury rules. But there is any number of different ways of approaching the problem of investing in the Tube, ranging from the conventional contracts run by London Transport to outright privatisation, a suggestion that sits uneasily with the failure of rail privatisation. The simplicity of Kiley's argument – let me raise the money and I will give you a new Tube – is attractive. So is the idea of securitising future income in order to raise a substantial capital sum (although the Tube's recent financial problems make this more difficult). All these alternatives could have been properly considered. Instead, in truth, for five years there has been no real consideration of any other plan. That in itself is a remarkable criticism of the way British governments develop and implement policy. Indeed, the PPP and the way it was developed is just another example of recent failures in British governance which include the poll tax, rail privatisation and, less seriously, nonsenses like the Dangerous Dogs Act. Londoners and the nation's taxpayers will be paying for this particular folly for at least thirty years to come.

As I revise this conclusion, a final nail in the coffin of the PPP's credibility arrives. At a public meeting in September 2002 about new runway capacity for the south east, a senior Department of Transport official says that the costs of the proposed airports in the government's consultation paper, have been calculated on the basis that the price of capital will be 6 per cent. This is, indeed, the rate used in the public sector comparator. But, he lets slip, because the cost of capital has been falling for a long time, the Treasury now says that such calculations should be based on 3.5 per cent. If the public sector comparator were calculated on the basis of guaranteed funding at that rate, it would be considerably cheaper than the PPP alternative. But, of course, the government is not going to go back and recalculate the whole basis of the unwieldy edifice that it has spent five years constructing.

Possibly the best point on which to end is that the PPP is, according to Susan Kramer, a misnomer which breaches the Trade Descriptions Act. The early documents about the PPP contain a lot of flannel about London Underground only wanting to work with companies in a spirit of partnership. Therefore, according to London Underground, there will not be any threats of litigation, disputes over the precise wording of or regular trips to the offices of an arbitrator. On the railways, Railtrack's rapaciousness as an aggressive company at the heart of the rail network led to the unravelling of the whole edifice created at privatisation. Like many critics, Kramer dismisses talk of partnership and cooperation as naïve, given the huge sums of money at stake and the fact that the companies taking over the contracts are conventional profit-maximising firms: 'Partnership? It is not a partnership. If it were a partnership, you would create a company to run the tube with both the private and public equally at risk. A partnership is two equals coming together and sharing, equally. This is not what has happened. How does the word partner come into this apart from the fact that it alliterates with public and private?'

So this book has been about something that does not really exist.

Glossary

ABATEMENT: The official term for the penalties incurred by infracos if they do not perform to the standard specified in the contract.

AMBIENCE: The perception of the environment in the stations and trains, one of the factors determining the level of payments to the infracos.

AVAILABILITY: A key measure under the PPP contracts. Under the PPP, contractors are 'incentivised' to ensure that the 'railway infrastructure is available and in a fit and proper condition'. Under the availability requirement, infracos must 'minimise asset-related delays measured in terms of "lost customer hours"'.

BAFO: Best and Final Offer.

BCV: Bakerloo, Central and Victoria lines, one of the three infraco contracts.

CAPABILITY: This is a measure of the potential performance of each line in terms of the number of people it can carry per hour. The higher the capability, the lower the average journey time can be.

CROSSRAIL: A proposed new main-line railway linking east and west London with a new tunnel between Paddington and Liverpool Street stations. No funding is yet available, although £154m has been allocated for preparatory work. The proposed Chelsea to Hackney line is now known as Crossrail 2.

CTRL: The Channel Tunnel Rail Link, a new 62-mile railway linking the mouth of the Channel tunnel with St Pancras.

DEEP TUBE LINES: The Underground lines built in tunnels bored under London, characterised by the limited height and width of the trains. They are the Bakerloo, Central, Jubilee, Northern, Piccadilly and Victoria lines.

DETR: The Department of the Environment, Transport and the Regions, which existed between May 1997 and 2001.

DTR: The Department for Transport, the stand-alone department created in June 2001.

DTLR: The Department for Transport, Local Government and the Regions, which existed between June 2001 and June 2002.

FAR: Final Assessment Report on the PPP, produced by London Underground in February 2002.

GREATER LONDON AUTHORITY: The new government of London, which includes both the mayor and the London Assembly created by the Greater London Authority Act 1999.

INFRACOS: Infrastructure companies; the three companies created by London Underground which are to be privatised.

JLE: The Jubilee Line Extension.

JNP: Jubilee, Northern and Piccadilly lines, one of the three infraco contracts.

JV: Joint Venture

LONDON REGIONAL TRANSPORT: The official but rarely used name of London Transport.

LONDON TRANSPORT: Historically, the term used for the organisation that ran both London buses and the underground. However, London Buses passed to Transport for London in 2000 and London Transport is now only the holding company for London Underground.

LONDON UNDERGROUND/LONDON UNDERGROUND LIMITED: Legally, a subsidiary of London Transport responsible for the Underground and which will pass to Transport for London once the PPP contracts are signed.

LOST PASSENGER HOURS: The delays caused to passengers through breakdowns in the system, used as a way of determining abatements to be paid by the infracos.

METRONET: The successful bidder for two of the infracos, BCV and Sub-Surface lines.

MOVING BLOCK: A new signalling system that dispenses with line side signals and theoretically allows trains to travel closer together.

NATM: The New Austrian Tunnelling Method, which is used to build tunnels.

PFI: Private Finance Initiative (explained in Chapter 8).

PPP: Public Private Partnership (explained in Chapter 8).

PUBLIC SECTOR BORROWING REQUIREMENT: In theory, simply the borrowing required by the government if its expenditure exceeds its income, but in practice there are major controversies over what is – and is not – included in this calculation.

PUBLIC SECTOR COMPARATOR: The estimate of what a scheme would cost in the future if a service were continued to be provided by the public sector; used as the basis of comparison for PFI and PPP schemes.

SERVICE POINTS: In order to place a value on the ambience.

SHADOW RUNNING: The restructuring of London Underground in preparation for the PPP by which the operations were separated from the infrastructure which was split into three companies still owned by London Transport.

SSL OR SUB-SURFACE LINES: The older Underground lines, built by the cut and cover method and which constitute one of the three infraco contracts. They are the Circle, District, Metropolitan, and Metropolitan and City lines.

TRANSPORT COMMISSIONER: The head of Transport for London appointed by the mayor. The post is currently held by Bob Kiley.

TRANSPORT FOR LONDON: Created by the London Government Act to run all London transport services, but which will not take on the Underground until the PPP is signed.

TSR: Temporary Speed Restriction, imposed on lines where repairs are needed.

TUBE LINES: The successful bidder for the JNP infraco.

TUBE: Technically, the deep tube lines, but used in this book interchangeably with 'Underground'.

VFM: Value for Money.

Notes

CHAPTER ONE

1 Peter Campbell. 'Why does it take so long to mend an escalator?', *London Review of Books*, 7 March 2002.
2 *Underground News*, magazine of the London Underground Railway Society, July 2002, p. 282.

CHAPTER TWO

1 Douglas F. Croome and Alan A. Jackson, *Rails Through Clay*, Capital Transport, 2nd edn, 1994, p. 6.
2 The best are probably the two-volume *History of London Transport* by T.C. Barker and Michael Robbins, George Allen and Unwin, 1963 and 1974, and *Rails Through Clay*, by Douglas F. Croome and Alan A. Jackson, 2nd edn, Capital Transport, 1994. There is also an excellent series of booklets on each line produced by Capital Transport Publishing.
3 Christian Wolmar, *Broken Rails, how privatisation wrecked Britain's railways,* Aurum Press, 2001.
4 William J. Pinks, *History of Clerkenwell*, London, 1865.
5 Stephen Halliday, *Underground to Everywhere*, Sutton, 2001, p. 13.
6 John Glover, *London Underground*, 9th edn, Ian Allan, 1999, p. 12.
7 Piers Connor, *Going Green, the story of the District Line,* Capital Transport, 1993, p. 8.
8 Halliday, *Underground to Everywhere*, p. 38.
9 *Railway Times*, 18 October 1884, p. 1332.
10 Halliday, *Underground to Everywhere*, p. 38.
11 Ibid., p. 49.
12 Ibid., p. 76.
13 Ibid., p. 76.
14 Barker and Robbins, *History of London Transport*, p. 248.
15 Glover, *London's Underground*, p. 39.

16 Barker and Robbins, *History of London Transport*, p. 273.
17 Ibid, p. 288.
18 The details of the scheme are to be found in *Improving London's Transport*, a Railway Gazette publication, 1946.
19 A small percentage of the borrowing went to the main-line rail companies to fund improvements to their suburban London services.
20 Barker and Robbins, *History of London Transport*, p. 290.
21 Halliday, *Underground to Everywhere*, Sutton, p. 99.
22 The BBC, a contemporaneous creation, is a similar construct which, of course, still thrives today.

CHAPTER THREE

1 Interview with author.
2 Douglas F. Croome and Alan A. Jackson, *Rails Through Clay*, Capital Transport, 2nd edn, 1994, p. 336.
3 Quoted in T.C. Barker and Michael Robbins, *A history of London Transport, vol. 2*, George Allen and Unwin, p. 338.
4 Ibid.
5 Stephen Halliday, *Underground to Everywhere*, Sutton, 2001, p. 177
6 Croome and Jackson, *Rails Through Clay*, p. 7.
7 Barker and Robbins, *A history of London Transport*, p. 344.
8 C.D. Foster and M.E. Beesley, 'Estimating the social benefit of constructing an underground railway', *Journal of the Royal Statistical Society* (A), 1963, pp. 46–92.
9 Halliday, *Underground to Everywhere*. p. 183. Under the PPP, incidentally, this calculation is made on the basis of £6 per hour.
10 Barker and Robbins, *A history of London Transport*, p. 347.
11 Croome and Jackson, *Rails Through Clay*, p. 324.
12 London Transport Executive, *Annual Report and Accounts for the year ended 31 December 1971*, p. 22.
13 Croome and Jackson, *Rails Through Clay*, p. 432.
14 Paul E. Garbutt, *London Transport and the politicians*, Ian Allan, 1985, p. 27.
15 Croome and Jackson, *Rails Through Clay*, p. 357.
16 Ibid., p. 358.
17 Garbutt, *London Transport and the politicians*, p. 74.
18 Croome and Jackson, *Rails Through Clay*, p. 447.

CHAPTER FOUR

1 *Your Disobedient Servant*, Penguin, 1979.
2 Horace Cutler, *The Cutler Files*, Weidenfeld and Nicholson, 1982, p. 145.

3 Interview with author.
4 Note to author.
5 Interview with author.
6 Cutler, *The Cutler Files*, p.150.
7 Interview with author.
8 Ibid.
9 Desmond Fennell QC, *Investigation into the King's Cross Fire*, Department of Transport, 1988, Cm. 499.
10 Note to author.
11 Interview with author.
12 Fennell QC, *Investigation into the King's Cross Fire*, p. 35.
13 Tunnicliffe became managing director before the departure of Ridley, who had realised that being both managing director and chairman was too much for one person.
14 Interview with author.
15 Fennell QC, *Investigation into the King's Cross Fire*, p. 63.
16 Ibid., p. 19.
17 Ibid., p. 128.
18 Interview with author
19 Fennell QC, *Investigation into the King's Cross Fire*, p. 30.
20 Ibid., p. 63.
21 Ibid., p. 125.
22 Ibid., p. 31.
23 Ibid., p. 31.
24 Interview with author.
25 Ridley adds: 'I did not ever believe that fires were an "occupational hazard on the Underground", I put it to Fennell they would not be totally eliminated.'
26 Interview with author.
27 Ibid.
28 Ibid.
29 Ibid.
30 Ibid.
31 London Underground Limited, *Company Plan, Summary November 1991: a new dawn for the heart of London*.
32 Interview with author.
33 House of Commons Transport Committee, Third report, *London's Public Transport Capital Investment Requirements*, 1992–3 session, HMSO, HC 754, p. 35.
34 Interview with author.
35 'Fire risk on Tube does not justify cost of changes', *Independent*, 9 September 1992.
36 Interview with author.

CHAPTER FIVE

1 Interview with author.
2 Ibid.
3 Ibid.
4 Ibid.
5 Ibid.
6 Monopolies and Mergers Commission Report, London Underground Limited, HMSO, June 1991, Cm. 1555, p. 1.
7 Ibid., p. 10.
8 Ibid., p. 2.
9 Ibid., p. 2.
10 Ibid., p. 10.
11 Interview with author.
12 Monopolies and Mergers Commission Report, London Underground Limited, HMSO, June 1991, Cm. 1555, p. 10.
13 Interview with author.
14 All figures in this paragraph are in 1993–4 prices.
15 Memo to author.
16 Ibid.
17 House of Commons Transport Committee, *London's Public Transport capital investment requirements*, 1992–3 session, third report, HC 754, p. 26.
18 Ibid., p. xv.
19 Interview with author.
20 Ibid.
21 A manager told me that he once went through the internal list of 250 top managers which showed their addresses and found that only one in seven was within walking distance of a Tube station.
22 Interview with author.
23 House of Commons Transport Committee, *London's Public Transport capital investment requirements,* 1992–3 session, third report, HC 754, p. 26.

CHAPTER SIX

1 Greater London Council/Department of the Environment, *London Rail Study,* 1973–4.
2 Department of Transport/British Rail Network SouthEast/London Regional Transport/London Underground Limited, *Central London Rail Study*, January 1989.
3 Halcrow Fox & Associates, *East London Rail Study* (commissioned by Department of Transport), September 1989.
4 Interview with author.

5 House of Commons Transport Committee, *London's Public Transport capital investment requirements*, 1992–3 session, third report, HC 754, p. 29.
6 The usual term is Net Present Value, which is an arithmetical method of adding up a future income stream and expressing the figure in terms of what it would be worth today as cash in hand.
7 Although London Underground confirmed that by mid-2002 some money had been paid over by O&Y, it was unable to say how much.
8 Interview with author.
9 Mike Horne, *The Jubilee Line*, Capital Transport, 2000, p. 58.
10 Speech to the Institute of Public Policy Research, 13 December 1999.
11 See Christian Wolmar, *Broken Rails, how privatisation wrecked Britain's railways*, Aurum Press, 2001, pp. 219–231 for a discussion of the cost overrun on the West Coast Main Line project.
12 Interview with author.
13 Ove Arup Partnership Ltd, *The Jubilee Line Extension, End of Commission Report by the Secretary of State's Agent*, presented to the DTLR July 2000, p. 7.
14 Interview with author.
15 Ibid.
16 Ibid.
17 Ibid.
18 Ibid.
19 Ibid.
20 Ove Arup Partnership Ltd, *The Jubilee Line Extension, End of Commission Report by the Secretary of State's Agent*, presented to the DTLR July 2000, p. 7.
21 Denis Tunnicliffe recalls how the Tory transport minister, Roger Freeman, had sought to make savings through reductions in the size of the stations but was easily rebuffed when the safety card was played.
22 See *Megaprojects and Risk* by Bent Flyvbjerg, Nils Bruzelius and Werner Rothengatter, to be published by Cambridge University Press in February 2003, for details of 'how the promoters of multi-billion projects systematically and self servingly misinform parliaments, the public and the media in order to get projects approved and built'.
23 Ove Arup Partnership Ltd, *The Jubilee Line Extension, End of Commission Report by the Secretary of State's Agent*, presented to the DTLR July 2000, p. 55.
24 Interview with author.
25 Ibid.
26 Ibid.
27 Ibid.
28 Ibid.
29 Ernst & Young, *London Underground PPPs value for money review, Independent review for the Secretary of State for Transport, Local Government and the Regions*, February 2002.

30 Draft of paper shown to author.
31 Memorandum to author from LU.
32 Interview with author.
33 Ove Arup Partnership Ltd, *The Jubilee Line Extension, End of Commission Report by the Secretary of State's Agent*, presented to the DTLR July 2000, p. 8.
34 Don Riley, *Taken for a Ride*, Centre for Land Policy Studies, 2001.

CHAPTER SEVEN

1 New Labour, *Because Britain Deserves Better*, 1997 election manifesto, Labour Party.
2 Department of the Environment, Transport and the Regions, *London Underground: Public Private Partnership, The Offer to Londoners*, 10 April 2001.
3 Roger Ford, 'Northern Line – Alstom's PFI success', *Modern Railways*, April 2002.
4 Interview with author.
5 Interestingly the first attempt at widespread use of such 'unconventional finance' was by the left-wing Labour councils of the 1980s who attempted to sell and lease back all kinds of capital assets ranging from town halls to parking meters. See Goss, Lansley and Wolmar, *Councils in Conflict*, Macmillan, 1990. The difference with PFI is that it usually involves the building of a new asset and requires risk transfer.
6 International Financial Services London, *Public Private Partnerships, UK expertise for international markets*, 2001.
7 Interview with author.
8 Jon Sussex, *The economics of the Private Finance Initiative in the NHS*, Office of Health Economics, 2001, p. 8.
9 Ibid., p. 38.
10 Sunita Kikeri, John Nellis and Mary Shirley, *Privatisation: the Lessons of Experience*, World Bank, Washington DC, 1992.
11 Brendan Martin, *In the public interest, privatisation and public sector reform*, Zed Books, 1993, p. 139.
12 Sussex, *The economics of the Private Finance Initiative in the NHS*, p. 37.
13 Treasury Taskforce Private Finance, *Partnerships for prosperity – the Private Finance Initiative*, HM Treasury, 1997.
14 HM Treasury, *Budget Report 2002*.
15 All Peter Hendy quotes are from an interview with the author.
16 *The PFI Report*, April 2001.
17 Quoted in Colin Brown, *Fighting Talk*, Simon and Schuster, 1997, p. 311.
18 Ibid., p. 312.
19 Ibid., p. 313.
20 London Underground, *The future for London Underground, evaluation of options*, September 1997.

21 Ibid., p. 4.
22 Ibid., p. 12.
23 Ibid., p. 14.
24 Ibid., p. 22.
25 Interview with author.
26 Ibid.
27 Ibid.
28 House of Commons, *Hansard*, 27 June 2002, col. 1002.
29 Department of the Environment, Transport and the Regions, 'Prescott announces deal to build Channel Tunnel Rail Link', press notice, 3 June 1998.
30 Interview with author.
31 The Transfer of Undertakings (Protection of Employment) Regulations 1981 (TUPE) ensure that workers retain certain rights when their company is privatised.
32 House of Commons, 20 March 1998, *Hansard*, col. 1540; and Department of the Environment, Transport and the Regions, 'John Prescott promises a first class Tube for everyone', press release, 20 March 1998.

CHAPTER EIGHT

1 All quotes from Martin Callaghan in this chapter are from an interview with author except where noted.
2 London Underground Limited, Public Private Partnership, *Final Assessment Report*, 7 February 2002, p. 17.
3 Ibid., p. 54.
4 Ibid., p. 53.
5 Ibid., p. 53.
6 Interview with author.
7 London Underground Limited, Public Private Partnership, *Final Assessment Report*, 7 February 2002, p. 10.
8 Ibid., p. 55.
9 Ibid., p. 57.
10 Ibid., p. 57.
11 Memo supplied to author.
12 London Underground Limited, Public Private Partnership, *Final Assessment Report*, 7 February 2002, p. 18.
13 Ibid., p. 15
14 Originally, it was £200m for every period, but this risk was, according to London Underground, too expensive to transfer to the private sector.

CHAPTER NINE

1 Interview with author.

2 House of Commons Environment, Transport and Regional Affairs, London Underground, seventh report, 1997–8 session, minutes of evidence, 29 April 1998, question 15.

3 During the rail privatisation of 1996–7 the main British Rail freight company was arbitrarily divided into three, but subsequently all were purchased by the same organisation. The rolling stock, too, was divided into three.

4 Michael Harrison, 'London Tube privatisation in jeopardy', *Independent*, 2 October 1998.

5 Stephen Glaister, Rosemary Scanlon and Tony Travers, *The way out: an alternative approach to the future of the Underground*, London School of Economics, 20 March 1999, p. 16.

6 And, incidentally, since London Buses were to transfer straight away to Transport for London, control of London's two main transport services was to be separated for the first time since the 1930s.

7 Standing committee A, debate on Greater London Authority Bill, *Hansard*, 25 February 1999.

8 Interview with author.

9 Standing committee A, debate on Greater London Authority Bill, *Hansard*, 23 February 1999.

10 Aurum Press, 2001.

11 *PPP for London Underground Progress Report*, London Transport, March 1999.

12 This has been variously called an arbitrator or arbiter, but the latter is the accurate term. However, as we saw in Chapter 8, the arbiter only deals with the financial arrangements at breakpoints, while routine disputes will go to a quite separate arbitrator.

13 Stephen Glaister, Rosemary Scanlon and Tony Travers, *The way out: an alternative approach to the future of the Underground*, London School of Economics, 20 March 1999.

14 This is very much a notional surplus since it does not service the capital of the Underground, nor does it cover the need for further investment; nevertheless, the economic performance of the Tube did, at the time, compare favourably with that of metros in other countries though, as we see later, the situation has deteriorated since the Underground began to be restructured for the PPP.

15 Glaister, Scanlon and Travers, *The way out: an alternative approach to the future of the Underground*, p. 15.

16 Ibid., p. 22.

17 *The Economist*, 20 November 1999.

18 'Why PPP is best for the Underground', *Financial Times*, letters to the editor, 25 November 1999.

19 *Observer*, 22 November 1999.

20 Rosemary Bennett, 'London Mayor business groups attack candidates speech', *Financial Times*, 7 October 1999.
21 Interview with author.
22 Quoted in Mark D'Arcy and Rory MacLean, *Nightmare: the race to become London's mayor*, Politico's, 2000, p. 133.
23 Interview with author.
24 Quoted in D'Arcy and MacLean, *Nightmare: the race to become London's mayor*, p. 110.
25 Quoted in Carol Millett, 'A rough ride ahead for the Tube', *Contract Journal*, 1 June 2000.
26 Interview with author.
27 House of Commons Committee on Environment, Transport and Regional Affairs, *Funding of London Underground*, 14th report, July 2000.
28 Comptroller and Auditor General, *The financial analysis for the London Underground Public Private Partnerships*, National Audit Office, HC 54, 2000–2001 session, 15 December 2000, p. 6.
29 Ibid., p. 8.
30 Ibid., p. 9.
31 Ibid., p. 9.
32 Ernst & Young, *London Underground PPPs Value for Money Review*, independent review for the Secretary of State for Transport, Local Government and the Regions, 5 February 2002, p. 51.
33 Transport for London, Interim Consultation Response to London Transport on PPP documents provided between 11 February 2002 and 15 March 2002, 21 March 2002, p. 4.
34 Ibid., p 36.
35 Ernst & Young, *London Underground PPPs Value for Money Review*, independent review for the Secretary of State for Transport, Local Government and the Regions, 5 February 2002.
36 The Industrial Society, now the Work Foundation, *The London Underground Public Private Partnership: an independent review*, September 2000.
37 Ibid., pp. 17–18.
38 Ibid., p. 136.
39 Simon Jenkins, 'Blair's troubles could be good for London', *Evening Standard*, 28 September 2000.
40 Seumas Milne, '"Safety at risk" in tube sell-off', *Guardian*, 18 August 2000.
41 See Christian Wolmar, *Broken Rails*, Aurum Press, 2001, Chapter 9 for a detailed account of the circumstances leading to the accident.
42 Quoted in Liam Halligan, 'Current Account', *Sunday Business*, 19 November 2000.
43 Charles Batchelor, 'London Underground contenders urge rethink of plans', *Financial Times*, 21 September 1998.
44 See Wolmar, *Broken Rails*, Chapter 8 for a detailed account of the Ladbroke Grove accident and the subsequent inquiry.

45 Department of Environment, Transport and the Regions press release, 1 December 1999.
46 *Financial Times*, 2 December 1999.
47 Quoted in *Building* magazine, 23 July 1999.
48 Quoted in *Independent*, 10 March 2000.
49 Quoted in *Building* magazine, 31 March 2000.
50 Alistair Osborne, 'Tube advisers on track for £100m', *Daily Telegraph*, 20 April 2000.
51 *Independent*, 1 December 2000.
52 *Lawyer*, 25 October 1999.

CHAPTER TEN

1 All direct Kiley quotes in this and subsequent chapters are from an interview with author except where specified otherwise.
2 Interview with author.
3 Ibid.
4 Ibid.
5 *Independent*, 20 December 2000.
6 *Evening Standard*, 5 February 2001.
7 Anthony Hilton, 'U-turn could send the PFI down the tubes', *Evening Standard*, 5 February 2001.
8 John Kampfner, 'Duel for the Tube', *New Statesman*, 9 April 2001.
9 Will Hutton, 'Don't make a mess of it, Mr Mayor', *Observer*, 4 March 2001.
10 Interview with author.
11 This letter was made public by the Department.
12 Note to author.
13 Interview with author.

CHAPTER ELEVEN

1 *Financial Times*, 12 April 2001.
2 It is worth noting that one of the failed bidders, who was highly critical of the PPP process, argued quite the opposite. Michael Cassidy, who headed the Linc bid, later told the Commons Transport Committee (28 November 2001, question 385) that he thought the move to preferred bidders was made too late.
3 Which also includes the Waterloo & City Line.
4 These incidents are examined in greater detail in Christian Wolmar, *Broken Rails*, Aurum Press, 2001, pp. 165–7.
5 Amtrak press release, 11 November 2001.
6 Interview with author
7 *Hansard*, 5 July 2001, col. 230W.

8 Quoted in *The Economist*, 28 July 2001.
9 Interview with author.
10 Ibid.
11 Polly Toynbee, 'Gordon's web: the Chancellor cannot escape his responsibility for this anti-democratic fiasco on the London Tube', *Guardian*, 20 July 2001.
12 Interview with author.
13 House of Commons, Transport Local Government and the Regions Committee, *London Underground*, second report of session 2001–2, question 374.
14 Ibid., question 374.
15 Ibid., question 378.
16 Ibid, question 585.
17 Interview with author.
18 Reliable source.
19 House of Commons, Transport Local Government and the Regions Committee, *London Underground*, second report of session 2001–2, question 588.
20 *Guardian*, 17 January 2002.
21 Quoted in *The Times*, 12 February 2002.
22 Ernst & Young, *London Underground PPPs value for money review, Independent review for the Secretary of State for Transport, Local Government and the Regions*, February 2002, introductory letter.
23 Patience Wheatcroft, 'When will there be light at end of Tube tunnel?', *The Times*, 8 February 2002.
24 Ernst & Young, *London Underground PPPs value for money review, Independent review for the Secretary of State for Transport, Local Government and the Regions*, February 2002, p. 6.
25 *Financial Times*, 11 February 2002.
26 House of Commons Transport, Local Government and the Regions Committee, *London Underground*, second report of session 2001–2.
27 Author's notes.
28 This stage is known as 'commercial close'.
29 *Financial Times*, 20 June 2002.
30 *Hansard*, 4 July 2002, col. 460W.
31 Interview with author.
32 Ibid.
33 Transport for London press release, 26 July 2002.

CHAPTER TWELVE

1 See Brendan Martin, *In the Public Interest: privatisation and public sector reform*, Zed Books, 1993.
2 Information obtained by author.
3 Cited in *The Case Against PPP*, published by Transport for London, 2002.

4 Interview with author.
5 Philip Stephens, 'Londoners' Descent into Hell', *Financial Times*, 6 July 2001.
6 Ever since the criticism over the sale of British Gas, the Treasury has insisted on having three of everything to ensure competition: there are three rolling stock companies, there were three freight companies when BR was sold, and three infracos.
7 This and subsequent quotes are taken from an interview with author.
8 Note to author from London Underground.
9 *Daily Telegraph*, 10 May 2002.
10 Interview with author.
11 Anatole Kaletsky, 'Don't let London go down the tubes', *The Times*, 29 March 2001.
12 My previous book, *Broken Rails*, Aurum Press, 2001, examines these accidents in great detail.
13 All the following is interview with author.
14 17 October 2001.

Index